# ESTEEMED
# COLLEAGUES

# ESTEEMED COLLEAGUES

## Civility and Deliberation in the U.S. Senate

BURDETT A. LOOMIS
*Editor*

BROOKINGS INSTITUTION PRESS
*Washington, D.C.*

Library of Congress Cataloging-in-Publication data
Esteemed colleagues : civility and deliberation in the U.S. Senate /
Burdett A. Loomis, Editor.
p. cm.
Includes bibliographical references and index.
ISBN 0-8157-5294-6 (alk. paper)
ISBN 0-8157-5293-8 (pbk. : alk. paper)
1. United States. Senate. 2. Civil society—United States.
3. Government etiquette—United States. 4. Representative government
and representation—United States. I. Loomis, Burdett A., 1945–
JK1161 .E77 2000                                    00-010381
328.73'071—dc21                                     CIP


9 8 7 6 5 4 3 2 1


The paper used in this publication meets minimum requirements of the American National Standard for Information Sciences—Permanence of Paper for Printed Library Materials: ANSI Z39.48-1984.

Typeset in Sabon

Composition by Cynthia Stock
Silver Spring, Maryland

Printed by R. R. Donnelley and Sons
Harrisonburg, Virginia

# Contents

# Acknowledgments

AS WITH ANY COLLABORATIVE EFFORT, *Esteemed Colleagues* owes many debts. The largest goes to the Pew Charitable Trusts, which, through its public policy program, funded the conference that commissioned these papers. In particular, I am indebted to Paul Light, Michael Delli Carpini, and Rebecca Rimel for supporting an examination of Senate deliberation. The Pew grant was administered by the Aspen Institute, and Aspen's Deborah Both was a delight to work with.

The University of Kansas's Robert J. Dole Institute for Public Service and Public Policy hosted a conference, "Civility and Deliberation in the U.S. Senate," July 16, 1999, in the Senate's Hart Office Building. The offices of Senators Pat Roberts and Sam Brownback proved instrumental in easing our path to using the Hart Building as the venue. Special thanks go to Senator Robert J. Dole and his law firm colleague Harry McPherson for providing wonderful sets of remarks at that conference. Heather Hoy, Dole Institute program assistant, and Chad Kniss were invaluable in setting up the conference. In addition, Sheila Burke, Richard Cohen, Keith Kennedy, Richard Baker, Bob Dove, and Wendy Schiller offered excellent commentaries on the papers and more generally on the nature of civility and deliberation in the Senate.

In addition to writing one of the articles for this volume, Jim Thurber, director of American University's Center for Congressional and Presidential Studies, gave us excellent advice on organizing a Washington conference. The Dole Institute is grateful for his assistance.

At Brookings, Nancy Davidson, Chris Kelaher, and Bob Faherty have welcomed this project, all the while offering constructive advice, even as we developed the conference program. They have been partners in this endeavor from the beginning. Moreover, the Press obtained the services of conscientious, insightful reviewers, whose comments helped improve our final collection of articles. On behalf of the Press, Vicky Macintyre edited the book, Carlotta Ribar proofread it, and Julia Petrakis indexed the pages.

Finally, and most profoundly, I want to thank the authors of the pieces that appear in this volume. They have produced an excellent, accessible grouping of original reflections and analyses on civility and deliberation in the Senate. They have turned a good idea for a conference into a first-rate book.

As the initial book from a Dole Institute initiative, *Esteemed Colleagues* is dedicated to Senator Robert J. Dole, whose thirty-six years of legislative experience demonstrate that one can stand strong as an individual and as a partisan, all the while practicing civility and promoting fruitful deliberation.

# ESTEEMED COLLEAGUES

# CHAPTER ONE

# Civility and Deliberation: A Linked Pair?

## BURDETT A. LOOMIS

We are, after all, a representative democracy—a mirror held up to America. . . . In a democracy differences are not only unavoidable— if pursued with civility as well as conviction, they are downright healthy.

—Former Majority Leader Bob Dole, July 16, 1999

HOWEVER MUCH WE MAY WANT TO romanticize the "world's greatest deliberative body," the cold fact remains that the 1980s and 1990s have witnessed a consistent growth in partisan behavior and position-taking in the U.S. Senate. Although eclipsed by the harsh rhetoric, strident partisanship, and occasional physical contact common to the House of Representatives, the Senate has become a less collegial body. The 1999 death of Rhode Island's moderate Republican John Chafee brought home how the chamber has changed. As Democratic centrist Senator John Breaux (D-La.) noted, "He was one who really put the country ahead of the party. I hoped the numbers [of such senators] would be increasing, but it looks like they are decreasing."[1] Indeed, with the retirement of fourteen veteran legislators in 1996, the Senate lost many important bridge-builders.

At the same time, the Senate remains a body that can encourage the fruitful exchange of ideas and the possibility for deliberation. Cross-party working relationships can flourish. As Ross Baker notes (chapter 2), the best such relationships may evolve between same-state senators from different parties, who need not compete for similar constituencies. More-

over, with just 100 members the Senate still encourages the forging of
cross-party personal relationships inside the chamber, ties that are especially useful in overcoming the frequent filibusters that threaten the viability of the legislative process.

This volume brings together a group of distinguished congressional scholars to consider the linkage between civility and deliberation in the U.S.
Senate. Although the writings are certainly scholarly, the issues of civility
and deliberation are anything but academic. Not only do many citizens
view the Congress with skepticism, if not outright hostility, but members
of both chambers often behave with "minimum high regard" for the institution and their peers. This focus on the Senate is valuable, for several
reasons. First, in comparison with the House, the Senate remains an un-
derstudied institution. Redressing the balance is worthwhile in and of itself. Equally important, the Senate occupies a unique role in American
politics. In a system that requires majorities to overcome many obstacles
to work their will, the Senate is indisputably the least majoritarian legislative body among our ninety-nine state and two federal chambers. All the
others are based on the principle of "one person, one vote." But the Constitution dictates that each state—whether Wyoming or California—is
entitled to two senators, a condition that can profoundly affect the
chamber's character, as Bruce Oppenheimer illustrates in chapter 7.[2]

In an era of divided government and ostensible gridlock,[3] understanding the Senate helps policymakers address broad issues of representation,
responsiveness, and capacity within governmental institutions. Finally, with
the retirement of many centrist senators and the growth of partisan voting
in the chamber, the question arises whether deliberation remains a reasonable expectation for the body. Perhaps pure position-taking and compromise under pressure have overwhelmed the institution's capacity to generate
coherent, productive dialogues on major issues.

## Civility, Deliberation, and Representation

At first blush, the connection between civility and deliberation seems
straightforward. Comity would seem a necessary, if not sufficient, condition for deliberation on the major issues of the day. And certainly a minimum level of civility is required, a level that could not be maintained back
in the 1850s, when slavery came to dominate the chamber's attention.[4]
More generally, the nineteenth century witnessed a "decline of restraint"
in the Senate that encouraged its members to employ more aggressively

procedural tools (such as the filibuster) that could hinder the free exchange of ideas.[5] Still, in 1885 Woodrow Wilson could conclude that, in contrast to the House, "the Senate is a deliberative assembly. [It is,] *par excellence,* the chamber of debate."[6]

The linkage between civility and deliberation remains open to question, in that extended debates—which become a strain on comity—have historically played a major role in the institution. Civility, in itself, it is argued here, is not the central issue. Rather, it is the relationships between levels of civility and two core elements of the legislative process: deliberation and representation. Hence the chapters are organized around four topics: the idea of civility in the Senate, the Senate as a deliberative institution, civility's ties to deliberation, and the practice of deliberation in the contemporary Senate and its linkage to representative government.

## The Senate in the American System

In contrast to the House, the Senate is often seen as free-flowing and informal.[7] Debate is less well structured, and floor activity proceeds through continuing negotiations between the parties' floor leaders, whereas House business is more structured and subject to time limits. Personal relationships become more important in the Senate, and committees are a bit less significant. Still, a few core constitutional requirements and internal rules/practices combine to shape the essence of Senate behavior and process.

### The Senate as Institution

The Senate, both through its rules and its constitutional role, often requires *supermajorities* to conduct business. The constitutional mandates for two-thirds majorities to ratify treaties, approve constitutional amendments, and convict on impeachment charges frame the conflict on a small number of important issues. Indeed, the Clinton impeachment trial generated relatively civil Senate behavior in large part because all senators knew that mustering the sixty-seven votes required for conviction was a virtual impossibility.[8]

In terms of affecting day-to-day business, the constitutional requirements for supermajorities pale before the Senate's own requirement of sixty votes to end extended debate by invoking cloture. Barbara Sinclair (chapter 4) observes that in recent Congresses (both Republican and Democratic) more than half of all major measures encountered a "filibuster problem" on the way to Senate approval.[9] This contrasts with 10 percent in the late 1960s and 20 percent or more in the 1970s. Routine filibusters have become a fact of Senate life. In untangling procedural knots, senators enter into detailed negotiation, but *this should not be confused with deliberation on the issues*. Rather, they are working out intricate compromises that protect any number of individual (and party) positions, so that the chamber's business can proceed.

In fact, as Sinclair and others have observed, the contemporary Senate combines both high levels of partisanship and individualism. Thus determined minorities of more than forty senators can block legislation, while an individual senator can exercise disproportionate influence in a chamber that depends on unanimous consent agreements (UCAs) to conduct its business. As Lawrence Evans and Walter Oleszek note (chapter 5), "For controversial legislation, getting 100 Senators to accept truly severe restrictions on their discretion requires broad consensus that a measure must not be filibustered, and a real sense of urgency about the timing of final passage." In short, obtaining unanimous consent is no mean feat in a chamber that continues to accord individual senators the capacity to slow, even stop on occasion, the legislative process.

Moreover, through the majority leader, the Senate allows its members to place "holds" on legislation and nominations. An informal courtesy that appears nowhere in the Senate rules, holds allow individual senators to slow down the process, to the point of grinding it to a halt, if the majority leader feels little pressure to work out the objections expressed by the given senator(s). In this instance, although individual senators may be inconvenienced by the "hold" practice, most do not want to remove this weapon from their arsenal, even if many of them rarely use it.[10]

All in all, partisanship and individualism within the Senate combine with the formal requirements of supermajorities and the informal practices of UCAs and holds to inhibit the ability of majorities to work their wills. No wonder that senators are often frustrated by their incapacity to move legislation in the face of determined majorities or, worse, a single senator who remains intransigent on a key (or pet) issue.

*The Senate and the Executive*

The Senate's role in a bicameral/separation-of-powers system also produces breaches in comity. Again, the Constitution sets the stage for many of the conflicts that play out both between the branches and within the Senate. Ratifying treaties, confirming a wide range of nominees, and trying impeachment cases offer the opportunity for confrontation between opponents and defenders of presidential actions inside the Senate. Roger Davidson and Colton Campbell observe in chapter 9 that "nearly all presidents have faced confirmation fights with the Senate."[11] Despite some high-profile, highly political disputes involving ambassadorial and judicial nominees, as well as the test-ban treaty ratification vote, Davidson and Campbell conclude, "it seems unlikely that Senate-executive relationships have deteriorated significantly over time." Still, the willingness to move from specific cases (a single ambassadorial or judicial nominee) to whole-sale disruption of Senate business (recall Justice Committee Chair Orrin Hatch's threat to block all judicial nominations) is an ominous development. Even more dangerous has been the Senate's practice of "hostage-taking." A major nominee, such as Richard Holbrooke, Clinton's choice for ambassador to the United Nations, was blocked from appointment by a single senator (Foreign Relations Chair Jesse Helms, backed by the Republican majority) with the strong desire to obtain a host of policy concessions from the administration.

Davidson and Campbell decry the practice of hostage-taking as poisoning interbranch relations. The question remains as to whether Senate-president conflicts carry over to affect relations within the Senate. The evidence here is sketchy, but many observers did paint the Senate's 1999 rejection of a nuclear test-ban treaty as a continuation of impeachment politics.[12] The Senate could have offered the administration a way out of an awkward situation, but Majority Leader Trent Lott joined with most of his Republican peers to force a vote that was destined to stand as a major foreign policy embarrassment for the president. At the same time, the Republican Senate did—however grudgingly—work with the president to produce a budget agreement in late 1999, even as most of the incentives for such a deal were political and not policy driven. The facts of discord and disagreement should not lead to the immediate conclusion that the Senate cannot function in a broadly responsive way to its constituents.

## The Special Case of Impeachment

On occasion, an exceptional event offers insights into the way an institution operates. The impeachment trial of President William Clinton (January–February, 1999) provides such an opportunity for the U.S. Senate. After an acrimonious, highly partisan struggle, the House surprised the Senate by voting to impeach the president. The Senate was thus confronted with a highly public test of its capacity to act in a civil manner that would defend the credibility of the Congress. The Senate worked through its early confrontations with flying colors, as Senators Phil Gramm (R-Tex.) and Edward Kennedy (D-Mass.) backed basic principles that led to a bipartisan agreement on procedure. The *New York Times* reported, "Senators held to the idea that the impeachment trial was a historic moment for the Senate and that they had to rise to the occasion" (see chapter 10).

To be sure, the Senate did behave with far more dignity than did the House, but largely because there was virtually no chance that the chamber would convict President Clinton on either article of impeachment. Rather, the senators constructed a well-scripted, highly ordered exit strategy, one that gave them a date certain (February 12) for final votes on the articles.[13] In this context, the need for a basic level of comity precluded any real possibility of deliberation; for example, only three witnesses were heard, all on videotape and with nothing new to offer beyond the information provided by the House managers (and indirectly, Independent Counsel Kenneth Starr). In the end, the Senate voted along partisan lines (with no Democratic defections on either article; five Republican defections on the obstruction article, ten on perjury) to find President Clinton not guilty.

As Norman Ornstein points out in chapter 10, the need for supermajorities in the Senate again defined its essence: "No conviction was possible without a significant number of members from the president's party. . . . A strictly partisan vote in the Senate . . . would mean failure, added to the costs of divisiveness." The Senate acted as a partisan institution as it failed to convict the president. Nor did it engage in anything that could remotely qualify as deliberation, although its members did work in concert to extricate the chamber from an uncomfortable, untenable position. On early procedural compromises all senators voted together.

In the end, the Senate's actions on impeachment shed only modest light on its civility and capacity for deliberation. Given the foregone conclusion of Clinton's acquittal, the chamber acted as well as it could in devising a way to get through the proceedings and put impeachment in the rearview mirror. But the overall congressional performance is scarcely hopeful. Ornstein concludes: "As long as the Senate is compared to the House, it will not be hard to look more civil and less corrosively partisan. But impeachment, a *high-water mark in the Senate's approach to institutional integrity in recent years*, may be met with fewer examples in the future" (emphasis added).

## The Senate in an Uncivil Society

According to congressional scholar Eric Uslaner, a less civil Congress has evolved precisely because it represents a society that has become less civil.[14] Although the path of causality is not always clear, one would be hard-pressed to argue with Uslaner's basic premise in the wake of post-1994 congressional behavior. The House and Senate are representative bodies, and they have become more partisan in the past two decades.

At the same time, in the post-Watergate era, the press has become more and more adversarial in its coverage of the Congress, and citizens have viewed the Congress with great skepticism and distrust.[15] This societal context scarcely encourages deliberation; rather, playing to one's base of activists becomes the order of the day.

### The Senate and the Media

As the collegial, textbook Senate of the 1950s gave way to the more individualistic, more partisan chamber of the 1980s–1990s, senators' relations with the press changed dramatically. The links between reporters and legislators did become more adversarial, especially with the adoption of Watergate-style reporting. As Timothy Cook (chapter 8) demonstrates, however, the changes have been far more profound and mixed than a simple movement from symbiotic relationships at midcentury to adversarial ones in the 1990s. Cook concludes, first, that "political agendas are increasingly reactive to news agendas, and policies have to be created with news values in mind," and second, that "political processes are sped up under the media spotlight." As legislators elbow each other (think of Phil Gramm and Robert Torricelli) for the media spotlight, these two trends can scarcely contribute to comity in the chamber. To the contrary, senators are more likely to take positions and hold to them, knowing that their constituents (geographical and financial) are watching, to say nothing of reporters who are waiting for a slip, a contradiction, a sign of weakness.

Legislators and journalists, Cook points out, continue to need each other. Relationships between reporters and their Senate sources produce "negotiated" news that reflects a continuing set of interactions between Washington elites.[16] In a sense, each senator cuts his or her own deal, or, increasingly, follows the party's orchestrated message, which stands as an attempt to overcome the journalist's capacity to shape the direction of the story.[17] Again, position-taking appears to trump the interpersonal communication that constitutes the basis for deliberation.

## The Senate as a Representative Body

Writing in 1993, Eric Uslaner looked for a culprit to blame for "the decline of comity in Congress." In the great tradition of Walt Kelley's Pogo, Uslaner concluded that the enemy is us.[18] If society has become less civil, should we be surprised that our representative institutions have followed suit? Although the conventional wisdom and most observers would label the House as less civil than the Senate, Uslaner warns us to be careful with our evaluations. Incivility may be less obvious, less pronounced in the Senate, but the chamber does represent the same citizens who have given us a closely divided and highly contentious House. As Uslaner reminds us, although the two chambers do differ, they are more alike than different.

More important, civility is not an end in itself. Highly contentious legislatures, such as the British House of Commons, can also be extraordinarily effective bodies. But the U.S. Senate, even with elevated levels of partisan voting, finds it most difficult to combine contentiousness with the capacity to deliberate. Given the replacement of deliberative centrists like John Chafee by deal-making centrists like John Breaux, the Senate in effect is sending the message that deliberation born of civility is less possible than compromise among position-takers, which requires only the bare minimum of civil discussion. Indeed, staff can do much of the heavy lifting, once the principals have agreed on the core elements of the deal. Ironically, deal making in an open, C-SPAN era may do little to build trust in Congress as a representative body.[19]

Uslaner (chapter 3) does find a couple of other contemporary culprits. First is the enhanced ideological extremism within both parties in both houses of Congress. Senate Majority Leader Trent Lott is no Newt Gingrich (House Speaker, 1995–99), but the legislators in the chambers act in relatively similar ways, especially in terms of high levels of party voting. Again, the strange combination of partisanship and individualism combines to make senators willing to take their own positions and yet vote in step with their parties.

Even more important than partisanship, says Uslaner, is a lack of trust, both within the society and within the Senate: "A less trusting citizenry leads to more incivility in Congress." In a society that incarcerates more and more of its citizens, that encourages litigation for resolving disputes, that builds increasing numbers of gated communities, there is little sense that trust will grow much stronger in the short term.

## The World's Greatest Deliberative Body

Congress is, by design, an institution which moves rather slowly in making law. This is especially true of the Senate, where the wishes of a cohesive minority hold considerable sway. This is so the passions of the moment are allowed to cool before laws are passed. Careful deliberation, analysis, and long-range thinking were important to the Founders, and these are usually necessary ingredients in legislating. If anything, the Congress . . . [does] not have enough of these ingredients. Few in their right mind will argue that it suffers from too much deliberation, analysis, or thought.

—Senator Howell Heflin (D-Ala.),
in his 1996 farewell address to the Senate

It may have been coincidence, or maybe not, that the fourteen senators who retired in 1996 were individuals who contributed mightily to the Senate as a deliberative body.[20] They did not all leave the chamber because of its contentiousness, but it is probably not a complete accident that their leave-taking occurred in the wake of the highly partisan, even raucous, 104th Congress. Even though these senators ranged from the acerbic Alan Simpson (R-Wyo.) to the southern moderate Sam Nunn (D-Ga.) to liberal Bill Bradley (D-N.J.) and conservative Hank Brown (R-Colo.), they were widely respected as individuals who could reach across party lines as they pursued their policy goals. As Senator Paul Simon (D-Ill.) once noted, the Senate was much more receptive than the House to the actions of a single legislator: "In the House, everything runs through the committees, and the parties. It's hard to move anything. In the Senate, even if I'm in the minority, all I have to do is convince one fellow Democrat and a couple of Republicans on a subcommittee and I can move ahead."[21] Deliberation can occur in many venues, but, as Simon reminds us, legislators must be open to discussion and the possibility of being convinced.

Above all, in line with Uslaner's findings, there must be trust. As James Thurber (chapter 11) concludes in his examination of the Budget Committee, increasing partisanship and declining levels of trust among committee members have led to a decline in the quality of budget policy deliberation.

There must be structures that allow for, even encourage, deliberation. Gerald Gamm and Steven Smith (chapter 6) examine the "struggle for order" in the nineteenth-century Senate, as the chamber sought to construct greater centralization of power in the office of the president pro tempore. Although the elevation of the majority-party floor leader to the position of Senate leader has addressed many of the order-based concerns, process and debate within the chamber (and on the floor, in particular) remain fluid, relatively informal, and susceptible to manipulation by a willful minority. As a condition for promoting deliberation, civility remains crucial, especially given the requirements for supermajorities and unanimous consent agreements (see chapter 5).

The Senate has long struggled with incivility. Such notable figures as Senate Historian Richard Baker and former Secretary of the Senate Sheila Burke responded to the sentiments expressed by some authors in this volume with cautionary warnings about historic comparisons and contemporary implications, respectively. In one direct comparison, however, the nineteenth-century Senate appears somewhat more civil than its contemporary counterpart. The rhetoric in the 1999 Senate impeachment trial of President Clinton proved "more nasty" than did the statements of senators in the wake of President Andrew Johnson's 1868 trial.[22] Even in such circumstances, the Senate did seem to act with civility in 1999, although it performed little actual deliberation that contained a thoughtful exchange of views.

As Howell Heflin notes, from time to time the Senate can carry out its deliberative role with great dignity and success. Still, declining trust, rising partisanship, and entrenched individualism are not the characteristics that ordinarily foster deliberation. Given the pervasiveness of information and the excellence of communication technologies, we must also face the question of whether deliberation can move beyond legislative chambers, save perhaps on the most important issues of a generation.[23]

The analyses in this volume should give us both pause and hope. Deliberation must be fostered, through structures, norms, and interpersonal relations. Yet it depends so much on the nature of society and how the legislators view the world beyond Capitol Hill. Wrapped in partisanship and individualism, perhaps the best we can expect of the Senate is for it to limp along, resolving the worst conflicts and producing a continuing flow of legislation via the politics of compromise.[24] Whether the body can regain enough civility to engage in the give and take of discourse designed to contribute to the public good remains an open question.

# Notes

1. Quoted in Richard E. Cohen, "John H. Chaffee, 1922–99," *National Journal*, October 30, 1999, p. 1350.

2. For a more detailed analysis, see Frances Lee and Bruce I. Oppenheimer, *Sizing Up the Senate* (University of Chicago Press, 1999).

3. David Brady and Craig Volden, *Resolving Gridlock* (Boulder: Westview Press, 1997); Sarah Binder, "The Dynamics of Legislative Gridlock, 1947–96," *American Political Science Review*, vol. 93 (September 1999), pp. 519–34.

4. For a brief, lively summary, see Robert C. Byrd, *The United States Senate, 1789–1989*, chap. 12, "The Turbulent 1850's" (Washington, D.C.: GPO).

5. Sarah Binder and Steven S. Smith, *Politics or Principle: Filibustering in the United States Senate* (Brookings, 1997), pp. 69–70.

6. Quoted in Joseph Bessette, *The Mild Voice of Reason* (University of Chicago Press, 1994).

7. In general, see Ross Baker, *House and Senate*, 2d ed. (New York: W. W. Norton, 1995).

8. See Ross Baker, "Examining Individualism v. Folkways in the Aftermath of Impeachment," and Burdett Loomis, "The Senate and Impeachment: Explaining the Unique Responsibility of the Exceptional Institution," papers presented at the Norman Thomas Conference on Senate Exceptionalism, Vanderbilt University, Nashville, Tennessee, October 21–23, 1999.

9. This subject has been addressed at length elsewhere, most notably in Binder and Smith, *Politics or Principle*.

10. See Roger Davidson and Walter Oleszek, *Congress and Its Members*, 7th ed. (Washington, D.C.: CQ Press, 2000), pp. 316–17.

11. See chapter 9 in this volume. The authors also provide data on ambassadorial nominations to show that the Democratic Senate of 1991–92 was more likely to hold up nominees than was the Republican Senate of 1995–96.

12. Chuck McCutcheon, "Treaty Vote a 'Wake-Up Call,'" *CQ Weekly Report*, October 16, 1999, p. 2435 ff.

13. Baker, "Examining Individualism v. Folkways"; Loomis, "The Senate and Impeachment."

14. Eric Uslaner, *The Decline of Comity in Congress* (University of Michigan Press, 1993).

15. John Hibbing and Elizabeth Theiss-Morse, *Congress as Public Enemy* (Cambridge University Press, 1995).

16. Aside from chapter 8 in this volume, see Timothy Cook's *Governing with the News: The News Media as a Political Institution* (University of Chicago Press, 1998); and Stephen Hess, *The Washington Reporters* (Brookings, 1981).

17. See, for example, Patrick Sellers, "Promoting the Party Message in the U.S. Senate," paper presented at the Midwest Political Science Association meetings, Chicago, April 15–17, 1999.

18. Uslaner, *The Decline of Comity in Congress*. His argument is more nuanced, of course, and his empirical linkages may be questionable, but little in the years since he wrote this work has suggested that the Congress does not

represent the contentiousness of society, especially as expressed by extreme partisans.

19. See, more generally, Stephen Frantzich and John Sullivan, *The C-SPAN Revolution* (University of Oklahoma Press, 1996).

20. The retirees were Bill Bradley (D-N.J.), Hank Brown (R-Colo.), William Cohen (R-Maine), James Exon (R-Nebr.), Mark Hatfield (R-Oreg.), Howell Heflin (D-Ala.), J. Bennett Johnston (D-La.), Nancy Landon Kassebaum (R-Kans.), Sam Nunn (D-Ga.), Claiborne Pell (D-R.I.), David Pryor (D-Ark.), Paul Simon (D-Ill.), and Alan Simpson (R-Wyo.); their farewell speeches are collected in Norman J. Ornstein, ed., *Lessons and Legacies* (Reading, Mass.: Addison Wesley, 1997). In addition, Senator Bob Dole resigned his seat in June 1996, in order concentrate on his ultimately unsuccessful presidential bid.

21. Paul Simon, personal communication, June 10, 1984.

22. Lee Sigelman, Christopher Deering, and Burdett Loomis, "Words, Words, Words," paper presented at the Midwest Political Science Association meetings, Chicago, April 26–29, 2000.

23. For the most extensive recent analysis of this question, see Bessette, *The Mild Voice of Reason.*

24. See Barbara Sinclair, "The Senate Leadership Dilemma: Passing Bills and Pursuing Partisan Advantage in a Non-Majoritarian Chamber," paper presented at "The Myth of 'Cool Judgment,'" conference held at Florida International University, Miami, January 21, 2000.

# PART I
## *Civility in the U.S. Senate*

CHAPTER TWO

# Constitutional Cohabitation

ROSS K. BAKER

ALONE AMONG ELECTED OFFICIALS of the U.S. federal government, senators share the representation of a constituency with another individual.
The decision, on the part of the Framers of the Constitution, as to the
number of senators accorded each state does not seem to have been a very
contentious one.[1] Giving each state a single senator was rejected because
the illness or death of a solitary senator would deprive a state of representation even if only temporarily. Moreover, travel was exceedingly uncertain, and this too argued for more than a single senator.

At the Constitutional Convention, Gouverneur Morris proposed that
each state be given three senators on the grounds that if a quorum were a
majority, only fourteen senators would be able to transact business, and
that would be vesting too much power in too few individuals. On the other
hand, a chamber in which three or more senators represented a state would
have violated the popular concept that the membership of the Senate not
be excessively large in order that the quality of deliberation be high.[2]

Members of the convention expressed concern about the extravagant
cost of maintaining three senators. The argument that the addition of new
states and the possible creation of others out of existing states would increase membership significantly seemed to be persuasive in holding the
number to two. The related decision that senators would cast their votes
as individuals rather than as a state unit was also adopted without extensive debate, with only Maryland dissenting.

The implications of this decision for the subsequent history of the Senate were more consequential than the number of seats each state would be
given. By abandoning the corporate principle—the voting scheme that
prevailed under the Articles of Confederation—the Framers ensured that

individual volition would be no less important an ingredient than loyalty
to one's state in the deliberations of U.S. senators.[3]

Had the Framers adopted the unit rule, the interpersonal relationships
that prevail between U.S. senators would be far different than they are
now. The necessity for a state's two senators to agree in order that their
state's vote be counted would have compelled consultation and, ultimately,
agreement. The arrangement agreed on by the Framers has yielded, instead, a system in which senators are independent actors with no constitutional obligation to interact with a state's other senator even in a pro
forma fashion.

As a consequence of this decision, senators are free to order their relationships with their state colleague—both political and personal—in whatever manner suits them. Hence relationships range across a broad spectrum,
from a few in which a state's two senators are close political allies and
personal friends to a small number in which the two conspire actively in
the downfall of each other, with most somewhere in between. Senate relationships within this middle range are not intimate. Rather, they can be
characterized as "institutional kinship."[4]

This chapter explores the nature of this relationship. It draws on interviews with fifty incumbent and former senators as well as journalists who
covered their state's congressional delegation, and on a survey of Senate
biographies and autobiographies. The evidence suggests that the relationship is both personal and political. Some measure of personal compatibil-
ity seems to be a precondition for any kind of cooperative relationship
between senators. However, the degree of liking and frequency of contact
between the two may be nominal.

## A Stipulation on Personality

The importance of personality in the forging of these relationships should
therefore be acknowledged. Typical of the initial reaction of senators to
the question of what factors contribute to satisfactory relationships between same-state senators was that of Senator Frank Moss (D-Utah, 1959–
77): "The relationship varies much according to the personality of the
senators." Senator Thomas Eagleton (D-Mo., 1968–87) also observed:
"Sometimes you just can't avoid conflict because of the nature of personalities involved."

Recognizing that personality, in some instances, may trump other factors does not mean that certain institutional, structural, or contextual forces

are not influential in shaping same-state senator relationships. These variables, which are not idiosyncratic in nature, interact with personality factors to either promote or inhibit the typical kind of relationship that prevails in the U.S. Senate.

There was an abiding temptation in the course of my research on same-state senators to attempt to identify variables that pointed conclusively to either cooperative or conflictual relationships. Most intriguing was the possibility that collegial relations are promoted by what would seem to be the most natural of bonds between American politicians: shared partisanship.

Even more provocative is the counterintuitive proposition that it is the senators from different parties who get along the best. But, like so much else in the Senate, the effect of partisanship on relationships is not clearcut. Inasmuch as partisanship and philosophy, with which partisanship often correlates, are such obvious forces in the Senate, I first examined the operation of shared and diverse party identity and ideology as they influence the relationships of same-state senators.

## The Role of Partisanship and Ideology

One of the most surprising responses among the senators interviewed was that shared partisanship is not a very important ingredient in establishing satisfactory relations. Indeed, there was considerable support for the view that it might be better to have a colleague from the opposite party and even one who is ideologically dissimilar. As tempting as it is to embrace an attractive counterintuitive, this one seems to hold only up to a point.

Certainly, the closest relationships that can be documented prevail between senators whose political characteristics are the closest. But some of the worst can also be found between senators matched in party and ideology. The best contemporary example of the former is the relationship between North Dakota's two senators, Kent Conrad and Byron Dorgan, both Democrats and so allied that Senator Conrad's wife is chief of staff to Senator Dorgan. A journalist who follows the North Dakota delegation refers to the two senators as "political soul mates."[5] In the recent past, others in the same category have included Democrats David Pryor and Dale Bumpers of Arkansas and Democrats John Breaux and Bennett Johnston of Louisiana, who shared staff members.

An example of notably poor relations between senators who share virtually every political characteristic can be found with New Jersey Democrats Frank Lautenberg and Robert Torricelli, whose chiefs of staff were reportedly not even on speaking terms. The interoffice softball game that had been held between the two staffs was canceled, and what was supposed to be a meeting with the two senators and two members of New Jersey's House delegation turned out to be two separate meetings because neither Lautenberg nor Torricelli wanted to go to the other's office.[6]

As might be expected, some same-state senators who are not identical in their political characteristics also remain distant. Senator Frank Moss (D-Utah, 1955–77) described his relationship with conservative Republican Wallace Bennett as follows:

> His political philosophy and mine were very different. There was no collaboration whatever at the staff level. He was a Mormon, and I'm a Mormon, but even when we'd go to church at the same time, and I came face to face with him, he'd just say "Hi," and then go right on. He wouldn't talk to me or anything. That party line was the thing that really lowered the shade.[7]

Moss's comments about the influence of personality mentioned earlier suggest strongly that it may be difficult to disentangle that variable from the more objective influences on these relationships.

Perhaps the media's penchant for paying attention to the feuds explains why they are much better documented than the satisfactory relationships. One such feud occurred between Mississippi Democrats Pat Harrison and Theodore Bilbo, who reportedly conspired actively—one might even say gleefully—in each other's downfall. Former Senator Clifford Case (R-N.J., 1955–79), reflecting on the animosities that can strain the ties between senators with similar political traits, mentioned another: "For a long time, [Bob] Packwood [R-Ore.] was not admitted to the Wednesday Club [of Republican senators] because Mark Hatfield [R-Ore.] said, 'You have to make a choice between me and Packwood.' Finally, Hatfield relented and Packwood was admitted." When Case was asked what the source of the conflict between the two liberal Oregon Republicans was, Case was blunt: "Hatfield just considered Packwood . . . unscrupulous."[8]

It is worthwhile exploring the reasons why relationships between senators whose characteristics are so similar can be so bad. Clearly, personality plays a role, but in the minds of senators interviewed, some less idiosyncratic factors are also at work. According to Senator John Danforth (R-Mo.), "The common view in the Senate is that it's easier to have good relations with somebody from the opposite party because you're not competing for exactly the same constituency."[9] Some members at least, Senator Paul Simon added, believe that when a state has two members from different parties, "people expect you to vote differently and there is not that kind of reaction that comes from having your voting records compared."[10] Senator Donald Riegle, a liberal Michigan Democrat like his counterpart Carl Levin, remarked: "There is a general belief that Democrats are generally going to vote the same way most of the time and that two Republicans will vote the same way most of the time. On high-profile votes, if you're in the same party and you come to different conclusions, that obviously can create fallout."[11]

According to a journalist who covered New Jersey's two Democratic senators, Frank Lautenberg and Bill Bradley, a president of the same party as the state's two senators adds a further complication. It has become tradition to have all federal appointments in the state approved by the senior senator of the president's party. Howard E. Shuman, who served as administrative assistant to Democrats Paul Douglas of Illinois and William Proxmire of Wisconsin observed that this tendency for senators of dissimilar partisanship to get along better than those who share party affiliation may be a curious phenomenon to the uninitiated: "There is a good reason for this. Senators from the same party vie with each other for support from people in the party. They vie with each other over judges and postmasters. They vie with each other to see who's going to get credit for projects for the state."[12]

These things do not pose a problem, of course, when there is diversity of partisanship. The senator whose party does not occupy the White House neither expects nor, in general, enjoys any presumptive right to senatorial courtesy. Yet some senators who share the president's partisanship do, as a courtesy, give the senator of the opposing party a certain number of judgeships and U.S. attorneys. This is the arrangement that prevailed in New York with Senators Daniel Patrick Moynihan and Alfonse D'Amato.

Inevitably, the matter of fund-raising tends to complicate the relationships between senators of the same party. As a New Jersey journalist asked, "Now when a senator wants to raise money in the legal community, which is a very fertile field for money, who is going to be more successful in fundraising, the senator who ultimately has the say as to whether one of them becomes a judge, or one who has no part in the process?" The larger question, however, is what happens when two senators who must raise $12,000 a week for six years to be competitive have to tap into the same sources of campaign money?

Presumably, two senators with similar or identical political characteristics would approach the same people for money, but this rivalry suggested by some senators was downplayed by others. Indeed, the quite plausible assumption that two senators who share partisanship and ideology will necessarily have congruent constituencies is open to question. When Robert Bernstein surveyed constituents to determine their attitude toward ideologically disparate senators from the same state, he found ideological distance had little impact on constituent support.[13] If anything, the perceived differences in supporting constituencies may be more distinct where same-state senators come from the same party.

Regardless of party, senators from the same state usually have different committee assignments and consequently have dealings with different policy constituencies both within and outside the state.[14] Different committee assignments allow senators to draw resources—most notably campaign contributions—from different policy domains. These interests may or may not have connections to the state. This is the case whether a state's two senators are of the same or of different parties.

Among the senators interviewed, those who share political traits stressed that their supporting constituency was different from that of their same-party colleague. Senator Gaylord Nelson said of Senator William Proxmire, also a Democrat from Madison, Wisconsin: "Our constituencies overlapped to a degree, but he had support in the business, conservative, money area that I never got. If it were an environmental matter, he would always vote whatever way I was voting because it hadn't been an interest of his."[15] Proxmire responded in the same vein: "Well, I think I was much more anxious than Gaylord to cut spending. Gaylord was a little less concerned about it than I was. On economic issues, he was considerably more liberal than I was. I was more conservative."[16]

Similarly, Donald Riegle of Michigan saw distinctions between his base of support and that of fellow Democrat Carl Levin, one emanating from geographical influences: "Carl came out of the city of Detroit. There are pluses and minuses that go with that in a statewide race in Michigan. I was seen as someone from the outstate area, although coming from an industrial city, Flint." Riegle had been a Republican at one time, he added, and had support in the business community that Levin didn't have. Another difference: "Carl being one of the Jewish members of the Senate . . . had a built-in constituency. The American Jewish community is quite politically active as you know, and they tend to be very supportive of senators who are Jewish. That created a bit of a fund-raising advantage for Carl."[17]

It appears, then, that same-party senators themselves perceive differences and may want to magnify them because greater differentiation will convey an image that the two senators are not carbon copies; therefore both are less susceptible to challengers who argue that the delegation is unbalanced politically. Perceived differentiation between senators of the same party may also enable them to raise fewer eyebrows when they part company on highly visible votes.

One senator's anxiety about being too similar to a colleague of the same party can be seen in the opposition of Connecticut Democrat J. Brien McMahon (1945–52) to the nomination of John Bailey to fill an unexpired Senate term. McMahon believed "it would not sit well with Connecticut voters to have another Irish Catholic represent them in the Senate."[18]

Intraparty factionalism can result from any number of forces: region, ideology, or personalism. This was observable in the Old South, where an appearance of Democratic uniformity cloaked significant differences. An important ingredient fueling the acrimony between Mississippi's Theodore Bilbo and Pat Harrison in the 1930s was that Bilbo had been a protégé of James K. Vardaman and Harrison a protégé of Vardaman's rival, John Sharp Williams.[19]

Even today, states that send nearly identical senators to Washington find tensions can emerge when the two represent different wings of the party. This intraparty factionalism may be based more on personal likes and dislikes than on less idiosyncratic factors such as ideology or regionalism. In recent Maine political history, William Cohen and Olympia Snowe appeared closely allied but represented distinct, and sometimes antagonistic, wings of the Republican party. According to one journalist who observed the Cohen-Snowe relationship,

> Moderate Republicans in Maine are divided between those who back Cohen and those who back Snowe's husband, the former governor John McKernan. There's a lot of personal animosity between those two guys and it goes back to Bangor and some personal slights in the early days when Cohen was a rising star and McKernan was basically a nobody. They have just basically never liked each other.[20]

Another Maine journalist added, "McKernan was Cohen's driver when Cohen was mayor of Bangor and . . . [i]t's all based on that petty stuff. Snowe people and Cohen people. They just can't stand each other, and they don't even try to hide it." Here again, the independent force of personality may be as influential as a more objective variable such as party factionalism.

With senators from the same party, there can often be a heightened likelihood that the junior-senior senator pecking order will trouble the relationship. In Senator Alan Cranston's view, "It seems generally that people of the same party may have more trouble getting along than people of the opposite party. Because of rivalries within the party, or top dog position, or patronage, or positions on issues, or whatever." Senator Donald Riegle elaborated:

> When you're in the same party, there's the question of the primacy of who is the most respected, who is looked to as able to get the most done. How does one carve out an identity and a stature and a standing for himself without having it seen in terms of: "If that's how I look, how does my colleague who's got the same job in the same party look?" . . . So when you've got two people competing directly for affection, commitment, and response, there's an inherently competitive situation going on there that's just inescapable.

While it may be the case, objectively, that the constituencies of two senators of the same party are distinct, and that the two may even be seen by voters and supporters as distinct players with widely different interests, comparison is inevitable. And competition for media coverage and political credit affects the relationship. A New Jersey journalist who covered Senators Bradley and Lautenberg argued that Lautenberg, who came to the Senate four years after Bradley, had to be even more aggressive in getting media coverage than the average senator: "If he let Bradley remain that well-known, it would be a mortal threat to Lautenberg's reelection, because they would compare the two and say, 'You're not a Bradley'. And that could be a fatal indictment to a junior senator." Summing up the media competition between the two Democrats, the journalist added, "It's two fannies fighting for the same stool."

## Agreeing to Disagree

In the case of same-state senators of opposing parties, they are generally expected to be in disagreement on issues. Certainly, those who hold widely different views on explosive social issues such as abortion rights are not likely to have a high level of agreement. Such senators simply acknowledge that they will part company.

## Credit Battles at Home

On issues relating to the state that both senators represent, a rather different attitude prevails. As Senator Alan Cranston described it: "The Republicans I served with—and I always had fairly conservative Republicans serving with me—we differed on the big national issues, but where we could get together on an issue was where it affected California. Then we were able to get things done." Differing with a colleague of the opposing party over macroeconomic issues and social issues while attempting to work in harmony on state issues appears to be an important ingredient in the maintenance of stable working relationships.

It is, however, the state issues that often contain the seeds of contention because of the natural desire on the part of politicians to claim credit for their accomplishments on behalf of the state. As Missouri's Thomas Eagleton put it, "There is always a tendency to want to grab the credit. You know, 'Senator so-and-so announces ten million dollars for such-and-such.'"

A former staff member for New Jersey's Bill Bradley who shared representation with fellow Democrat Frank Lautenberg expressed strongly the importance of claiming credit: "It's the ink back home and who gets credit for what. These guys feel, and with good reason, that they break their ass and nobody knows about it."

Credit is only part of the problem with state issues. Senators may, of course, disagree on the substance of a measure that affects the state. Even when Alan Cranston and John Tunney generally worked well in the face of differences, as they did on the Desert Bill, it was, Cranston said, "difficult not having a fellow Democrat to go along with on that bill."

In like manner, Wisconsin Democrats William Proxmire and Gaylord Nelson disagreed on the construction of a dam on the Kickapoo River. "It was a bad project," Nelson said. "I came out against it and Proxmire strongly supported it . . . but when the newspapers came out against it, he changed his mind. We never had any disputes about that. He had his position and I had mine. We didn't even bother to discuss it."

## Friction Induced by Staff and Supporters

Senators do not interact with one another as individuals, but rather as the center of a small universe that contains political supporters, representatives of interest groups, and personal and committee staffs. Because so much senator-to-senator interaction is conducted through intermediaries and because, especially in the case of same-state, same-party senators, some supporters may be common to both, the danger is considerable that the principals will be dragged into a quarrel by their agents.

To a surprising degree, the senators I interviewed pointed to supporters and staff as a major complicating factor in senator-to-senator relationships. Paul Simon volunteered: "You want to stick up for your staff, and so things can get pretty prickly. It can be something really trivial, but usually there's been a background of relationship that's not so good, so a trivial little thing can kick it off." More colorfully, Senator Eugene McCarthy (D-Minn., 1959–71) quipped: "It's like the knights and their squires. Even though the knights got along all right up in the banquet hall, the squires would be down in the stable cuffing each other around."

Senator Chuck Hagel (R-Neb.) pointed to another source of outside interference. "There are supporters who have been close to you during your campaign, not necessarily your inner circle but the inner ring of people who advise you and feel protective toward you, and who came to you before they came to the other senator from your party. There's a lot of edginess there in the party when you're in the same party."[21]

## The Etiquette of Institutional Kinship

Gaylord Nelson and William Proxmire, quite independent of one another, characterized their relationship in much the same way. Nelson said, "There was never any problem at all between Bill and me. During the 18 years I was there we never had any personal clashes of any kind. He followed his course and I followed mine. Frequently they were together, frequently they weren't." Proxmire did not recall "any real conflict of any kind" either: "When Gaylord disagreed with me, I thought, 'Fine, Gaylord has his reasons and from his own standpoint he may even be right.' I'm sure he felt the same way about me."

The relationship of the two Wisconsin Democrats comes close to being an archetypal institutional kinship: not intimate but respectful, tolerant of difference, and, if not enthusiastically supportive, certainly not averse to helpful gestures. The etiquette of institutional kinship shows how the concept operates. For same-party senators, the following behavior tends to be associated with institutional kinship:

—Taking no active role in a primary election against a colleague.

—Coordinating fund-raising activities so that they do not conflict with those of the colleague facing the closest reelection contest.

—Agreeing, either formally or informally, on the announcement of federal projects beneficial to the state.

—Agreeing, either by active coordination or acquiescence, on patronage nominations.

—Giving cues on issues and votes (these flow from the senator who is better acquainted with the issue to the less well-informed senator).

One "rule" of etiquette often referred to in the interviews pertains to colleagues of the opposite party, namely, that a senator refrain from harsh, negative attacks on a colleague of the opposing party and that the senator not facing reelection play a limited role on behalf of the challenger of his own party. This particular practice appears so prominent that it warrants a closer look.

Missouri Republican John Danforth summarized the etiquette of campaigning against a colleague of the opposing party: "My own situation with Senator Eagleton [Danforth's Democratic colleague] was that I would really lie low. It was really the minimal amount of going through the motions: never criticizing the other guy, maybe signing a fund-raising letter for the Republican, but it was very low visibility for each of us when the other person was running."[22] Similarly, Dennis DeConcini (D-Ariz.) recalled:

> The last time [Barry] Goldwater [R-Ariz.] was up, a guy by the name of Bill Schultz ran against him. . . . Schultz and I were pretty friendly and he wanted me to do a commercial against Goldwater and I would not do it. I did appear with Schultz at a rodeo and there was a picture of us on the front page of the paper, but I was also quoted as making some positive remarks about Goldwater. It was the closest race Barry ever had and he called me after the election and thanked me for staying out of his race.[23]

An even higher standard of bipartisan campaign etiquette was found in the relationship of Maine's Democratic Senator George Mitchell and his Republican counterpart Bill Cohen. As described by a Maine political journalist,

> The last time George Mitchell ran, it so happened that the guy running against him—Jasper Wyman—had gotten Cohen to be his honorary campaign chairman. Now Cohen and Mitchell had co-authored a book about Iran-Contra and were having joint book signings during the campaign. At one of them, Jasper Wyman shows up and there is his honorary chairman signing books with his opponent.

Even more notable are bipartisan gestures such as New York Republican Al D'Amato's criticism of Democrat Pat Moynihan's 1994 Republican opponent Bernadette Castro or Republican Senator Gordon Smith's tour of his own area of Eastern Oregon with Portland Democrat Ron Wyden. Typical institutional kinship relationships do not go that far, however.[24]

Just holding one's fire against a colleague is usually sufficient. As Illinois Democrat Paul Simon noted, "You know, these guys are pros. If you get up and say, 'Joe Smith is a great guy and I'm happy to be here supporting him,' your colleague of the other party understands and nothing will be said about it. If you get up and start lambasting him, that's a different situation."

## Senatorial Prenuptials

There is evidence that some senators, anticipating that strife may erupt between them, go to the trouble of signing what amounts to a treaty or a prenuptial agreement that sets the ground rules for cooperation. Such an agreement was formalized by Senators Ron Wyden and Gordon Smith of Oregon. The two had opposed one another in the 1995 special election to replace Bob Packwood, who had resigned. In a campaign marked by especially harsh television advertising, Wyden, the Democrat, won narrowly. In 1996 Smith, a Republican, won the seat of the retiring Mark Hatfield. The two former opponents were to be colleagues.

> Shortly after the November election, Wyden and Smith agreed to talk. They met for breakfast in a corner booth at the Pazzo Restaurant in downtown Portland . . . and quickly resolved lingering hard feelings. . . . Wyden and Smith also recognized a political reality: They had run their last campaigns against each other. Although both pledged to serve all Oregonians, each could cater to the distinct constituencies who elected them.[25]

Wyden and Smith have established a kind of model for collegial cooperation in the Senate. Wyden, with his base in the more liberal Portland area, has welcomed Smith onto his turf, and Smith, from Pendleton in conservative eastern Oregon, traveled through his region with Wyden at his side to introduce the Democrat to his core constituency.

A similar agreement was made between Nebraska Democrat Bob Kerrey and his newly elected Republican colleague, Chuck Hagel. The two actually formalized their agreement in a five-page document. Hagel, the newcomer to the Senate, noted wryly that the agreement was concluded in the office of the senior senator.

## The Dynamics of Senate Relationships

Interviews with incumbent senators on the subject of their relationship with their same-state colleague are generally not very enlightening. Most of the interviews I conducted elicited platitudes or "false positives": professions of friendship that simply did not square with the reports of those who had observed the relationship.

The same-state senator relationship is among the most delicate in American politics. Incumbents are reluctant to go on the record with candid comments about the relationship, especially if they are negative. The Lautenberg-Torricelli relationship was a notable recent exception.

Even for those senators whose relationships are icy, public behavior rarely betrays any hint of rancor. In the manner of a married couple who can barely stand the sight of one another but who do not bicker in public, senators are adept at presenting a positive face to the world. Speaking of the chilly relationship between Maine's two senators, a political reporter from the state remarked that

> Cohen and Snowe don't like each other. The fight here in Maine almost feels like the fight in Ireland. Everything goes back to something that frigging William of Orange did three hundred years ago. It doesn't make a whole lot of sense, but it continues and it's real. . . .
> I think you see the same situation with [Susan] Collins and Snowe, but neither one will let it show up in public in any way.

While many of the relationships, both good and bad, take on a kind of stability over time, neither enmity nor accord is permanently encoded in them. Ohio Democrats John Glenn and Howard Metzenbaum nursed a feud that went back to a Democratic primary in 1970 in which the relatively unknown Metzenbaum narrowly defeated the celebrity astronaut. The bad feelings persisted until 1984, but by 1988 Glenn was defending Metzenbaum against an unfair media attack during the latter's reelection campaign.[26]

Even the disputatious Democrats from New Jersey, Frank Lautenberg and Robert Torricelli, managed a temporary truce in May 1998 when Lautenberg invited his colleague to share a chartered plane from Washington to an event in East Brunswick. An observer of the two men on the flight quipped: "They flew up and back together and nobody was thrown out of the plane. Was that peace? I don't know, but it was a completed flight."[27]

The truce did not last a year. By early 1999, the relationship had deteriorated to a level of public vituperation with few precedents in the history of the U.S. Senate. That these relationships are subject to change, both for the better and also for the worse, alerts us to the changing contexts in which senatorial pairs operate and also to the protean nature of human behavior.

## Payoffs for Cooperative Relationships

I had hypothesized that when asked about the payoffs of cooperative relationships with their same-state colleague, senators would emphasize the benefits cooperation would bring to the state. Remarkably, no senator stressed state benefits. For the most part, the emphasis was on personal satisfaction and a more serene quality of life.

The answer of Charles Percy (R-Ill.) was typical: "The payoff [was] just getting along. You'd sooner have a friend than an enemy." This sentiment was echoed by Gaylord Nelson: "If you don't find ways to work things out with the other senator, life would be pretty miserable down here." Thomas Eagleton was even more emphatic:

> The payoff is peace of mind. You know, there are enough annoyances that go with the job in terms of a staggering amount of mail, constituent requests, do this, do that, demands on you when you go back to the state, go here, go there, speak here, speak there, sessions that last until three in the morning, and all these demands take a toll on a senator. Why add to that list of grief a nasty relationship with the colleague from your own home state. It's in everybody's best interest.

## Conclusions

Senators have numerous incentives to maintain the kind of cooperative relationship found in the institutional kinship described in this chapter. At the same time, drawing on the theory of minimum winning coalitions, one can say they have little incentive to go beyond what it takes to coexist tolerably with a colleague. Few senators look to colleagues for intimacy.

Those who seek true friends tend to find them outside the highly competitive realm of politics.

Cooperative relationships appear to be formed out of a keen sense of self-interest and self-preservation. Even when the political histories of a state's two senators point to a future of strife, they can take active steps to avoid clashes because it is in their interest and convenient to do so.

Accordingly, when Republican Gordon Smith takes Democrat Ron Wyden to his own area of Oregon and speaks well of him to his own core constituency, his motives may be less altruistic than what meets the eye. Knowing that Wyden's 1998 opponent was regarded as a weak challenger and that Wyden was likely to be his colleague for the next six years, Smith took out a kind of insurance policy on his own peace of mind.

Pat Moynihan might, at one time, have been privately contemptuous of Al D'Amato, as one journalist suggested, but his junior senator was a known quantity who meddled little in the areas that Moynihan cared about. A Democrat with interests closer to Moynihan's or someone more apt to be an intellectual soul mate might also turn out to be a trespasser on Moynihan's most cherished issues. The senatorial calculation seems straightforward and unsentimental.

Agreement pays off most conspicuously for senators when it concerns the state they jointly represent. Differences on national or international questions—especially when two people of opposing parties are concerned—can be dismissed as normal disagreement. Strife on state issues is readily picked up by media in the state and conveyed to the people that both senators want to keep happy, the voters.

Though senators appear to define payoffs in terms of their own personal comfort, a public good may indeed arise out of cooperative relationships. Evidence to indicate that states with cooperative senators receive more benefits than states whose senators are at odds is difficult to muster, but it makes intuitive sense that such is the case. Anecdotal evidence suggests that enmity, at the very least, makes for a less cohesive and less effective congressional delegation and that the transaction costs for hostile senators become unacceptably large.

## Notes

All unattributed quotations are from interviews conducted by the author.

1. Daniel Wirls and Stephen Wirls, "The Senate and American Democracy," unpublished ms. (draft of October 18, 1996), pp. 42–43. See also George H. Haynes, *The Senate of the United States* (Boston: Houghton Mifflin, 1938), p. 10.

2. *Federalist* No. 62.

3. The importance of individual volition in the Senate in the deliberations of the Constitutional Convention was argued forcefully by Elaine K. Swift in "The Making of an American House of Lords: The U.S. Senate in the Constitutional Convention of 1787," *Studies in American Political Development*, vol. 7 (1993), pp. 177–224.

4. Ross K. Baker, *Friend and Foe in the U.S. Senate* (New York: Free Press, 1980), pp. 44–46.

5. Albert Eisele, "Lucy Calautti, Low Profile Power on the Hill," *The Hill*, Wednesday March 8, 1995.

6. Adam Piore, "N.J. Senate Delegation Finds Two Is a Crowd," *The Record*, November 16, 1997. The climax of the Lautenberg-Torricelli feud came in early March 1999 at a meeting of Democratic senators at the Library of Congress. The senators were being briefed by Torricelli, who was serving as chairman of the party's Senate campaign committee. Furious that Torricelli had omitted any mention of the New Jersey seat that he would be vacating in 2000, Lautenberg denounced Torricelli. See Jane Mayer, "Wind on Capitol Hill," *New Yorker*, March 15, 1999.

7. Interview with Frank Moss, December 5, 1996.

8. Interview with Clifford R. Case, February 5, 1979.

9. Interview with Senator John Danforth, November 19, 1996.

10. Interview with Senator Paul Simon, October 16, 1997.

11. Interview with Senator Donald Riegle, September 30, 1997.

12. Interview with Howard E. Shuman, Oral History Interviews, July 22 to October 22, 1987, U.S. Senate Historical Office, Washington, D.C., pp. 299–300.

13. Robert A. Bernstein, "Determinants of Differences in Feelings towards Senators Representing the Same State, "*Western Political Quarterly*, vol. 45 (September 1992), pp. 701–21.

14. Wendy J. Schiller, "States as Two-Member Districts: The Effect of Dual Representation on Senate Behavior and Constituent Awareness," paper presented at the annual meeting of the American Political Science Association, San Francisco, August 29–September 1, 1996, p. 18. This paper was a condensation of Schiller's later book, *Partners and Rivals: Representation in U.S. Senate Delegations* (Princeton University Press, 2000).

15. Interview with Senator Gaylord Nelson, November 24, 1997.

16. Interview with Senator Donald Riegle, September 30, 1997.

17. Interview with Senator William Proxmire, October 7, 1997.

18. Sidney Hyman, *The Lives of William Benton* (University of Chicago Press, 1969), p. 407.

19. Martha H. Swain, *Pat Harrison, The New Deal Years* (University of Mississippi Press, 1978), pp. 4–5.

20. *The Washingtonian*, June 1998, stated that "Defense Secretary Bill Cohen and Olympia Snowe snarled at each other when he was senator from Maine." This statement brought a rejoinder in the form of a jointly signed letter from Cohen and Snowe in the next issue stating, "Throughout the years, we have enjoyed an excellent working relationship as well as a close personal friendship, and

contrary to the completely unfounded characterization in *The Washingtonian*, neither of us can recall even a single instance in which a disagreeable word passed between us."

21. The distinctions made by Hagel reflect the same kind of complexity of perception described by Richard F. Fenno Jr. in *Homestyle* (New York: HarperCollins, 1978).

22. Interview with Senator John Danforth, November 19, 1997.

23. Interview with Senator Dennis DeConcini, December 20, 1996.

24. See Todd S. Purdum, "G.O.P. Contender Asserts D'Amato Is Undercutting Her Bid," *New York Times*, October 18, 1994; and Jim Barnett, "Oregon's Senators Are a Complimentary Couple," *Portland Oregonian*, January 4, 1998.

25. Jim Barnett, "Unlikely Partners," *Sunday Oregonian*, January 26, 1997.

26. Richard F. Fenno Jr., *The Presidential Odyssey of John Glenn* (Washington, D.C.: CQ Press, 1990), pp. 14, 255.

27. Robert Cohen and Scott Orr, "Look Who's Talking Again," *Star Ledger*, May 15, 1998.

# CHAPTER THREE

# Is the Senate More Civil than the House?

## ERIC M. USLANER

THE DEBATE ON IMPEACHING President Bill Clinton in the House of Representatives was marked by a "distrust [that] is so deep-seated and enduring that there are only downticks in the steady rise in animosity."[1] Representative Jose Serrano (D-N.Y.) admonished the Republican majority that voted to impeach the president on an almost strict party-line vote: "Bullies get theirs and you're going to get yours!" Representative Albert Wynn (D-Md.) warned: "There's raw feelings. It's going to take a long, long time to heal and there's not going to be any love fest." Representative David Skaggs (D-Colo.) said: "Nobody knows whether this place is going to be pulled apart so much that we can't do our business." And Representative David Obey (D-Wis.) summed it up: "We are on the short route to chaos."[2]

The Senate trial of the president did have its low points, notably when the senators went into closed session with no cameras to bring the proceedings to the public.[3] Overall, the Senate conducted its business in a much more civil manner than the House. It papered over partisan differences by unanimously adopting vague rules of procedure. Although Senate votes on procedure were often partisan, senators met in informal groups and worked out compromises that prevented the sort of outbursts that occurred in the House. Eventually, the Senate did not convict the president on either of the two counts before it. Senator Christopher J. Dodd (D-Conn.) pointed to "the other body" and said, "It's so acrimonious there. It's so sad."[4]

The House impeachment proceedings were nonstop partisan warfare, with members casting aspersions about each other's motives. The carnage included admissions by Speaker-designate Bob Livingston (R-La.) and House Judiciary Committee chair Henry Hyde (R-Ill.) that they had had extramarital affairs in the past. Livingston subsequently gave up both his new leadership position and his seat in the House. Calls for restraint were regarded as frontal attacks. Representative Tony P. Hall (D-Ohio), who has long worried about the decline in civility in Congress, lamented: "We have real partisanship, and I would like to move beyond that." Representative John Lindner (R-Ga.) took "personal affront" at the implication that Republicans were to blame for the partisanship.

Senators and journalists attributed the Senate's civil deliberations to its long-standing tradition of courtesy, to the bipartisan friendships that permit senators to reach agreement even in the face of policy disagreements, to the six-year term that gives senators more freedom to repel outsiders who would push them to extremes, and to a simple fear of replicating the contentiousness of the House debate.[5] According to Joel Achenbach of the *Washington Post*:

> The Senate has always been clubby. There is little chance that two Senators would have a dust-up like that of congressmen Bob Barr [R-Ga.] and Patrick Kennedy [D-R.I.] on the day of the House impeachment vote. Needing to win election statewide, few senators are ideologically as extreme as the representatives, who can emerge from a smaller and more homogenous congressional district. In recent years, when new members have come on too strong and thrown too many elbows, said Patrick Leahy [D] of Vermont, "they were quickly taken aside by senior members of both sides and told, 'The Senate's different.'"[6]

Senators boast of their ability to work with members of both parties. The compromises on impeachment were worked out by bipartisan teams such as Slade Gorton (R-Wash.) and Joseph Lieberman (D-Conn.), Dianne Feinstein (D-Calif.) and Robert Bennett (R-Utah), Tom Harkin (D-Iowa) and Susan Collins (R-Maine), and even the unlikely pair of Edward Kennedy (D-Mass.) and Phil Gramm (R-Tex.).[7]

So the Senate is different? Not so fast. Over a century ago, Woodrow Wilson cautioned that "the Senate is just what the . . . conditions of public life in this country make it to be. . . . The Senate can have in it no better men than the best men of the House of Representatives." The upper chamber, then, is "a small, select, and leisurely House of Representatives."[8] And, as I shall argue below, understanding the limits of civility requires heeding the words of Richard Nixon's attorney general, John Mitchell: "Watch what we do, not what we say." Civility alone, to paraphrase former vice president John Nance Garner, isn't worth a warm bucket of spit. Civility matters because it is part of comity, a more general syndrome of treating others with respect both in language and in deed. And the Senate shows that there is plenty of reason to be wary of restricting our attention to words spoken on the floor. Senators obstruct. Representatives can't block legislation so easily, so they make a lot of noise instead. Legislators, like young children, only create a scene when they can't get their way.

Wilson makes two key arguments that help us understand comity in the House and the Senate. First, whatever differences we find between the two chambers are of degree rather than of kind. It is a fundamental mistake to talk about a House of Representatives out of control and a Senate that keeps the republic on an even keel. Second, the behavior of both representatives and senators is *not* simply posturing among elites. The name-calling in the House on impeachment reflects deeper conflicts between the two parties that were about to take over the Senate as well, until it became clear that the public was growing weary of the whole enterprise.[9] While the public was critical of the way the House and the Senate conducted the impeachment hearings, popular attitudes were also polarized along partisan lines.[10]

I shall lay out my framework for looking at comity in Congress and then consider arguments as to why the Senate should have more comity than the House, and why the senators can speak softly and still carry the big stick of obstructionism. Then I shall review a bit of impressionistic evidence on the House and the Senate and move to a consideration of "harder" statistical evidence, supporting my argument.

## Civility and Comity, House and Senate

The Senate *is* more civil than the House, but civility is not an end in itself.[11] Debate in the Congress is full of flowery language such as "I yield to my good friend, the distinguished gentleman (gentlelady) from _____, who is my good friend."[12] This civility or, as Donald Matthews called it, "courtesy," is a key norm of the Senate.[13] Courtesy involves treating others with respect, even—or especially—if they disagree with you. William S. White wrote more than four decades ago: "To grant to one's opponent in high political discussion and maneuver each and all of the rights that one demands for oneself—this is . . . a Senate rule."[14] The mark of a good senator, according to White, is "the absence of petty exhibitionism" and "amicable association with other minds and with the interests of others."[15] Personal attacks on other members are prohibited by Senate (and House) rules. The logical extension of courtesy is friendship. In a chamber with only 100 members—and less than that for most of American history—and a historically weak party system, personal connections mean a lot. As Ross K. Baker has argued in his study of friendship patterns in the Senate, "the slender threads of common experience, fellowship, trust, and mutuality—the components of institutional kinship—serve to provide an important, perhaps indispensable, force for cohesion."[16]

Senatorial politics often makes strange friendships. Former senator Alfonse D'Amato (R-N.Y.) often had few charitable words for his colleagues; he called Kennedy "an extreme, disingenuous partisan," Howard Metzenbaum (D-Ohio) "a dictator," and the collective members of Congress a "bunch of turkeys." He saw nothing wrong with bringing the entire Senate to a halt through a filibuster. Yet D'Amato had nothing but kind words for his Democratic colleague from New York, Daniel Patrick Moynihan, who "has served New York with distinction."[17]

Civil language makes friendship possible. When people are denouncing each other, they are not likely to become friendly. And friendship makes compromise across partisan and ideological lines possible, for two reasons. First, friends have confidence in each other and will be willing to take each other at their word. Second, and more critically, legislators form friendships across party lines only when it is politically safe to do so, when members believe that they have something in common.

Strong friendship circles across party lines signify a legislature marked by trust. This is where civility turns into comity. Comity is more than being civil to others. It also involves reciprocity, which simply means that people must respect their promises and obligations to others. They must also recognize that another point of view is legitimate. Reciprocity involves respecting other people *and their expertise*. It means willingness to make deals and committing oneself to sticking with the agreement. Without reciprocity, you get either rule by a partisan majority or stalemate.

It is natural to think of senators huddling together in the well of the chamber and making deals with one another other. The Senate is, above all, a chamber of individuals. The Senate has few rules, and routine legislative business is usually accomplished through unanimous consent agreements.[18] A single senator can tie the Senate up in knots and a minority (forty-one) can sustain a filibuster even in the face of a determined majority. Without a commitment to reciprocity, the Senate could well come to a complete halt.

The House, on the other hand, is more majoritarian. It has an elaborate set of rules that in recent years has been increasingly used to restrict minority party rights. The House membership is four and a half times as large as the Senate's. Individual members cannot bring the House to a halt. The two-year election cycle means that members have less time to chat with their colleagues since they must spend more time courting the folks back home.

Nevertheless, the norms of courtesy (or civility) and reciprocity have also been central to House deliberations. It was a Speaker of the House— Sam Rayburn (D-Tex.)—who coined the phrase that has become the hallmark of reciprocity in Congress: "To get along, go along." Personal friendships among House leaders—Rayburn and Republican Joseph Martin (R-Mass.) and Speaker Thomas P. "Tip" O'Neill (D-Mass.) and Minority Leader Bob Michel (R-Ill.)—are more legendary than close relationships among Senate leaders. Rayburn would court other members by inviting them to his "Board of Education," a daily strategy meeting in an unmarked hideaway office in the Capitol where members shared bourbon and water mixed by the Speaker himself. Members came only at the invitation of the Speaker, who made it his business to be as inclusive as he needed or wanted to be.[19] In those years, good relations were just as important to junior members. Representative Clem Miller (D-Calif.) summed up his freshman experience in a 1962 book: "One's overwhelming first impression as a member of Congress is the aura of friendliness that surrounds the life of a congressman. . . . The freshman congressman is being constantly made aware of the necessity, even the imperative, of getting along with his fellow congressmen."[20] Members of the House have traditionally depended upon reciprocity just as senators have.[21]

## The Waning of the Norms

The classic discussions of the norms of courtesy and reciprocity were written in the 1950s and the 1960s.[22] By the 1970s Congress was becoming a less civil place. Watergate, the two energy crises, the continuing conflict in Vietnam, and especially the economic turbulence of the 1970s made American social and political life far more contentious. The core American belief that the future will be better than the past gave way to a pessimism about the future, not just next year, but the longer term. There is good reason for recent pessimism: the gap between the rich and poor has been growing larger over time, so the poor have less prospect of faring well in the future. When people are pessimistic, they look out for themselves first and see others as doing the same. In such a world, it makes less sense to trust other people and to be willing to make the compromises that underlie reciprocity.

The 1970s saw an outbreak of incivility in both Congress and in public life. The freshman class of House members of 1975 were weaned politically in the civil rights and anti-Vietnam protest movements. Many members were at least as comfortable with strategies of confrontation as with norms of civility and reciprocity.[23] Every House freshman responding to a 1969 survey said that friendly relations with other members were important. By 1976 only 63 percent of new freshmen agreed that "personal cordiality" was important, and four years later just 37 percent took this position. In 1969 72 percent of freshmen said that they were likely to trade votes. By 1976 and 1980 just about half of new members said that "ability to compromise" was essential.[24]

Uncivil language knew no bounds at first. The mild-mannered Bob Michel (R-Ill.) attacked Jack Kemp (R-N.Y.) over their positions on Contra aid in 1987, while Guy Vander Jagt (R-Mich.) likened his challenger for chair of the National Republican Congressional Committee, Don Sundquist (R-Tenn.), to Iraqi dictator Saddam Hussein in 1990.[25] However, most of the attacks, even initially, were partisan.

A serious confrontation took place in 1985 when Representative Bob Dornan (R-Calif.) grabbed Representative Thomas Downey (D-N.Y.) by his tie and accused him and other Democrats of being weak on defense. Five years later, Representatives Bob Walker (R-Pa.) and Craig Washington (D-Tex.) had to be restrained from battling over intemperate remarks from Henry Hyde (R-Ill.) to Barney Frank (D-Mass.). One can construct a litany of diatribes from the collected speeches of Dornan, Frank, and Representative Maxine Waters (D-Calif.), mostly addressed to members of the other party.

Incivility became increasingly partisan in the 1980s. Sometimes barely more than a handful of House members succeeded in bringing the House to a halt. These self-proclaimed kamikazes, the Conservative Opportunity Society, used obstructionist tactics and a plethora of controversial amendments to block even routine legislation. An upstart junior Republican named Newt Gingrich organized the rebels. The Senate might be helpless in the face of such an onslaught. The House majority leadership simply tightened the screws by adopting more restrictive rules against minority ob-structionism.[26] Gingrich in turn launched attacks on the personal morality of Speaker Jim Wright in 1989 (successful) and Speaker-designate Tom Foley shortly thereafter. When civility mattered more, a Gingrich would have been relegated to the back benches and treated as a pariah. Instead, his attacks on Wright and Foley (and even on Dole, whom he once called "the tax collector for the welfare state") led to his rise to minority whip of the House, and to the Speakership itself in 1995.[27]

Once the Republicans took over the House in 1995, there was no effec-tive majority party in the lower chamber. The Republicans could not shed their guerrilla tactics in favor of a more disciplined leadership style. The Democrats began to act like the old GOP minority. Their actions were both purposive (giving the Republicans a dose of their own medicine) and involuntary (they did not know how to behave as a responsible opposi-tion). Venom became the order of the day. Representative Sam Gibbons (D-Fla.), the seventy-five-year-old erstwhile chair of the Ways and Means Committee, believed that new subcommittee chair Bill Thomas (R-Calif.) was stalling a hearing on health legislation. He called Thomas and his GOP colleagues "a bunch of fascists." Republican members taunted him, and Gibbons grabbed Thomas's tie. Thomas got revenge by shutting off House microphones when Democrats were speaking one Saturday, and then closing House restaurants when the Democrats showed up to eat.

Representatives James P. Moran (D-Va.) and Randy "Duke" Cunningham (D-Calif.) challenged each other's patriotism on military in-terventions, which led Moran to shove Cunningham and half a dozen other members to join in the wrestling match.[28] Republican Whip Dick Armey (R-Tex.) called Frank, an openly gay member, "Barney Fag" in 1995, and three years later Cunningham made an obscene hand gesture and a crude remark about Frank's sexuality in a speech to a group of prostate cancer patients.[29] In 1998 House Rules Committee chair Gerald Solomon (R-N.Y.) asked on the floor: "Is it appropriate in this House for a Member to accuse other Members, even without mentioning a name, of being religious wackos?"[30]

The mood in Congress has gotten so bad that an outside agency, the Pew Foundation, has tried to restore comity by sponsoring two retreats in Hershey, Pennsylvania, to get members of the House talking to each other. The 1997 getaway was marked by good spirits all around, but the cheer-fulness quickly faded. About a month later, the House Rules Committee Subcommittee on Rules and Organization of the House saw the depth of the problem and held hearings on what might be done to restore civility. The initial hearings were called to a halt when the members had to scurry to the House floor to vote on a motion to censure a House Democratic leader for insulting the Speaker.[31] The 1999 meeting came after each party had inflicted further wounds on the other during the debate on the impeachment of President Clinton. Two weeks before the retreat, one of the Democratic party's leaders (Steny Hoyer, D-Md.) said that the gathering would be a good opportunity to lecture the Republicans on how to behave more civilly.

The world of courtesy had been turned upside down. Civility gave way to unrestrained partisanship and to a frontal assault on reciprocity. The new members of the House no longer accepted committees as experts on policy. Instead, they took more of the action directly to the floor. Members became more likely to offer amendments to bills even if they did not serve on the originating committees. Members of both the House *and the unreformed Senate* became more likely to adopt amendments offered by committee outsiders.[32] The share of amendments in the House that came from outside the originating committee increased, as did the number of senators offering amendments outside their committee.[33]

The waning of reciprocity and courtesy signaled more than a new breed of member and a more contentious agenda. Senator Joseph Biden (D-Del.) summed up the new mood that engulfed the upper chamber in the late 1970s and early 1980s:

> There's much less civility than when I came here ten years ago. There aren't as many nice people as there were before. . . . Ten years ago you didn't have people calling each other sons of bitches and vowing to get at each other. The first few years, there was only one person who, when he gave me his word, I had to go back to the office to write it down. Now there's two dozen of them. As you break down the social amenities one by one, it starts expanding geometrically. Ultimately you don't have any social control. . . . We end up with 100 Proxmires here. One . . . makes a real contribution. All you need is 30 of them to guarantee that the place doesn't work.[34]

Ross K. Baker noted almost two decades ago that "the Senate is verging on a system in which each senator is his own judge of acceptable behavior in a colleague."[35]

The Senate was hardly more civil than the House. Moderate Republican Senator Lowell Weicker (Conn.) called his centrist GOP colleague

John Heinz (Pa.) "devious" and "an idiot." Capitol police carried Bob
Packwood (R-Oreg.) feet first into the chamber after "arresting" him for
boycotting a Senate session and depriving Democrats of a quorum on a
cloture vote in 1988.[36]

Dole and Ernest Hollings (D-S.C.) got into a sharp exchange the next
year over whose personal attacks were more bitter. Dole suggested what
seemed to be an old-style playground brawl:[37] "I say to my friend from
South Carolina, I will be glad to discuss this with him privately, or maybe
he wants to go out and make that statement when not protected by speaking from the Senate floor."

The Senate, unlike the House, has always tolerated "outsiders" who go
their way and do not always observe the norm of reciprocity. Wisconsin's
William Proxmire (D) and Oregon's Wayne Morse (R-I, and then D) are
prime examples of senators who did not play by all the rules but made a
difference anyway.[38] The contemporary Senate—even more so than Biden's
Senate of the early 1980s—has a rather healthy complement of members
who disdain the niceties of the old Senate norms. More than a handful of
today's Republican senators cut their teeth in the House, where they learned
first-strike tactics from the master guerrilla turned leader, Newt Gingrich:
Tim Hutchinson (Ark.), Wayne Allard (Colo.), Larry Craig (Idaho), Michael
Crapo (Idaho), Jim Bunning (Ky.), Rod Grams (Minn.), Rick Santorum
(Pa.), Sam Brownback (Kans.), Jim Inhofe (Okla.), Mike DeWine (Ohio),
Judd Gregg (N.H.), Bob Smith (N.H.), and Connie Mack (Fla.) all served
under Gingrich's tutelage as either assistant minority leader or Speaker.
This baker's dozen (though not a Baker's dozen) of senators has pushed
the GOP Senate conference sharply to the right. Several vocally protested
the Senate's refusal to call witnesses before television cameras in the impeachment trial.[39]

Senate rhetoric is generally not as shrill as the voices in the House. Yet
senators sometimes step over the line, as Majority Leader Trent Lott did in
1997 when he said that two freshman Democratic senators—Robert Toricelli
(N.J.) and Tim Johnson (S.Dak.)—deceived their constituents and were dishonest.[40] Senators are hardly restrained in using the guerrilla tactics that
House rebels could only dream about. Incivility in the House may be a
mark of members' frustration that they cannot control the legislative process. A determined majority can work its will against even the most determined and vocal minority, especially in this era of strong partisanship.

Senators follow the advice of President John F. Kennedy: Don't get mad,
get even: obstruct business. Filibusters have become more common in re-

cent years, rising sharply since 1965. The number of cloture votes—attempts to shut off filibusters—has risen from 3 a year during 1960–73 to 6 in the late 1970s, 7.4 in the early 1980s, 10.8 in the late 1980s, and 17.6 from 1990 to 1994. The filibuster used to be employed primarily for major legislation, particularly civil rights bills. Now all manner of legislation, much of little consequence, is subject to extended debate. D'Amato bragged about how he filibustered proposals to cut funding for a military aircraft built on Long Island and a bill without an antidumping clause that would assist a typewriter manufacturer in upstate New York.[41]

The filibuster is the tool of a minority, and tiny minorities can rule in the Senate. Individual senators have increasing power to block legislation and face no sanctions for doing so. Senators can put "holds" on legislation. Originally designed to let senators indicate that a proposed schedule for consideration of a bill was inconvenient, this practice has been transformed into an effective veto. Senators put holds on bills anonymously (though often leaders can guess who has done so), and the legislation can remain bottlenecked indefinitely. The hold is now a major source of obstructionism in the Senate.[42]

Individual senators can wreak havoc with policy in other ways, too. As chair of the Foreign Relations Committee, Jesse Helms has blocked ambassadorial nominations from both Democratic and Republican administrations, sometimes to extract other policy concessions from administrations, sometimes because he simply does not like the nominee (as in the case of moderate Republican William Weld, nominated by Clinton as ambassador to Mexico, and James Hormel, nominated as ambassador to Luxembourg, but objectionable because he is gay). Orrin Hatch, chair of the Judiciary Committee, has blocked many of Clinton's nominations for judicial positions, again sometimes to advance his own agenda (to name a Republican judge in Utah to the federal bench) or sometimes because he disapproves of nominees' ideologies.[43]

Many senators, including sitting and former leaders, have taken to the floor or to public forums such as op-ed articles in major newspapers to decry the lack of civility in the Senate. Among those who have done so are former majority leaders Mike Mansfield (D-Mont.), Howard Baker (R-Tenn.), and Robert Byrd (D-W.Va.), as well as Nancy Landon Kassebaum (R-Kans.) and Gary Hart (D-Colo.). So concerned were Senators David Pryor (D-Ark.) and John Danforth (R-Mo.) that they established a "Quality of Strife" caucus in 1985 to improve life in the Senate, but it was to no avail. A recent volume of senatorial farewell addresses contains pleas for civility by Bill Bradley (D-N.J.), William S. Cohen (R-Maine), Howell Heflin (D-Ala.), Claiborne Pell (D-R.I.), and Paul Simon (D-Ill.). Similarly, in his farewell address Bob Dole went out of his way to praise Democratic members of the Senate (and especially their leaders) and to extol the benefits of bipartisanship.[44]

One reason for the rise of incivility is the collapse of the congressional party system and the increased polarization between Republicans and Democrats. In the early 1970s only about 27 percent of House roll calls and 35 percent of Senate votes divided a majority of Democrats from a majority of Republicans. Members looked out for themselves and there was no sense of collective responsibility, making attacks on other members fair game. By the mid-1980s, the cumulative effects of the Conservative Opportunity Society in the House and the overall polarization of politics during the Reagan years led to a sharp increase in party-line voting. In 1995, 73 percent of House roll calls and 69 percent of Senate votes saw party majorities opposing each other.[45] Members now reserved their bile for legislators of the other party. What started off as a Hobbesian "war of each against all" turned into a battle between the congressional parties.

## Why Congress Has Become Less Civil

Only a cockeyed optimist would have expected caucuses, hearings, retreats, or the structural reforms that were supposed to come out of such meetings to restore comity to the Senate or to the House. The nasty mood in the Congress reflects the growing hostility in the country. Since the 1970s, American society has become far more contentious than it used to be. Witness the explosion in litigation rates, the frequency of air rage and road rage, the popularity of "shock jocks" on the radio, and the way talk show guests attack each other on television. Stores now advertise polite service as it if were something reserved for special occasions.

Congress isn't insulated from the public. Instead it is first and foremost a representative institution. Wilson was right: the members of Congress take their cues from the public. As the public has become less civil, so has the Congress. The public does not mimic Congress (even though Jerry Springer was a politician before he became a referee on his television talk show).

The most telling indicator of the public's sour mood is responses to the survey question: "Generally speaking, do you believe most people can be trusted, or can't you be too careful in dealing with people?" The question was first asked in a national survey in 1960, when 58 percent of Americans were trusting. By the mid-1990s, barely more than a third of Ameri-

Figure 3-1. *Trends in Trust over Time, 1960–98*

Most people can be trusted (percent)

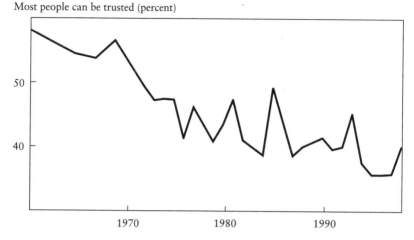

Source: For 1972, 1973, 1975, 1976, 1980, 1983, 1984, 1986, 1987, 1988, 1989, 1990, 1991, 1993, 1994, 1996, and 1998 the General Social Survey; for 1964, 1966, 1968, 1974, and 1992, the American National Election Studies; for 1960, the Civil Culture survey; for 1971, the Quality of American Life survey; for 1979, the Temple University Institute for Survey Research (reported in the Roper Poll data base on Lexis-Nexis); for 1981, the World Values Survey; and for 1995, the *Washington Post* trust in government survey.

cans had faith in others, before a slight upward bounce to 40 percent in 1998 (see figure 3-1).[46]

People who trust others have a positive view of human nature. They feel comfortable with people who are different from themselves and are willing to compromise when necessary. They do not look at people from different groups, religions, or races as rivals, much less apostates. People with faith in others believe that underlying any differences they have is a common set of values. Thus they possess the very ideals essential to comity in all forms of human relations: civility and reciprocity. Dole stressed the importance of this assumption in his farewell address: "I do not believe we (Republicans and Democrats) ever had any real disagreements."[47] Trusting people are tolerant of others' views and take an active role in doing good works, especially giving to charity, and volunteering their time. They believe that a common set of values transcends those different political views.

That sense of trust is fading from our civic life. We give less of our national income to charity, we spend less time volunteering (at least for the Red Cross), we are more apt to question the motives of people who look and think differently from ourselves, and we are less likely to compromise with people on the other side of the political divide. We are becoming less and less connected to one another. As our national mood becomes more nasty, a civil Congress would be very much out of touch with the public. If pro-life and pro-choice (or fundamentalist Christian and more secular) people do not trust each other, they will put heavy pressure on their elected representatives not to compromise with the other side. Instead of thinking about our shared fate with others, we think primarily about ourselves.

Another related, though analytically distinct, reason for the decline in civility is the weakening of the center in American electoral politics. The reciprocity norm in Congress smoothed over differences between Democrats and Republicans. All legislators could claim credit for bills passed with the support of both parties, especially the pork barrel projects that legislators believe are popular with their constituents (and that make it possible for legislators to win by overwhelming margins and secure safe seats for themselves). Since 1994, however, almost 90 percent of Democrats and a similar share of Republicans have voted for House candidates from their own party.[48] Democrats are thus pulled to the left (and Republicans to the right) when they cannot get Republican (Democratic) votes in the general election.

Democrats and Republicans are also polarized by their regional patterns of representation. Traditionally, the East has been the bastion of liberal Democrats and moderate Republicans, while the South has been home to conservatives, regardless of party, and some Democratic moderates. Southern Democrats and eastern Republicans have traditionally pulled the two parties to the center, making compromise (and good relations) with the other party necessary. However, the once-"solid" (Democratic) South has become more competitive, even tilting toward the Republicans, in House and Senate elections. In the 80th Congress (1947–48), 55 percent of Democratic senators and 49 percent of Democratic House members came from the eleven states of the old Confederacy. By the 105th Congress (1997–98), just 28 percent of Democratic senators and 16 percent of Democratic House members were southerners. There were no southern Republican senators until John Tower's victory in a special election in Texas in 1961, but by 1997 they constituted 27 percent of the Senate GOP conference. Southern strength grew from 1 percent of the House GOP conference in the 80th Congress to 32 percent in the 105th. Southerners were particularly important in the Democratic party because they held a disproportionate share of committee leadership positions. In 1965 southerners held 67 percent of committee chairs in the House and 56 percent in the Senate. By 1993–94, the last years of Democratic control, southerners held only a third of committee chair positions in either house. As the southerners became less influential within the Democratic party, committee chairs became more representative of the full Democratic caucus, and thus more liberal.[49]

As the South became more Republican, the Northeast became more Democratic. Between the 80th and 105th Congress, easterners increased from 16 percent to 26 percent of the Democratic House caucus.[50] Easterners now represent just 15 percent of House Republicans, down from 37 percent in the 80th Congress. The story is much the same for the Senate, where members from New England and the Middle Atlantic states now constitute 22 percent of the Democratic caucus (up from 11 percent in the 80th Congress), but just 18 percent of the Republican conference (down from 29 percent).

There is thus less pressure for Democrats to move to the center and greater pressure for the GOP to tilt toward the party's right. More easterners mean a more liberal Democratic party and more southerners mean a more conservative Republican party. More and more southern Democrats who remain in the party are elected by majority minority districts, and their members are ideologically indistinguishable from northern Democrats.[51] The moderates have been at the forefront of drives to restore comity to both chambers. One of the few southern moderates left in either party, Representative John Tanner (D-Tenn.), summed up the dilemma: "Democratic districts become more Democratic and Republican districts become more Republican. There are fewer and fewer districts in the middle. We are the roadkill. We are the yellow line in the middle of the road that gets hit on both sides. Because the districts in Congress are more and more one-party dominant, the American Congress is more extreme."[52]

The decline in trust and the changing regional basis of partisan representation are *not* alternative explanations for the waning civility in Congress. The partisan polarization in the South and the Northeast reflects a hardening of political stands that is part and parcel of the movement in modern society that treats compromise as a four-letter word. Indeed, as the country has become less trusting, it has been more willing to elect more southern Republicans and fewer eastern Republicans in both chambers. As trust has gone down, there have been fewer southern Democrats in both chambers and more eastern Democrats (but only in the Senate).[53]

Many quantitative indicators of waning civility track interpersonal trust rather well. I have shown elsewhere that committee reciprocity in both the House and Senate weakened as interpersonal trust declined. In both chambers, members were more willing to offer amendments to bills from outside their committees, and the chambers were more likely to adopt these amendments. As trust fell, the level of partisanship on special rules for the consideration of legislation rose. And the level of trust in other people was the most important factor shaping the number of cloture motions filed (and, indirectly, the number of filibusters) in the Senate. Perhaps most critical, as trust declined, Congress passed fewer major laws.[54]

Hostile words on the floor tell only a small part of the story of comity, since the nastiest words may occur when there is the least chance they will be taken down: in committees, in the cloakrooms, to reporters, or to public audiences. And my House-Senate comparisons so far indicate that you can have plenty of incivility even with restrained language.[55] Obstructionism and minority rights are notoriously difficult to measure. We lack basic public information on holds, who files them, and how many there are.[56]

I thus sought an indirect measure of incivility. I started with two simple assumptions. First, comity presumes a willingness to compromise. Second, strong ideologues are less likely to accept compromises than are moderates. With stronger ideologues in the Congress, there should be less civility. My surrogate measure for civility is a measure of the ideological homogeneity of each congressional party. A very liberal party and a very conservative party, each with few moderates, will have fewer incentives to cooperate with the opposition. There are fewer restraints in a homogeneous party to bring members to the center or, in a polarized environment, even to socialize with one another. It is hard to imagine a contemporary Republican leader of either House bragging, as did GOP chief Joe Martin (R-Mass.) in the 1950s, of "my long and close friendship" with Democratic leader Rayburn that "enabled me to obtain for our side more patronage, such as jobs around the Capitol, than we, as the minority, ever would have got otherwise."[57] Indeed, it was Michel's close relationships with O'Neill and Foley that led Gingrich to form the Conservative Opportunity Society to press for a more ideologically distinctive and strident agenda.

The measure of ideological homogeneity I employ is the standard deviation of ideology in the House and Senate (by party). The larger the standard deviation within each party, the more moderates there should be. A strictly liberal Democratic or an overwhelmingly conservative Republican party will have a small standard deviation of ideology scores.

Figure 3-2. *Trends in Standard Deviations of DW-Nominate Scores*

Standard deviation

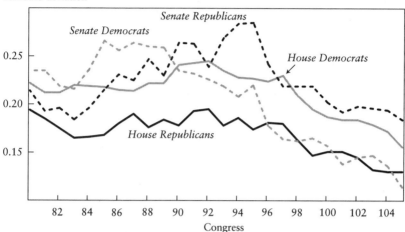

Source: Personal communication with Keith T. Poole. DW-Nominate scores are based on the methodology developed in Keith T. Poole and Howard Rosenthal, *Congress: A Political-Economic History of Roll Call Voting* (Oxford University Press, 1997).

I use the DW-NOMINATE scores developed by Keith Poole and Howard Rosenthal as my measure of ideology.[58] I present the standard deviations for each congressional (House and Senate) party from the 80th to the 105th Congress in figure 3-2.

If there were a simple downward trend in civility, we should see four parallel lines—for House and Senate Democrats and House and Senate Republicans—all sloping ever downward. We don't. There seems to be a somewhat jumbled pattern, especially in the early years of the time series. But appearances can be deceiving. For all but Senate Republicans, there *is* an overall downward trend from the 80th Congress to the 105th. The correlations of the standard deviations with time are –.611 for House Democrats, –.712 for House Republicans, –.864 for House Democrats, and just –.078 for Senate Republicans. But it might not make sense to look back quite so far.

A more careful inspection of figure 3-2 shows that there is a powerful downward trend for all four congressional parties beginning with the 89th Congress (1965–66). Now, three of the four correlations with time are greater than –.90, and the fourth comes close to it.[59] At least since the mid-

1960s, then, *there is a single syndrome of incivility for all four congressional parties. Ideological extremism shows the same basic time path in the Senate as it does in the House for both parties.*

I estimated a series of statistical models to determine what drives this surrogate measure of incivility for the four congressional parties. First, a note of caution. Since the first survey question on trust was not asked until 1960, the analyses do not begin until the 86th Congress. Second, there are no measurements for trust for either the 87th or 91st Congresses, so these cases are omitted from models with trust. Third, the other major source of incivility, regional patterns of representation, are generally highly correlated with each other, since representation is like a seesaw: when the Democratic House contingent from the South goes down, the share of eastern seats in the party's caucus goes up virtually in lockstep. And most of the measures of party regional representation, as noted above, are also strongly correlated with trust. I also examined (and dismissed) several other possible causes of incivility: divided control of the legislative and executive branches, the relative seniority levels in each chamber, and both the absolute difference in party membership percentages and the share of seats held by each party in the two chambers.[60]

The models focus on trust and regional representation, but I include another variable for all four estimations: James A. Stimson's measure of public mood, which is a summary indicator of how liberal (high scores) or conservative (low scores) public opinion is.[61] Congressional parties should respond to ideological trends in the country, as well as to the more general atmosphere of trust and distrust. I expect that Democrats would have smaller standard deviations when public opinion is pushing them to the left (the public mood is liberal) and Republicans would be most conservative when public attitudes tilt rightward.

Briefly, the multivariate statistical analyses suggest that social trust has the most pervasive effects on the surrogate measure of incivility for all four congressional parties. A less trusting citizenry leads to more incivility in Congress. Trust matters in the Senate, but its effects are stronger in the House. This is not surprising, since the disruptions in the House are more on public view and House constituencies are more homogeneous, and thus are more likely to push members away from compromise. For both House parties, trust is the stronger of two significant predictors in the statistical models.

Regional representation is not quite so powerful or ubiquitous. It is statistically significant only in the model for Senate Democrats. As northeastern Democrats became a greater force in the Senate Democratic caucus, Democratic senators became more ideologically extreme (and thus more likely to be less civil).

Finally, public attitudes play a major role in shaping ideological extremism, but the relationship is not always as simple as we might expect. The Democrats behave as predicted: the more liberal the country is, the lower the standard deviation of ideology for both House and Senate Democrats. When the country is liberal, Democrats tilt more sharply to the left and clearly see no need to compromise with Republicans. However, Republicans in both the House and the Senate are clearly *countermajoritarian*. When the country is liberal, congressional Republicans circle the wagons and become increasingly *conservative*. These are not minor effects. They are easily significant by any conventional standards (even using two-tailed tests). The powerful effects for trust and the countermajoritarian finding for public mood tell a consistent story of a minority party that believed that it had to develop a clear-cut alternative to the dominant majority in order to have any hope of gaining power. And this is precisely what the Republicans, especially those in the House, did. They turned away from the optimal political strategy of the moment to develop support in their core constituencies.

The weak results for the regional representation variables likely stem from their interrelationship with trust. Consider the case of House southern Republicans. As southerners became a more powerful force in the House Republican conference, the party became increasingly conservative and monolithic. The culmination of this trend was the ascension to power of three southerners—Gingrich (Ga.), Majority Leader Dick Armey (Tex.), and Majority Whip Tom DeLay (Tex.)—when the GOP took control of the House in 1995. But the southern road to power in the GOP was not a sudden phenomenon. It had been developing at least since the Republicans made major inroads in the South in the 1964 presidential election. The correlation between the House Republican standard deviation and the southern share of GOP House seats is .901 from the 89th to the 105th Congress. When I reestimate the model to begin with the 89th Congress, trust drops out (owing to its high correlation with the southern share of House Republican seats) and the regional variable dominates the equation.

Overall, the statistical analyses suggest that incivility has the same roots in the House and the Senate, and that the most consistent effects relate to trust in other people. The Democratic party seems more majoritarian than the Republican party, which may be why Republican obstructionism generally shows up as less popular in public opinion polls than Democratic tactics. But this is of little solace, since the Republicans have been able to maintain majority status in both houses.

## A Plague on Both Your Houses?

Is the Senate, then, more civil than the House? If the criterion is the decibel level, the answer is yes. If the criterion is handling important national issues such as impeachment, the answer is less reassuring. Were the Constitution different and had the Senate acted first, it is far from clear that the widely heralded center would have held. The northeastern moderates who held the balance of power on the first article of impeachment are a weak reed on which to hinge an overall image of moderation for the Senate GOP. The Republicans have a five-seat majority in the 106th Senate. Three of the four northeastern moderates who vote with their party less than two-thirds of the time—three of whom voted against impeachment— are either gone (D'Amato, N.Y.) from the Senate, deceased (John Chafee, R.I.), or facing stiff competition in the year 2000 (Jim Jeffords, Vt.). D'Amato has already been replaced by a Democrat and Chafee's successor might be a Democrat. Two others who also voted against impeachment, Maine's Olympia Snowe and Susan Collins, vote with their party about two-thirds of the time, so that their relatively infrequent defections might be balanced by moderate Democrats who will vote with the GOP.[62] The slim Republican majority in the Senate nevertheless remains a working majority, even if by just one or two votes.

Unless the moderates can exert enough influence to swing victories to the Democratic minority on key issues, they are in effect powerless. By voting with their party two-thirds of the time, Maine's moderates are ensuring that the more conservative members of their party will be able to dominate the legislative process in the Senate. And this means that moderates have no effective sanctions to exert over more extreme members who seek to obstruct the legislative process. The pull of party unity has gotten so strong that members who look moderate by their voting record might use the same tactics as their more extreme colleagues (on the right or the left), as D'Amato's braggadocio about filibustering shows.

There may be a ray of hope, however. If obstructionism and uncivil language reflect a society in distress, the good times of the mid- to late 1990s may make the public more public spirited. Throughout the early to mid-1990s, interpersonal trust continued to fall even as the economy boomed. Americans still worried about the longer term. But now there are signs of a turnaround, however small. Today Americans are more upbeat about the longer-term future, and there was an upward blip in trust in 1998 (it moved from 36 percent to 40 percent in the General Social Survey, and up to 46 percent in the American National Election Study). If this spurt upward is the beginning of a trend, then there is hope for more civility in Congress. After all, a trusting citizenry will not tolerate a Congress that seeks to divide the nation against itself.

A polarized politics cannot survive in a trusting environment. The 1998 elections saw some interruptions in the seemingly inexorable growth of conservative Republicanism in the South (even as eastern Republicans struggled to retain their positions). Moderate Democrats defeated incumbent Republicans in the Alabama governor's race and the North Carolina Senate contest. If there is to be a rebirth of civility in the Congress, it will start from the ground up.

## Notes

I am grateful to the Pew Charitable Trusts for sponsoring the conference and to the Everett McKinley Dirksen Center for Congressional Leadership and the General Research Board of the Graduate School of the University of Maryland–College Park for providing support for this research. Keith Poole, Sarah Binder, Gary Jacobson, Richard Beth, and John Owens provided much of the data used in this paper. Burdett Loomis, the participants at the conference on "Civility and Deliberation in the Senate," and two anonymous referees for the Brookings Institution provided very helpful comments. Other data come from the Inter-University Consortium for Political Research, which is not responsible for any interpretations. Readers can obtain more details on the data analysis by contacting me at euslaner@gvpt.umd.edu.

1. Guy Gugliotta and Terry M. Neal, "Republicans and Democrats Ponder Ever-Widening Chasm," *Washington Post*, December 20, 1998, p. A3.

2. Ibid., p. A3.

3. Francis X. Clines and Frank Bruni, "Behind Closed Doors, Senators Spoke Plainly and Pointedly," *New York Times*, Washington edition, February 14, 1999, p. A30.

4. Lizette Alvarez, "Of 100 Senators, Only 6 Attend Unity Gathering," *New York Times*, Washington edition, February 26, 1999, p. A15.

5. Ibid.; David Von Drehle, "Protecting Propriety in the Club," *Washington Post*, January 9, 1999, p. A10; Spencer S. Hsu, "Senate's Partisan Lines Don't Foreclose Partnerships," *Washington Post*, January 31, 1999, p. A20; Joel Achenbach, "The Proud Compromisers," *Washington Post*, January 9, 1999, pp. A1, A11.

6. Achenbach, "The Proud Compromisers," p. A11.

7. Hsu, "Senate's Partisan Lines." Senator John McCain (R-Ariz.) commented: "Stranger things have happened in politics . . . but the Kennedy-Gramm alignment is one of the strangest" (quoted in Helen Dewar and Peter Baker, "Senate Votes Rules for President's Trial," *Washington Post*, January 9, 1999, p. A11).

8. Woodrow Wilson, *Congressional Government* (Boston: Houghton Mifflin, 1913), pp. 193, 194, 210. Originally published in 1885.

9. Senator Paul Wellstone (D-Minn.) said: "What's driving us is how awful the House looked." Quoted in Achenbach, "The Proud Compromisers," p. A11.

10. Richard L. Berke and Janet L. Elder, "Damaged by Trial, Senate's Standing Sinks in New Poll," *New York Times*, Washington edition, February 3, 1999, pp. A1, A14.

11. This section draws heavily on Eric M. Uslaner, *The Decline of Comity in Congress* (University of Michigan Press, 1993), chap. 1.

12. The repetition is designed to make people believe the remark, even when it lacks immediate plausibility.

13. Donald Matthews, *U.S. Senators and Their World* (University of North Carolina Press, 1960), pp. 97–99.

14. William S. White, *Citadel: The Story of the U.S. Senate* (New York: Harper and Brothers, 1956), pp. 56–57.

15. Ibid., p. 117.

16. Ross K. Baker, *Friend and Foe in the U.S. Senate* (New York: Free Press, 1980), p. 12.

17. Senator Al D'Amato, *Power, Pasta, and Politics* (New York: Hyperion, 1995), pp. 140, 146–48, 153. D'Amato's friendship with Moynihan is not atypical. A state's two senators are more likely to be rivals if they come from the same party. Senators often get along better with their state colleague if he or she represents the other party. See Wendy Schiller, *Rivals and Partners* (Princeton University Press, 2000); and Ross K. Baker, "Factors Influencing the Political Relationships of Same-State Senators," paper presented at the Annual Meeting of the American Political Science Association, September 1998, Boston.

18. Keith Krehbiel, "Unanimous Consent Agreements: Going Along in the Senate," *Journal of Politics*, vol. 40 (August 1986), pp. 541–64.

19. William S. White, *Home Place: The Story of the U.S. House of Representatives* (Boston: Houghton Mifflin, 1965), pp. 45–46.

20. Clem Miller, *Member of the House*, edited by John Baker (New York: Charles Scribner's Sons, 1962), p. 93.

21. For the classic study of how subcommittees defer to one another's expertise in the House, see Richard F. Fenno Jr., "The House Appropriations Committee as a Political System: The Problem of Integration," *American Political Science Review*, vol. 56 (June 1962), pp. 310–24.

22. This section relies heavily on Uslaner, *The Decline of Comity in Congress*, chaps. 1–2.

23. On the new members, see Burdett Loomis, *The New American Politician* (New York: Basic Books, 1988), esp. p. 28.

24. The 1969 survey results are reported in Herbert B. Asher, "The Learning of Legislative Norms." *American Political Science Review*, vol. 67 (June 1973), pp.

499–513. The 1976 and 1980 surveys come from Loomis, *The New American Politician,* p. 48.

25. Heinz is quoted in Barbara Sinclair, *The Transformation of the U.S. Senate* (Johns Hopkins University Press, 1989), p. 89. For the other quotations, see Rowland Evans and Robert Novak, "The Kemp-Michel Row," *Washington Post,* April 1, 1987, p. A23; and "Vander Jagt Compares Foe to Saddam Hussein," *Washington Post,* November 2, 1990, p. A3.

26. Barry Weingast, "Fighting Fire with Fire: Amending Activity and Institutional Change in the Postreform Congress," in Roger H. Davidson, ed., *The Postreform Congress* (New York: St. Martin's Press, 1992).

27. Helen Dewar, "Republicans Wage Verbal Civil War," *Washington Post,* November 19, 1985, pp. A1, A5.

28. Robin Toner, "Angry Opposition Attacks the Process," *New York Times,* September 22, 1995, p. A26; and Guy Gugliotta, "Taking Decorum Down," *Washington Post,* January 2, 1996, p. A13.

29. Associated Press, "Cunningham Apologizes for Curse, Gesture, Crude Remark," *Washington Post,* September 8, 1998, p. A6.

30. *Congressional Record,* daily ed., June 5, 1998, p. H4181.

31. The leader was Representative John Lewis (D-Ga.). I was scheduled to testify at this hearing in April. It was rescheduled for May.

32. Steven S. Smith, *Call to Order* (Brookings, 1989), chap. 5; Sinclair, *Transformation of the U.S. Senate,* chap. 6.

33. The measures come from Smith, *Call to Order,* p. 145, and Sinclair, *Transformation of the U.S. Senate,* p. 82. The correlation between the two time series is .830 (N = 9).

34. Quoted in Alan Ehrenhalt, "In the Senate of the '80s, Team Spirit Has Given Way to the Rule of Individuals," *Congressional Quarterly Weekly Report,* September 4, 1982, pp. 2176, 2181.

35. Baker, *Friend and Foe in the U.S. Senate,* p. 40.

36. Uslaner, *The Decline of Comity in Congress,* chap. 1.

37. *Congressional Record,* daily ed., March 7, 1989, p. S2241.

38. Ralph K. Huitt, "The Outsider in the Senate: An Alternative Role," *American Political Science Review,* vol. 55 (September 1961), pp. 566–75.

39. Former Majority Leader Howard Baker (R-Tenn.) had a very different style and remains one of the former leaders most committed to restoring comity.

40. Eric Piannin, "Lott Slams Pair over Budget Switch," *Washington Post,* March 1, 1997, p. A4.

41. Sarah A. Binder and Steven S. Smith, *Politics or Principle? Filibustering in the United States Senate* (Brookings, 1997), chaps. 2 and 4; Sinclair, *Transformation of the U.S. Senate,* 94–97; Richard S. Beth, "Filibusters in the Senate, 1789–1993," Congressional Research Service, Library of Congress Memorandum, February 18, 1994; and D'Amato, *Power, Pasta, and Politics,* 147–53. The figures on cloture votes come from Beth's memorandum.

42. Binder and Smith, *Politics or Principle?* pp. 11–12.

43. Joan Biskupic, "Hatch, White House at Impasse on Judgeships," *Washington Post,* June 5, 1999, pp. A1, A6.

44. Juliet Eilperin, "Comity Hour with Mike Mansfield," *Washington Post*, March 25, 1998, p. A19; Howard Baker, "Civility: The Secret to Leading the Senate," *The Hill*, September 2, 1998, p. 16; Robert Byrd, "Civility in the Senate," *Congressional Record*, daily ed., December 20, 1995, pp. S18964–S18971; Nancy Landon Kassebaum, "The Senate Is Not in Order," *Washington Post*, January 27, 1988, p. A19; Gary Hart, "Stuart Symington's Senate," *Washington Post*, January 10, 1999, p. A23; Norman J. Ornstein, ed., *Lessons and Legacies* (Reading, Mass.: Addison-Wesley, 1997); Robert J. Dole, "Farewell Address of Senator Robert J. Dole," *Congressional Record*, daily ed., June 11, 1996, pp. S6043–S6046.

45. Norman J. Ornstein, Thomas E. Mann, and Michael J. Malbin, comps., *Vital Statistics on Congress, 1997–1998* (Washington, D.C.: American Enterprise Institute, 1998), p. 210.

46. See Eric M. Uslaner, "The Moral Foundations of Trust," unpublished manuscript, University of Maryland–College Park, 1999, chap. 1. The next several paragraphs are based on this manuscript.

47. Dole, "Farewell Address of Senator Robert J. Dole," p. S6046.

48. "A Look at Voting Patterns of 115 Demographic Groups in House Races," *New York Times*, Washington edition, November 9, 1998, p. A20.

49. The data on regional representation come from *Roster of United States Congressional Officeholders and Biographical Characteristics of Members of the United States Congress, 1789–1993: Merged Data*, 9th ICPSR ed., September 1993, Inter-University Consortium for Political and Social Research Study 7803. The data on southern committee chairs come from Ornstein, Mann, and Malbin, *Vital Statistics on Congress 1997–1998*, p. 126; and Sinclair, *Transformation of the U.S. Senate*, p. 107.

50. The growth of the eastern share of Democratic House seats is actually less than it seems, since the 80th Congress was a low point (under GOP control). When the Democrats regained control in the 81st Congress (1949–50), the eastern share rose to 21 percent. It also reached its current height of 26 percent in the late 1960s (1967–70), before falling slightly.

51. David Rohde, *Parties and Leaders in the Postreform House* (University of Chicago Press, 1991).

52. Quoted in James G. Gimpel, *Fulfilling the Contract* (Needham Heights, Mass.: Allyn and Bacon, 1996), p. 123.

53. The average absolute value of the correlation between trust and the share of southern and eastern Republicans (Democrats) is .842, excluding the insignificant (and incorrectly signed) correlation for the share of eastern Democrats in the House caucus. See the discussion in n. 50 to learn why the latter correlation is not strong.

54. See the analyses in Uslaner, *The Decline of Comity in Congress*, chaps. 4–6. For discussions of filibusters using data collected by Richard S. Beth and an updated measure of amendments from noncommittee members in the House developed by John Owens, see also Uslaner, "The Moral Foundations of Trust," chap. 5.

55. For an attempt to measure incivility through textual analysis of floor proceedings, see Kathleen Hall Jamieson, "Civility in the House of Representatives," Annenberg School of Communications, University of Pennsylvania, 1997.

56. Binder and Smith, *Politics or Principle?* p. 11; Sarah A. Binder, *Minority Rights, Majority Rule* (Cambridge University Press, 1997), chap. 2.

57. Joe Martin, *My First Fifty Years in Politics*, as told to Robert J. Donovan (New York: McGraw-Hill, 1960), pp. 8–9.

58. For a discussion of the general methodology, see Keith T. Poole and Howard Rosenthal, *Congress: A Political-Economic History of Roll Call Voting* (Oxford University Press, 1997). Poole graciously provided the standard deviations. He notes (personal communication) that the ideology scales are constant for members across their service in the House or Senate so that all changes in means and standard deviations reflect membership change in the congressional parties. And he cautions that the House and Senate scores are derived from separate scaling analyses and that cross-chamber comparisons should be done cautiously. I do not find this argument damning, since I am interested precisely in how the chambers differ. The measures I use are for the Poole-Rosenthal first dimension, which is a general measure of ideology.

59. The correlations are –.970 for House Democrats, –.933 for House Republicans, –.965 for Senate Democrats, and –.874 for Senate Republicans.

60. One might hypothesize that incivility would be greater under divided control, when there are greater pressures to stick with your own side rather than to compromise. And we might also expect that as aggregate seniority falls, we sould find members with less of a stake in the system and thus more incivility. Finally, we might hypothesize that as the overall partisan balance in the chamber grows smaller, there might be greater pressures to stick with your own party. None of these hypotheses were supported. The models below were estimated first using ordinary least squares and then reestimated by ARIMA (autoregressive integrated moving average) models to control for time-series correlations (always using first-order autoregressive processes, since higher-order processes and moving average parameters were never significant).

61. James A. Stimson, *Public Opinion in America*, 2d ed. (Boulder, Colo.: Westview Press, 1998). The updated data set is available at http://www.unc.edu/~jstimson/ann5296.prn.

62. The seventh least loyal Republican, William Roth (Del.), may also be replaced by a Democrat who would be more loyal to his own party. See "Leading Scorers: Party Unity," *CQ Weekly*, January 9, 1999, p. 81. A Mason-Dixon poll taken more than a year before the election gave Governor Tom Carper (D) a ten-point lead over Roth. See http://www.mason-dixon.com/states/Delaware/main.htm (accessed March 5, 2000).

# PART II
## A Deliberative Institution

# CHAPTER FOUR

# Individualism, Partisanship, and Cooperation in the Senate

## BARBARA SINCLAIR

THE SENATE IS UNIQUE AMONG legislative chambers; no other legislature grants its members as individuals so much latitude in the legislative process. Extended debate allows any senator to hold the floor as long as he or she wishes unless cloture is invoked, which now requires a supermajority of sixty votes. The Senate's permissive amending rules enable senators to offer any and as many amendments as they please to almost any bill, and those amendments need not even be germane. Senators' prerogatives have their origins in decisions made—or more accurately, not made—in the nineteenth century.[1] Yet, as the Senate's membership and its political environment have changed, so has the way senators use their prerogatives and consequently the legislative process. This chapter examines the development of the individualist Senate in the late 1960s and 1970s, the resurgence of partisanship in the late 1980s and 1990s, and the impact of these trends on the legislative process in the chamber.

## Development of the Individualist Senate

The Senate of the 1950s was a clubby, inward-looking body governed by constraining norms; influence was unequally distributed and centered in strong committees and their senior leaders, who were most often conservatives, frequently southern Democrats.[2] The typical senator of the 1950s was a specialist who concentrated on the issues that came before his committees. His legislative activities were largely confined to the committee room; he was seldom active on the Senate floor, was highly restrained in his exercise of the prerogatives the Senate rules gave him, and made little use of the media.

The Senate's institutional structure and the political environment rewarded such behavior.[3] The lack of staff, for example, made it hard for new senators to participate intelligently right away; so serving an apprenticeship helped prevent a new member from making a fool of himself early in his career. Meager staff resources also made specialization the only really feasible course for attaining influence. Restraint in exploiting extended debate was encouraged by the lack of the sort of time pressures that would later make extended debate such a formidable weapon; when floor time is plentiful, the leverage senators derive from extended debate is much less.[4] Furthermore, the dominant southern Democrats had an enormous constituency-based interest in restricting and thus protecting the filibuster for their one big issue: opposition to civil rights. The Senate of the 1950s was an institution well designed for its generally conservative and electorally secure members to further their goals.

Membership turnover and a transformation of the political environment altered the costs and benefits of such behavior and induced members to change the institution; over time, norms, practices, and rules were altered.[5] The 1958 elections brought into the Senate a big class of new senators with different policy goals and reelection needs. Mostly northern Democrats, they were activist liberals and most had been elected in highly competitive contests, in many cases having defeated incumbents. Both their policy goals and their reelection needs dictated a more activist style; these senators simply could not afford to wait to make their mark. Subsequent elections brought in more and more such members and, in the 1960s, the political environment began a transformation. A host of new issues rose to prominence, politics became more highly charged, the interest group community exploded in size and became more diverse, and the media— especially television—became a much bigger player in politics.

This new environment offered tempting new opportunities to senators.[6] The myriad interest groups needed champions and spokesmen, and the media needed credible sources to represent issue positions and to provide commentary. Because of the small size and prestige of the Senate, its members fit the bill. To take on those roles, however, senators would have to change their behavior and their institution.

From the mid-1960s through the mid-1970s, senators did just that. The number of positions on good committees and the number of subcommittee leadership positions were expanded and distributed much more broadly.

Staff, too, was greatly expanded and made available to junior as well as senior senators. Senators were able to involve themselves in a much broader range of issues, and they did so. Senators also became much more active on the Senate floor, offering more amendments and to a wider range of bills. The typical senator in the mid-1950s, over the course of a Congress, offered and pushed to a roll call vote two amendments; by the 1970s, the typical senator was offering and pushing to a roll call three times as many amendments.[7] Senators exploited extended debate to a much greater degree, and the frequency of filibusters shot up; the number of filibusters averaged less than one per Congress over the period 1955–60; in the 1970s the average was 11.4 filibusters per Congress.[8] The media became an increasingly important arena for participation and a significant resource for senators in the pursuit of their policy, power, and reelection goals.

## The Resurgence of Partisanship in the Senate

The 1980 elections made Ronald Reagan president and, to almost everyone's surprise, brought a Republican majority to the Senate. As president, Reagan was more conservative and confrontational than his Republican predecessors of the post–World War II era, and his election signaled an intensification of ideological conflict that came to fall increasingly along partisan lines.

Realignment in the South, the Proposition 13 tax-cutting fever, the rise of the Christian Right, and the development of the property rights movement were changing the political parties. In 1961 not a single senator from the eleven states of the old Confederacy was a Republican; by 1973, seven were, and by 1980 that number had risen to ten. It dropped to seven in 1991 but rose back to ten in 1993. With the 1994 elections, the number of southern Republican senators rose to thirteen and with the 1996 elections to fifteen. In 2000 the number stands at fourteen, which represents 64 percent of the senators from the once solidly Democratic old South. As conservative southern Democrats were replaced by even more conservative southern Republicans, the congressional Democratic party became more homogeneously liberal and the Republican party more conservative.

Outside the South as well, Republican candidates and activists were becoming more ideologically conservative. The 1980 elections brought into the Senate southern conservatives such as Jeremiah Denton of Alabama and Paula Hawkins of Florida, but also Steve Symms of Idaho, Dan Quayle of Indiana, Don Nickles of Oklahoma, and Roger Jepsen of Iowa.

Figure 4-1. *Party Votes in the Senate, 90th–105th Congresses*[a]

Percent

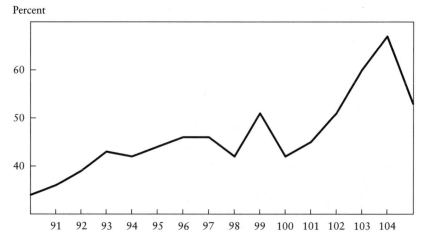

Congress

Source: *Congressional Quarterly Almanac* and *Weekly Report,* various issues.
a. Figure reports percent of roll call votes that pitted a majority of Democrats against a majority of Republicans.

The Republican senators elected subsequently tended to be more conservative than their predecessors, whatever the predecessor's party. Rick Santorum (R-Pa.) and James Inhofe (R-Okla.), both Gingrichite House Republicans, replaced Democrats, but conservatives Rod Grams (R-Minn.) and John Ashcroft (R-Mo.) replaced moderate Republicans Dave Durenberger and John Danforth, respectively. In 1996 Sam Brownback (R-Kans.), an activist member of the conservative House class of 1994, replaced Bob Dole, and Michael Enzi (R-Wyo.), running on a strong anti-abortion platform, replaced Alan Simpson, another conservative pragmatist like Dole. Thus the character of the Senate Republican party changed, though the long Senate terms meant the change was more gradual than in the House.

Voting on the Senate floor became increasingly partisan. At the low point in the late 1960s and early 1970, only about a third of Senate roll call votes pitted a majority of Democrats against a majority of Republicans (see figure 4-1). By the 1990s, half to two-thirds of roll calls were such party votes. In addition, the frequency with which senators voted with their partisan colleagues on party votes increased significantly. Figure 4-2 graphs the mean party support score for Democrats and the mean support score for Repub-

Figure 4-2. *Party Polarization in the Senate, 90th–105th Congresses*

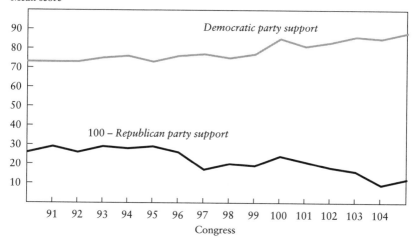

Source: See figure 4-1.

licans subtracted from 100. The greater the distance between the lines, the less Democrats and Republicans vote together. Clearly, the Senate parties in the 1990s were more internally homogeneous and more polarized than in previous decades.

A similar though somewhat earlier change in the character of the parties in the House of Representatives led to a strengthening of party leadership in that body.[9] Senators, in contrast, have not given their leaders new powers. Granting the majority leader true control over the flow of legislation to and on the floor would require senators to give up their extraordinary prerogatives, and that they are not willing to do. Thus Senate majority leaders must lead by accommodation. Senate majority leaders have always had to be negotiators, brokers, and persuaders. They have to work closely not only with the members of their own party but with the minority leader and often with other individual minority party senators as well.

Partisan polarization has made participation through their parties more attractive to senators than it was when the parties were more heterogeneous and there was less ideological distance between them. Partly in response to their members' demands, recent Senate party leaders have sought to provide more channels for members to participate in and through the party. On both sides of the aisle, the party organization and party processes have been much elaborated to provide services to members and to include members in all aspects of party functioning.[10] Each party holds a weekly senators-only lunch, which provides an opportunity for policy discussion and for communication between leaders and members. Democratic Leader George Mitchell and even more so his successor Tom Daschle increased the number of members in party leadership positions and regularly shared floor management duties with these senators, the whip, and other colleagues. The Democratic whip system and other party organs became more active. Under Trent Lott, who was elected Republican whip in late 1994, the Republican whip system became larger, more structured, and more active.[11] When in mid-1996 Lott won election to succeed Bob Dole as majority leader, he instituted a similar form of leadership at the top level, relying on and sharing duties with other elected leaders more, attempting to provide more structure but also more openness to leadership endeavors, and striving to include as many senators as possible in party-based activities. In early 1999, for example, he formed five "working groups," each chaired by two senators, to develop communications strategy on the five main issues Senate Republicans intended to emphasize.[12]

The increase in partisanship has transformed the preferred Senate leadership style from that of solo operator to majority leader as head of a party team. Previous leaders like Robert Byrd (D-W.Va.) and Dole were in effect solo operators; they (along with their top staff) carried out most of the leadership's tasks themselves; they did not rely on other leaders. In an atomistic chamber, this modus operandi provided maximum flexibility. George Mitchell (D-Maine) started delegating and decentralizing the organization, though he himself was inclined to a solo leadership style. Lott and his minority counterpart Tom Daschle (D-S.Dak.) have much more inclusive leadership styles, both in terms of organization and in terms of actual operations; they are heads of party teams. Still, individual senators exercise a great deal more discretion about when and under what conditions to participate on the party team than House members do; they have available attractive alternative channels for participation, and they pay little price when they go off on their own. Individualism and intense partisanship coexist in the Senate, often uneasily.

In recent years, junior Senate Republicans, a number of whom previously served in the House, have been particularly frustrated with the barriers to party government and thus to nonincremental policy change in their chamber. Individualism by their more senior and often more moder-

ate party colleagues at the expense of the position held by the party majority has riled them even more than minority Democrats' exploitation of
Senate prerogatives. It was the defection of a moderate Republican on a
key vote in 1995 that first brought their frustration to a head. After the
House had approved it, the constitutional amendment requiring a balanced budget failed in the Senate by one vote, with Mark Hatfield, the
chairman of the Appropriations Committee, casting the only Republican
vote against it. The amendment was a part of the Senate Republicans'
agenda, and the ideologically driven junior Republicans, many of whom
were Gingrich admirers and allies, believed that, on such a crucial vote, a
senior committee chair should not be allowed with impunity to vote against
the party to which he owed his chairmanship. They proposed stripping
Hatfield of his chairmanship but were placated with a reform task force
to which three freshmen were appointed.

The provisions proposed by the task force that the Senate Republican
conference adopted included limiting chairs and party leaders (except the
top leader) to three terms, requiring a secret ballot vote on committee
chairs both in committee and in the conference, and providing for the
adoption of a Senate GOP agenda in the conference by a three-quarters
vote. The new rules went into effect at the beginning of 1997 and were
intended by the junior conservatives to make their senior and often more
moderate party colleagues more responsive to the predominantly conservative party membership as a whole.

## The Legislative Process in an Individualistic and Partisan Senate

What effect has the combination of individualism and partisanship had
on the legislative process in the Senate? Certainly by the mid-1970s the
Senate had become a body in which every member, regardless of seniority,
felt entitled to participate on any issue of interest for either constituency
or policy reasons. Senators were well equipped with resources—both good
committee assignments and generous staff—to participate broadly. Because senators were stretched thin, committees became less work groups
in which senators participated day in and day out than discretionary are-
nas for participation *when* an issue of special interest to a senator was
under consideration. Staff played a more important role in the legislative
process. The floor became a more active decisionmaking arena as senators
offered an increasing number of amendments, often to legislation from

Table 4-1. *Increase in Filibusters and Cloture Votes per Congress, 1951–98*

| Years | Congresses | Filibusters | Cloture votes | Successful cloture votes |
|-------|-----------|-------------|---------------|--------------------------|
| 1951–60 | 82–86 | 1.0 | 0.4 | 0 |
| 1961–70 | 87–91 | 4.6 | 5.2 | 0.8 |
| 1971–80 | 92–96 | 11.2 | 22.4 | 8.6 |
| 1981–86 | 97–99 | 16.7 | 23.0 | 10.0 |
| 1987–92 | 100–02 | 26.7 | 39.0 | 15.3 |
| 1993–94 | 103 | 30 | 42 | 14 |
| 1995–96 | 104 | 25 | 50 | 9 |
| 1997–98 | 105 | 29 | 53 | 18 |

Sources: Data for filibusters are from "A Look at the Senate Filibuster," DSG Special Report 103-28 (June 13, 1994), appendix B (compiled by Congressional Research Service); and for cloture votes, from Norman Ornstein, Thomas Mann, and Michael Malbin, *Vital Statistics on Congress 1993–1994* (Washington, D.C.: CQ Press, 1994), p. 162. Data for 103d Congress are from Richard S. Beth, "Cloture in the Senate, 103rd Congress," memorandum, Congressional Research Service, June 23, 1995. Data for the 104th and 105th Congresses are from the *Congressional Quarterly Almanacs* (1995–98).

committees on which they did not serve. Senators became increasingly willing to exploit their prerogative of unlimited debate. The number of filibusters increased, the range of issues on which extended debate occurred expanded, and, more and more, senators were willing to employ filibusters on minor and parochial as well as on momentous issues. As Congress was rushing to adjourn in October 1992, for example, Senator Alfonse D'Amato (R-N.Y.) held the floor for fifteen hours and fifteen minutes to protest the removal from an urban-aid tax bill of a provision he said could have restored jobs at a New York typewriter plant.[13]

As table 4-1 shows, cloture votes became a routine part of Senate procedure. By the 1990s, there were attempts to cut off debate on over twenty-five different matters (legislative measures and nominations) per Congress. The consequences of senators' willingness to exploit extended debate reached well beyond actual filibusters. The Senate's big workload and limited floor time made threats to filibuster a potent weapon, and senators increasingly employed such threats. "Holds," senators' notifications to their leader that they object to a measure or nomination being brought to the floor, also became a routine part of the process. Major legislation was ever more frequently subject to problems related to extended debate, as table 4-2 shows.[14] With increasing frequency, to pass a measure or approve a nomination in the Senate took sixty votes.

How did escalating partisanship affect the legislative process in the individualist Senate? The 1990s have seen the emergence of the filibuster-

Table 4-2. *The Increasing Frequency of Extended Debate-Related Problems on Major Legislation*[a]

| Congress | Years | Filibuster problem (percent) |
|---|---|---|
| 91 | 1969–70 | 10 |
| 95 | 1977–78 | 22 |
| 97 | 1981–82 | 24 |
| 101 | 1989–90 | 30 |
| 103 | 1993–94 | 51 |
| 104 | 1995–96 | 52 |
| 105 | 1997–98 | 53 |

Source: Author's calculations.
a. Percentage of "filibusterable" major measures subject to such problems.

centered partisan strategy. In the past, filibusters were often partisan in the sense that the obstructionists were predominantly of one party. In some cases, the obstructionists were led by party leaders. Not until the 103d Congress, however, did obstructionism based on extended debate emerge as a systematic partisan strategy. Actually, Bob Dole, as minority leader in the 100th Congress (1987–88), did pursue a filibuster strategy for much of 1987; Republicans had just lost control of the Senate, Reagan was a lame duck without an agenda, and the congressional Democrats were aggressively pursuing their own agenda. However, Dole's run for the presidential nomination distracted him and led to the strategy's demise.

The 103d Congress marked the return of unified control of the presidency and both houses of Congress for the first time since the late 1970s; the new Democratic president had a big and ambitious agenda; yet he had been elected with only 43 percent of the vote and in an era of popular distrust of politicians and government. Those circumstances combined with the increased ideological polarization of the congressional parties made it possible and profitable for Senate Republicans under Bob Dole's leadership to pursue a systematic filibuster strategy. In the 103d Congress, about half of all major legislation encountered some problem related to extended debate that can be identified from the public record (see table 4-2). A Republican filibuster killed Bill Clinton's stimulus package; Republicans used the filibuster or a threat thereof to extract concessions on a number of bills, two being voter registration legislation ("motor voter") and the national service program. Such attempts were not always successful, of course. For example, the Republican filibuster of the Brady bill imposing a seven-day waiting period for buying a hand gun collapsed when a number of Republican moderates began to fear the political price of their participation.

Time pressure makes obstructionism based on extended debate an especially effective weapon at the end of a Congress, and Republicans were determined to deprive Clinton and congressional Democrats of legislative victories. At the end of the 103d Congress, Republican filibusters killed campaign finance and lobbying reform bills. Although unsuccessful in the end, Republicans filibustered and tried to prevent passage of a massive crime bill, the California Desert Protection Act, and a comprehensive education bill. In some cases, filibusters were waged to prevent legislation from being sent to conference and, more frequently, on the approval of the conference report. Republican threats of obstructionist floor tactics contributed in large measure to the death of important bills revamping the superfund program, revising clean drinking water regulations, overhauling outdated telecommunications law, and applying federal labor laws to Congress.

In the 103d Congress, the filibuster was used as a partisan tool to an extent unprecedented certainly in post–World War II American history. In the 104th, Democrats, now in the minority, returned the favor; 52 percent of major legislation encountered problems related to extended debate, and by the end of the Congress Democrats had managed to block much of the Contract with America. In the 105th, again about half of all major measures ran into filibuster problems. Through filibusters, actual or threatened, Democrats killed bankruptcy reform, the Republicans' comp time bill, and property rights legislation. Republicans used "holds" to deny President Clinton even a vote on many of his nominees.

In the hands of a determined and organized minority, Senate prerogatives can be employed to do much more than simply kill legislation or nominations. The Senate minority party now frequently uses extended debate and the Senate's permissive amending rules to attempt to seize control of the agenda from the majority. Procedure-based strategies are often combined with a public relations campaign. Usually the minority's aim is to pass legislation if possible, but certainly to score political points in a political process that is carried out more and more on the public stage and by vying for the public's support.

Democrats' successful effort to raise the minimum wage in 1996 illustrates the strategy at its most effective. After their enormous electoral victory in 1994, congressional Republicans totally dominated agenda setting.[15] President Clinton advocated raising the minimum wage in his 1996 State of the Union address; but despite the proposal's popularity with the American public, strong Republican opposition was expected to ensure that the proposal would be dead on arrival in Congress. Majority Republicans would not even allow the legislation to be considered.

To prevent that outcome, Senate Democrats determined to offer the minimum wage increase as an amendment to whatever legislation the majority leader brought to the floor. Lacking the votes to kill the minimum wage or impose cloture on legislation he did want to pass, Majority Leader Dole was forced to pull bill after bill off the floor, prompting news stories of Senate gridlock. House and Senate Democrats, the White House, and organized labor all worked to keep the issue in the news and to put pressure on moderate Republicans. Public approval of a minimum wage increase went up to 85 percent. With an election approaching, Senate and House Republicans capitulated and both chambers passed legislation raising the minimum wage.

In the 105th Congress, Democrats attempted the same strategy on campaign finance reform and tobacco control legislation. In neither case did they manage to pass legislation, but, with the help of Republican Senator John McCain, they did force the Senate to devote considerable floor time to issues the majority would rather not have had highlighted and reaped great media attention therefrom. In 1999 Democrats again succeeded in seizing the agenda with gun control measures in the wake of the Columbine High School shootings. In that case, public pressure was so intense that Majority Leader Lott did not make an all-out effort to prevent the issue from being debated on the floor, a stance for which he was criticized by some of his more conservative members. In response, Lott replied, "You don't *allow* debate to happen. It happens!"[16]

Majority leaders use a variety of strategies to counter such minority party efforts. They now more frequently attempt to impose cloture early since, post-cloture, amendments must be germane.[17] On campaign finance reform in the 105th, Majority Leader Lott responded to the Democrats' strategy with other hardball tactics. He brought the bill to the floor with no prior notice to its supporters. Lott then "filled the amendment tree"— that is, he used the majority leader's prerogative of first recognition to offer an amendment that Democrats considered antilabor and strongly opposed, and then offered enough other second-degree amendments so that his amendment could not be further amended. His purpose was to prevent the Democrats from amending his amendment and thus to force them to filibuster. Stalemate ensued; the bill was on the floor for several days, but neither side could muster the votes to impose cloture. Lott then pulled the bill. This was, of course, the outcome he had hoped for.

The bill's proponents were furious and still had plenty of ammunition to continue the battle. Democrats started blocking everything except appropriations bills by threatening to offer the McCain-Feingold campaign finance bill as a nongermane amendment, and the Senate ground to a halt. Finally Lott gave in and made a deal; he promised a full debate on campaign finance the following year, including an up-or-down vote on McCain-Feingold. Republicans eventually succeeded in preventing passage of the bill but at a considerable price in bad publicity.

Robert Byrd had attempted the same tactic of filling the amendment tree in the 103d Congress to protect President Clinton's stimulus program from hostile amendments. In the end, that bill was killed by a filibuster, and Republican rage at Byrd's tactics may have contributed to that outcome. Although no data are available, it appears that majority leaders use that tactic more than in the past. Lott used it again on the Ed-Flex bill early in the 106th Congress, but again the tactic was not successful in preventing Democrats from getting votes on their amendments.

Certainly the control that the majority leader and the Senate majority party exercise over the floor agenda is even less secure than it used to be. A concerted campaign by an organized minority party is a greater threat than the efforts of an individual senator or small group, and the costs of losing control tend to be higher. A Jesse Helms uses nongermane amendments to force Democrats—and some of his fellow Republicans—to go on record on hot-button issues they might rather avoid, and Nevada's senators employ extended debate to block nuclear waste from being stored in their state. When the same tactics are used by an organized partisan minority—the Republicans in the 103d Congress and the Democrats in the 104th and 105th, for example—party images and legislative outcomes on major legislation can be severely affected.

Demonstrating again the peculiar combination of individualism and partisanship in the Senate, the minority party often receives aid from a dissenting majority party member. Thus the vocal opposition of Senator Sam Nunn, Democratic chairman of the Armed Services Committee, to President Clinton's policy on gays in the military and senior Republican Senator John McCain's support for a stiff tobacco control bill and for Democratic-supported campaign finance reform legislation gave the minority's campaigns a bipartisan aura and yielded more and better media coverage.

In the current context of policy-polarized parties, the more ideologically driven senators tend to press their leaders to pursue hardball partisan tactics and to avoid compromise. Republican leaders are under greater pressure than Democrats because, in recent years, a larger number of ideologically driven senators have been elected on the Republican side and because, as the majority, Republicans are more dissatisfied with the restraints the Senate imposes on majority decisionmaking.[18] Some committee leaders have come under attack; thus Orrin Hatch (R-Utah), hardly a moderate, has been chastised for working too closely with Ted Kennedy, for being too accommodating to the Clinton administration on judicial nominees, and for being insufficiently enthusiastic about impeachment. Junior conservatives even made several attempts to reduce his powers. Majority Leader Lott has been criticized for allowing Democrats to get the upper hand, as in the gun control debate. Not only did he "allow" floor debate on the issue, his attempt to blunt the Democratic attack by artfully crafted amendments failed, and he then did not prevent a situation in which Vice President Gore cast the deciding vote on a key amendment. The fall 1998 budget deal between the Republican Congress and Clinton, negotiated by Lott and Gingrich, also provoked a storm of criticism. Conservatives, in and out of the chamber, charged that Lott had made too many concessions to Clinton, and twenty Republicans, including Whip Don Nickles, voted against the agreement.[19]

The greater intensity of partisan conflict has led to some hot words and occasionally some lapses of civility. When two Democrats switched their position on the balanced budget amendment, thus ensuring its defeat again, a frustrated Lott blasted them on the floor of the Senate—though not by name—as dishonest and deceptive.[20] Minority Leader Daschle decried Lott's use of the tactic of filling the amendment tree as "undemocratic and unfair," to which Lott responded, "They don't get to set the agenda."[21]

## Skirting Gridlock

Yet, despite its rules, the Senate does manage to pass legislation and usually does so while maintaining civility in its committee rooms and on the floor. Senators may not be best friends—especially across the aisle—but they seldom express open hostility, as House members do.[22] Furthermore, even senators of very different ideological persuasions—Senators Kennedy and Hatch, for example—manage to work together.

The Senate's handling of impeachment illustrates how the contemporary Senate functions and provides clues to how this individualist, partisan body with permissive rules avoids breaking down. What is notable about impeachment in the Senate is that neither side went for broke, as their counterparts in the House did. When the House of Representatives sent impeachment articles against President Clinton to the Senate, the Senate Republican majority and its leadership, although they knew their chances of reaching the two-thirds vote necessary to convict were slim at best, needed to satisfy the Republican party's core supporters and the House managers who wanted a full-scale and vigorous trial. Democrats, of course, wanted as truncated a process as possible. Yet Lott and Daschle worked together closely to keep the process as civil and consensual as they could; other senators worked across the aisle too, including, notably, the unlikely duo of Ted Kennedy and Phil Gramm. On the question of witnesses, Lott made a deal that gave Daschle veto power over further witnesses when he could have forced through a much tougher set of ground rules on a majority vote. Daschle and Senate Democrats, for their part, did not systematically pursue their obvious strategy of portraying the Senate process as similar to and as partisan as that in the House and, thus, as illegitimate. Certainly both sides had immediate reasons for their decisions. Lott and Senate Republicans wanted to avoid the public black eye the House had given itself by its strident partisanship. Daschle and the Democrats did not want to damage the chamber in which they served either. Yet the awareness of both sides that, for anyone to attain their legislative goals, they would have to work together in the future seems to have played a considerable part as well.

Although senators as individuals and as party groupings now exploit Senate prerogatives to a much greater extent than they did in the 1950s and 1960s, they do not, in fact, frequently push them to the limit. The Senate is regularly able to reach unanimous consent agreements to carry out much of its work. The course of hot partisan battles—those over the Ed-Flex bill, gun control, and the "Patients' Bill of Rights" in 1999, for example—is studded with unanimous consent agreements between the parties on timing, to accommodate individual senators (an amendment will seldom be taken up when a strong opponent cannot be present), and even to limit amendments to some extent. And tough partisan battles are still usually conducted in civil language. When the Republicans attempted to use a cloture vote on another bill to get the issue of gun control off the floor, Majority Leader Daschle responded mildly, "Surprises are never welcomed, and this was a surprise that was disappointing. Nonetheless, we will work through that."[23]

Since the full exploitation of Senate prerogatives by many of its members as individuals or by a sizable organized minority would lead to total gridlock, senators do have an interest in maintaining some restraint. For senators to further their goals, the chamber must be capable of legislating. Most senators advance their goals, at least in part, through legislating; even those who do not depend on the Senate's relevance as a legislative body. The climate of restraint and cooperation that allows the Senate to legislate despite its permissive rules is, however, a collective good: all senators benefit from it whether or not they "contribute," because one senator pushing his or her prerogatives to the limit will not make the chamber unworkable. So each senator would seem to have an incentive to "cheat" or "free-ride," to push his or her prerogatives to the limit, while others continue to act so as to allow the chamber to function. Analyses of such situations suggest that concern about the future can induce individuals to cooperate, to forgo the current benefit of noncooperative behavior in return for the future benefits of cooperation.[24] Those analyses also show the fragility of such tacit arrangements. Especially now that the Senate parties are ideologically polarized and sufficiently organized to make systematic strategic use of Senate prerogatives, how is the minimum necessary cooperation and restraint maintained?

Individual members are, to some extent, restrained by concern about the future impact of their present behavior. Senators, staff, and informed observers questioned about what prevents senators from pushing their powers to the limit uniformly responded that almost all senators want to "get something done" and they are aware that if many senators exploited their prerogatives to the limit, that would be impossible. As one knowledgeable insider phrased it, "I like to think of the Senate as a bunch of armed nuclear nations. Each senator knows he can blow the place up, but most of them came here to do something, and if he does blow things up, if he does use his powers that way, then he won't be able to do anything." Norms of "comity and courtesy" were mentioned by several aides; "there are unwritten rules that say you shouldn't abuse these powers, and if you really go too far, you're likely to be ostracized within your own party." No one, however, argued that norms were sufficient to ensure other-regarding behavior. Using one's prerogatives aggressively entails concrete short-run costs, most argued. "If you do object [to a unanimous consent request], it's going to hurt someone and maybe more than one person," a senior staffer explained, "so the next time you want something, it may very well happen to you." Senators do not put holds on every bill or nomination they oppose, another experienced aide said, "because people will put a hold on their stuff then." In the Senate, individuals can exact retribution swiftly and often quite easily on those they believe have harmed them. Because of that, a junior senator reported, "in the Senate, you don't go out of your way to hack people off." In the House, there is less such concern, he explained. The likelihood that some retaliation will be forthcoming forces the wise senator to be selective in the employment of his or her prerogatives.

The importance of guarding their reputations also constrains senators. Placing a hold or objecting to a unanimous consent request is inexpensive in terms of senator or staff time; following through and actually employing delaying tactics on the floor costs a great deal of time. "Threats are taken seriously in the Senate," a senior staff aide said, "but they depend on a perception that you'll carry out your threat, so you need to do it selectively." A senator's reputation influences the leadership reaction to a senator's threat. As a leadership aide explained, "When you get a letter [putting on a hold], you ask what is his track record in order to judge how seriously you need to take it."

The restraint necessary to allow the Senate to function is not, then, purely a public good. Senators do have some individual incentives to avoid repeatedly pushing their prerogatives to the limit. Yet they also have in numerous individual instances considerable incentives to use their prerogatives aggressively. The incentives that constrain individual senators do not by themselves seem sufficient to allow the Senate to function.

The party leaders seem to play a critical role in maintaining the necessary cooperation. For the party leaders, a breakdown in Senate functioning is a direct threat to their own goals: if they allow a situation to develop in which their members cannot further their legislative goals, the leaders are in danger of losing their positions. And they are almost certainly more aware than other senators of how fragile the conditions for Senate functioning are.

In the Senate, the majority leader and the minority leader work together closely. The Senate leaders confer daily, and they consult most frequently when the parties are locked in combat on a big issue. During the impeachment process, Lott and Daschle talked multiple times a day. The leaders work hard at maintaining a good relationship. Lott goes out of his way to comment on how frequently he talks to Daschle and how good their relationship is: "as good as any Majority and Minority Leader . . . probably since Johnson and Dirksen."[25] On the second anniversary of Lott's becoming majority leader, Daschle said, "I think he's doing a good job," and, after the impeachment trial, he praised Lott effusively. Other Democrats, both senators and staff, complain that Lott "can't control his right wing and so can't deliver on promises he makes," that, therefore, his word is not good. Republicans, in turn, gripe that Daschle is not serious about legislating or that he is not really in charge but rather that Ted Kennedy is; and therefore his word is not good. Lott and Daschle, in contrast, know they must deal with each other and reportedly actually defend each other behind closed doors. Both know that each must pursue his party's policy and electoral aims vigorously, but they also know that both will suffer severe damage if the chamber ceases to function. What happened when Bob Dole decided to run for the presidency from his position as Senate majority leader provides an exception that illustrated the strategic considerations involved. In this case, Dole's stake in the Senate functioning well became much higher than that of his opposite number; in fact, Democrats had a much stronger interest in depriving Dole of legislative victories during the few months in question than in scoring ones of their own.

For the Senate to function successfully as a legislature requires some restraint and cooperation on the part of senators. The party leaders, who act as coordinators, seem to be instrumental to maintaining that condition. Of course, for success, they are dependent on cooperation from their members. Self-interest restrains individual senators to some extent. Leaders also have favors they can do and threats they can use. A long-time observer of the Senate explained, "I think I remember every majority leader saying at one point or another, 'I think we're going to have to work through Christmas,' and that's obviously a threat. Get things done or we'll be here forever. Members are dependent on the leaders to have any sort of predictability to their schedules though even so, it's extremely unpredictable when, how long people will be in. And you hear a Majority Leader saying, 'Well, we won't be in on Friday if we finish this bill on Thursday,' and it's remarkable how that works to get people to come to closure." The greater partisanship and sense of party team spirit may actually increase party leaders' clout over individual members who want to go off on their own; the leaders will often have peer pressure on their side.

In a highly partisan era, on the other hand, party leaders are also under pressure from their members to vigorously pursue partisan ends. Maintaining the conditions necessary for the Senate legislative process to function is a delicate enterprise, so the process itself is fragile. Major legislation is, in fact, more likely to die in the Senate than in the House.[26] Perhaps what leads to the reestablishment of the minimum necessary restraint and cooperation after an impasse is reached is the immediacy of the negative consequences of failing to do so.

## Notes

All unattributed quotations are from interviews conducted by the author.

1. Sarah Binder, *Minority Rights, Majority Rule: Partisanship and the Development of Congress* (Cambridge University Press, 1997).

2. Donald E Matthews, *U.S. Senators and Their World* (New York: Vintage Books, 1960).

3. Barbara Sinclair, *The Transformation of the U.S. Senate* (Johns Hopkins University Press, 1989); Ralph Huitt, "The Internal Distribution of Influence: The Senate," in David Truman, ed., *The Congress and America's Future* (New York: Prentice-Hall, 1965).

4. Bruce Oppenheimer, "Changing Time Constraints on Congress: Historical Perspectives on the Use of Cloture," in Lawrence C. Dodd and Bruce I. Oppenheimer, eds. *Congress Reconsidered*, 3d ed. (Washington, D.C.: CQ Press, 1985).

5. Sinclair, *Transformation of the U.S. Senate*; Michael Foley, *The New Senate* (Yale University Press, 1980); David Rohde, Norman Ornstein, and Robert Peabody, "Political Change and Legislative Norms in the U.S. Senate, 1957–1974," in Glenn Parker, ed., *Studies of Congress* (Washington, D.C.: CQ Press, 1985).

6. See also Burdett Loomis, *The New American Politician* (New York: Basic Books, 1988).

7. Sinclair, *Transformation of the U.S. Senate,* p. 84.

8. Ibid.; Barbara Sinclair, *Unorthodox Lawmaking* (Washington, D.C.: CQ Press, 1997).

9. See Barbara Sinclair, *Legislators, Leaders and Lawmaking* (Johns Hopkins University Press, 1995).

10. Donald Baumer, "Senate Democratic Leadership in the 100th Congress," in Ronald Peters and Allen Herzke, eds., *The Atomistic Congress* (Armonk, N.Y.: M. E. Sharpe, 1992); Steven S. Smith, "Forces of Change in Senate Party Leadership and Organization," in Lawrence C. Dodd and Bruce I. Oppenheimer, eds. *Congress Reconsidered*, 5th ed. (Washington, D.C.: CQ Press, 1993).

11. Mary Jacoby, "Waiting in Wings, a Kinder, Gentler Lott?" *Roll Call*, March 9, 1995, p. 22.

12. John Bresnahan and Jim VandeHei, "Leaders Set to Meet with Clinton," *Roll Call*, February 18, 1999, p. 15.

13. Phil Kuntz, "Drawn-Out Denouement Mirrors Character of 102nd Congress," *Congressional Quarterly Weekly Report*, October 10, 1992, p. 3128.

14. Major legislation is here defined as those measures included in the *Congressional Quarterly* in its list of major legislation, augmented by those measures on which there were key votes, again according to *Congressional Quarterly*.

15. Dean McSweeney and John E. Owens, eds., *The Republican Takeover on Capitol Hill* (London: Macmillan, 1998).

16. *Congressional Quarterly Weekly*, May 22, 1999, p. 1205.

17. Greg Thorson and Tasina Nitzschke, "When the Majority Won't Listen: The Use of the Senate Filibuster by the Minority Party," paper delivered at the Midwest Political Science Association meetings, April 15–17, 1999, Chicago.

18. Dan Blatz and Ronald Brownstein, *Storming the Gates: Protest Politics and the Republican Revival* (Boston: Little, Brown, 1996).

19. John Bresnahan, "Lott Tries to Fix Budget Damage," *Roll Call*, October 26, 1998, p. 22.

20. *Los Angeles Times*, March 1, 1997.

21. *Congressional Quarterly Weekly*, May 6, 1999, p. 1056.

22. Ross Baker, *Friend and Foe in the U.S. Senate* (Acton, Mass.: Copley, 1999).

23. *Congressional Record*, daily ed., May 14, 1999, p. S5335.

24. Robert Axelrod, *The Evolution of Cooperation* (New York: Basic Books, 1984); James Morrow, *Game Theory for Political Scientists* (Princeton University Press, 1994).

25. John Bresnahan, "Senate Leader Defends His Performance," *Roll Call*, June 11, 1998, p. 34.

26. Barbara Sinclair, "Institutional Structure, Political Context and Policy Making," paper delivered at the 1999 Midwestern Political Science Association Meetings, April 15–17, 1999, Chicago.

# CHAPTER FIVE

# The Procedural Context
# of Senate Deliberation

## C. LAWRENCE EVANS
## WALTER J. OLESZEK

"I THINK WE ARE DEALING HERE with sort of a Molotov minuet. Everything we have tried to do, we are being met with, 'No. Nyet.'"[1] So complained a frustrated Senate Majority Leader Trent Lott (R-Miss.), in late June 1999, as he sought agreement with Democratic leaders on a procedure for considering managed health care reform on the Senate floor.

Throughout the 1990s, the managed care issue sharply divided the two political parties, with Republicans generally favoring a market-based approach to change and Democrats emphasizing more governmental oversight and extending patients' legal rights. After two procedural votes were taken on June 22, 1999, it became clear that the Republican version of managed care reform would prevail in a head-to-head contest with the Democratic proposal, the so-called Patients' Bill of Rights. But both sides also recognized that portions of the Democratic substitute were highly popular with the public. If considered on the Senate floor as free-standing amendments, these provisions might pass. At the very least, Senate Republicans would have to cast a series of politically dangerous votes. Thus, as often occurs in Congress, a decision about procedure would have potentially important implications for floor deliberations on a major policy matter.

The standing rules of the Senate are cumbersome, and they provide individual lawmakers with a range of tools to delay or even block the flow of legislation. As a result, floor action on important bills is usually governed by unanimous consent agreements (UCAs), in which senators unanimously waive the rules and adopt instead specific guidelines designed for the consideration of a particular measure. On the evening of June 23, 1999, for instance, GOP leaders proposed a UCA that would have made either the Republican or Democratic managed care plan the "pending business at 1 p.m. on Monday, July 12," with a final vote scheduled for three days hence. All amendments would have to be substantively relevant to managed health care (or propose a health care tax cut), and the consideration of individual amendments would be limited to two hours each. Among other restrictions, the right to offer the last amendment would be reserved for Majority Leader Lott. And no other proposals relevant to managed care would be in order on the Senate floor for the rest of the year.

Minority Leader Tom Daschle (D-S.Dak.) immediately rejected the GOP offer and quipped, "If this is a Molotov minuet, there's only one side dancing."[2] Under the proposed UCA, Daschle argued, Republicans would be able to introduce a plethora of amendments, each consuming two hours of debate. Insufficient time might remain to consider the main Democratic amendments. He also objected to the provision giving Lott the final amending opportunity, warning that the Mississippian could "wipe out all that we've done."[3] Instead, Democrats wanted a UCA that would guarantee them the ability to offer at least twenty amendments and also ensure that Republicans would not block a vote on final passage if the legislation were amended toward the minority party's position. They increased the pressure on GOP leaders to make such concessions by blocking legislative action in the full chamber for an entire week.

Finally, on June 29, as the traditional July 4 recess approached, Lott, Daschle, and other interested senators struck a procedural accord for the managed health care legislation that left GOP conservatives privately fuming and Democrats declaring victory. Under the new UCA, four days of managed care debate would occur in mid-July, with a final vote scheduled for Thursday, July 15. Debate on individual amendments would be limited to just fifty minutes, ensuring that Senate Democrats would have sufficient time to offer all twenty amendments on their priority list. No filibustering would be allowed.

The intense parliamentary wrangling over managed care illustrates the important linkages that exist between procedure and policymaking in the U.S. Senate. It also raises some fundamental questions about the procedural context of Senate deliberation.

—*Procedure* is a broad term that encompasses the formal standing rules of the Senate, the precedents compiled and interpreted by chamber parliamentarians, temporary agreements such as UCAs, and even informal understandings between interested lawmakers. How do the various forms of Senate procedure relate to one another and to the deliberative process?

—Procedural arrangements shape policymaking by assigning parliamentary rights and otherwise constraining the range of permissible actions. But many aspects of Senate procedure, including the UCAs that structure so much legislative work, are themselves determined as part of the deliberative process. How are procedures developed and how do they change?

—According to most observers, the Senate has become more partisan and ideologically polarized over the past two decades. Has the use of procedure on the Senate floor been affected by the heightened partisanship? What are the consequences for deliberation?

This chapter takes up these questions by exploring the historical development and contemporary usage of UCAs in the U.S. Senate. Our broader goal is to shed light on the role of procedure in the Senate, especially the consequences of procedure for the institution's deliberative capacity.

## Nuts and Bolts

Our focus on UCAs is appropriate because, in the Senate, practice often dominates over formal rules. In 1876 the president pro tempore of the chamber stated that "rules are never observed in this body; they are only made to be broken. We are a law unto ourselves."[4] Over a century later, a lawmaker remarked that "the way the Senate conducts its business hour after hour, day after day, week after week, and year after year, is senators voluntarily waive the rights which they possess under the rules."[5]

It is hyperbole to assert that the Senate "never follows its rules." Many provisions of the chamber's standing rules influence day-to-day legislative work, while others have been mostly superseded by precedent or are routinely waived by unanimous consent. Of the formal Senate rules that are most directly associated with floor deliberations (see table 5-1), one that has not been overtaken by precedent or practice is Rule 22, which delineates the steps necessary to invoke cloture, that is, to secure the sixty votes necessary to end a filibuster and bring debate to a close.[6] Its various provisions remain a binding and pervasive feature of legislative work in the chamber. In contrast, most provisions of Rule 30, which pertains to the chamber's constitutional prerogative of treaty ratification, have been overtaken by practice. The two-thirds requirement for Senate passage is still

Table 5-1. *Observance of Senate Rules Directly Relevant to Floor Consideration*

| Rule number | Rule content | Usually followed | Followed in part | Mostly overtaken by precedent, practice, or consent |
|---|---|:---:|:---:|:---:|
| IV | Start of daily sessions | | X | |
| V | Suspension and amendment of rules | | | |
| | Motion to suspend | | | X |
| | Continuous rules | X | | |
| VI | Quorums | X | | |
| VII | Morning business | | | X |
| VIII | Order of business | | | X |
| X | Special orders | | | X |
| XII | Voting procedure | X | | |
| XIII | Reconsideration | | | |
| | Senator on prevailing side | X | | |
| | Measure transmittal to House | | | X |
| XIV | Bills, joint resolutions, etc. | X | | |
| XV | Amendments and motions | | | |
| | Written motions | X | | |
| | Withdrawal of motions | X | | |
| | Amendment procedure | | | X |
| | Lay on the table | X | | |
| | Committee amendment and jurisdiction | X | | |
| XVI | Appropriations and amendments to appropriations | | X | |
| XVII | Reference to committees | X | | |
| XIX | Debate | X | | |
| XX | Questions of order | X | | |
| XXII | Precedence of motions (cloture) | X | | |
| XXVIII | Conference | | | |
| | Presentation of reports | X | | |
| | Insertion of new matter | | | X |
| | Conference substitute | | | X |
| | Printed reports | X | | |
| | Debate time | X | | |
| | Open conferences | | | X |
| XXX | Treaties | | | X |
| XXXI | Nominations | | | X |

binding, but the actual process of treaty consideration is largely governed by UCAs, rather than the formal strictures of the relevant rule.

Precisely what is a unanimous consent agreement? Basically, it is a device used to establish procedural ground rules for the consideration of legislation and to impose time limits on debate and amendments. Textbooks distinguish between *simple* and *complex* UCAs. According to one account, "Simple requests are made from the floor by any senator; these almost always deal with routine business or noncontroversial motions." In contrast, complex UCAs, also known as *time agreements,* "set the guidelines for floor consideration of major bills."[7]

Such a classification is of limited practical value, however, because complex agreements themselves differ so much in content and coverage. The UCA for managed health care, to take one example, is a relatively comprehensive agreement that sets a deadline for the vote on final passage and also places significant limitations on the amendment process. Far more common are UCAs that deal with just one portion or aspect of a bill's consideration. Indeed, most major contemporary measures are subject to a dozen or more discrete UCAs, all of which would be deemed complex according to the standard definition. We can distinguish complex UCAs along two general dimensions: scope and restrictiveness. Scope refers to the proportion of floor debate on a measure that is covered by a UCA, restrictiveness to the degree to which a UCA actually constrains the procedural prerogatives of individual members.

Some UCAs are relatively narrow in scope and fairly unrestrictive (figure 5-1). In May 1999 the Senate adopted a number of UCAs to help structure floor debate on S.254, the juvenile justice bill. At one point, Judiciary Committee Chairman Orrin Hatch (R-Utah) requested unanimous consent that no second-degree amendments be in order to a pending "code of conduct" amendment (offered by Sam Brownback, R-Kans.) until thirty minutes of debate had occurred. Later, Chairman Hatch requested unanimous consent to lay aside a pending amendment so that Barbara Boxer (D-Calif.) could offer a different amendment. Both UCAs dealt with just one or two amendments, and neither was particularly constraining.

Other UCAs are narrow in scope but provide more precise restrictions on portions of the amendment process. On the juvenile justice bill, for instance, Majority Leader Lott received unanimous consent to limit debate on four amendments and to also take a two-hour detour to work on a supplemental appropriations bill. The time limits and other debate restrictions here were more significant than in the case of the other two juvenile justice agreements.

Notice that in figure 5-1 the more constraining UCAs are referred to as "moderately restrictive." Highly restrictive UCAs seldom surface in the Senate except on noncontroversial measures, in which case their restrictiveness is mostly illusory. For controversial legislation, getting 100 sena-

Figure 5-1. *Differences among Complex Unanimous Consent Agreements (UCAs)*

| | | Restrictiveness | |
| --- | --- | --- | --- |
| | | Moderate | Low |
| Scope | Broad | Comprehensive accords with major amendment limitations; typically reference germaneness or relevance; extensive time limits or time certain on amendments; typically a time certain for final passage vote. | Large number or portion of amendment process covered, but there are few possible amendments not in order; many amendments without time limits; perhaps a provision for final passage vote, but generally no time certain. |
| | Narrow | Precise debate limits on one or a few amendments; typically includes debate limitations and time certain for votes; speaking time may be precisely allocated to individual members. | Schedule an amendment or procedural motion; set pending amendment aside; other minor limits on debate. |

tors to accept truly severe restrictions on their discretion requires broad consensus that a measure must not be filibustered and a real sense of urgency about the timing of final passage.

A third category is UCAs that are broad in scope but not especially restrictive. These agreements may encompass a large portion of the amendment activity on a measure, but members give up little discretion in accepting them. During consideration of the juvenile justice measure, Lott requested and received unanimous consent that "the following amendments be the only first degree amendments in order, with relevant second degree amendments in order, only after a vote on, or in relation to the amendment." This accord may sound restrictive, but Lott's list included sixty-eight amendments to be offered by thirty-seven senators, and time limitations were included for just two of the amendments. For the most part, the UCA was an attempt by the majority leader to pin members down about the amendments they planned to offer. Lott described the agreement as "a pathetic accomplishment."[8]

The fourth category in figure 5-1 consists of UCAs that are broad in scope but more restrictive than the juvenile justice accord just mentioned. Lott's original proposal for managed health care reform is an example. The amendments to be offered were not delineated, but Democrats felt that the general time limits on amendments combined with the date certain for final passage would keep them from offering many of their proposals. According to most accounts, the final agreement for managed care was less constraining.

How are unanimous consent agreements devised? On major bills, UCAs typically are the product of informal negotiations among interested senators, with party leaders and relevant committee leaders playing major roles. The majority leader generally prefers a comprehensive agreement, including overall limitations on debate and a deadline, or time certain, for final passage. But on controversial measures, such an agreement usually will not be feasible "up front." As a result, floor action on a bill often begins subject to a series of narrow, piecemeal UCAs aimed at facilitating consideration of individual amendments. As time passes and the pressure to speed action builds, the majority leader will request broader UCAs that encompass greater portions of the remaining amendments, with an eye toward limiting the total number of proposals to be offered and nailing down a deadline for final passage.

Even for relatively comprehensive agreements, only a select number of members and staff are active participants in the negotiation process. When a tentative agreement has been achieved among the active participants, the relevant party cloakroom informs Senate offices of that party via a telephone "hotline," which has a distinctive ring. Three or four staff persons in each member office are linked to the hotline. When a UCA request has been cleared at the leadership level, a tape recording of the contents will be relayed via the hotline, along with instructions that any office objecting to the request must notify the relevant party leadership within a certain period. Examples of typical hotline messages are presented in box 5-1.[9]

If a proposed UCA is comprehensive and related to controversial legislation, the deadline for registering an objection might be a number of days. For narrower agreements on pending items, the time available for objection might be as little as fifteen or twenty minutes. Obviously, if an individual senator objects to a proposed UCA, it is not an enforceable order of the Senate. As Majority Leader George Mitchell (D-Maine) once said, "I regularly propound unanimous consent requests on the floor, and I can assure [the Senator from Ohio] when Senators object we hear within seconds—within seconds. Frequently when I am in the middle of a sentence, the phone rings and staff comes running out [of the cloakroom] to say, 'Senator so and so objects.'"[10]

Usually, the majority leader, or his designee, will propose a UCA orally and, if it is accepted, the agreement is printed not only in the *Congres-*

Box 5-1. *Sample Hotline Messages from the Senate Democratic Cloakroom*

"In the event that the Senate considers the Social Security lock box issue and that it is amendable, the Cloakroom is attempting to generate a list of amendments. Please call the Cloakroom if the Senator has any amendments to this issue." (July 13, 1999, 3:50 p.m.)

"The Majority Leader asks unanimous consent that at a time to be determined by the Majority Leader and no later than Tuesday, October 12, 1999, the Senate proceed to the immediate consideration of the McCain-Feingold campaign reform bill. The Majority Leader asks further consent that the reform bill be put on the calendar by Wednesday, September 14, 1999, and that debate on the bill prior to a cloture vote be limited to three hours and that only amendments related to campaign finance reform be in order." (July 20, 1999, 4:29 p.m.)

"The Majority Leader asks unanimous consent that all first degree amendments [to the Commerce, Justice, State Appropriations Bill] must be offered and debated tonight followed by final passage." (July 22, 1999, 5:34 p.m.)

"The Majority Leader asks unanimous consent that the Senate take up and pass S.305, Calendar 161, a bill to provide for changes in the boxing industry, with three additional amendments. (1) A McCain amendment to add changes requested by the Attorney General. (2) A Reid amendment pertaining to additional regulation regarding the broadcasting of the sport. (3) A Moynihan amendment requiring a CAT Scan and physical for all fighters every two years. If there are objections, call the Cloakroom." (July 27, 1999, 5:07 p.m.)

*sional Record* but also in the *Senate Journal*. UCAs that carry over from one day to the next also are printed in the Daily Calendar. Technically, a request for unanimous consent is not debatable, but this precedent is routinely obviated by senators stating that they "reserve the right" to object; they then gain the right to discuss their reservation about the proposal.

## UCAs: The Early Years

Because procedure shapes policy, the nature of Congress as a representative body can be understood by looking at the direction in which its procedures have evolved. How do congressional procedures change—incrementally, as a by-product of day-to-day legislating, or through periodic efforts at "congressional reform?" Are procedures primarily designed to promote the policy agenda of the majority party? Are they designed to help powerful interest groups? Or do the internal arrangements of Congress serve the interests of the membership as a whole? Because members of the Senate have used UCAs to structure floor action since the mid-1800s, these devices serve as a useful base from which to explore these questions.[11]

Senators came to rely on UCAs because of the cumbersome nature of Senate rules and the absence of a previous question motion. It was certainly apparent early on that individual lawmakers could use dilatory tactics to block the flow of legislation. And if all members pushed their procedural prerogatives to the limit, the outcome would be gridlock on the Senate floor, as is increasingly likely today. Senators as a group would be worse off than if, as individuals, they had all exercised some restraint.

Consider one late-night session in February 1917. Senator Furnifold Simmons (D-N.C.) proposed a UCA for a revenue measure; Senator Henry Ashurst (D-Ariz.) promptly objected, threatening his colleagues that he would continue to block all legislation until the conference report for an Indian appropriations bill he favored was scheduled for floor action. Warned Ashurst, "You made me the promise two years ago and you did not keep it. You are going to pass that Indian bill, or you will not have any legislation."

*Mr. Smoot.* May I suggest that Thursday morning—

*Mr. Ashurst.* No sir; no, sir. . . . No; you sang me that kind of a song two years ago—"Wait, wait, wait"—and we waited forever. Now, the iron hand: You will pass the Indian bill, or you will get nothing. . . .

*Mr. Simmons.* After this bill is disposed of on Wednesday, at the next session we will take up the conference report on the Indian appropriation bill.

*Mr. Ashurst.* Mr. President, Wednesday is not satisfactory to me. I want it done to-night.

*Several Senators.* Oh, no!

*Mr. Simmons.* You can not do it to-night. It is 12 o'clock now.

The senators then came up with a proposal, acceptable to Ashurst, in which the Indian appropriations report would be considered immediately following a pending flood control measure. But as Simmons began to make the unanimous consent request, Senator John Shafroth (D-Colo.), who wanted yet another bill scheduled, interrupted him and stated, "I wish to have some kind of an understanding as to the Puerto Rican civil-government bill."[12] The result was bedlam on the Senate floor.

Now fast-forward eight decades to summer 1999, and consider again the willingness of Democrats to shut down the Senate floor until a UCA was devised for managed health care reform. Majority Leader Lott posed in front of four tractors on the Capitol lawn to dramatize the potential damage from delaying the agriculture appropriations bill and other spending measures. But Minority Leader Daschle and other Democrats simply responded, "We'll get votes [on managed care]. It's either that, or we'll sit on the Senate floor looking at each other."[13]

One way to contain the dilatory potential of Senate rules is to regularize the process through which the agenda is set and floor action is structured. Individual senators are less likely to push their obstructionist powers to the limit if they can influence the procedure for considering a bill, and if they know their parliamentary rights are fully protected.[14]

Following the Civil War, the workload and policymaking role of the Senate expanded significantly. As a result, it became increasingly important for senators as a collectivity to devise mechanisms for rationalizing floor deliberations and bringing matters to a vote. But it also became increasingly tempting for individual senators to make systematic use of the dilatory potential in Senate rules. Unanimous consent agreements emerged as an informal adaptation aimed at balancing this need for legislative efficiency against the individual prerogatives of senators.

For the most part, early UCAs were not treated as binding orders of the Senate, but as informal agreements among individual members.[15] As UCAs became more common, norms and guidelines concerning their use emerged incrementally over time. In February 1902, *Gilfry's Precedents* recorded an early UCA precedent, which reinforced long-standing tradition that the procedural accords were informal gentlemen's agreements: "The responsibility for violating the agreement must rest with the senators themselves. The chair has no power to enforce it."

By the 1910s, however, it was apparent that precedent and practice were no longer sufficient to make the unanimous consent process fair and predictable. A formal rule change was necessary. In 1913 a bitter floor fight erupted when a senator who planned to object to a request for unanimous consent was momentarily distracted and failed to offer a timely "I object." Two days of debate ensued about the legitimacy of the existing unanimous consent process and the conditions under which a UCA could be modified. In the end, the Senate voted to resubmit the UCA under question, there was an objection, and another accord was quickly propounded and accepted. The following year, Rule 12 was amended to stipulate that no unanimous consent request to take a final vote could be submitted without a quorum present, that UCAs would be treated as enforceable orders of the Senate, and that a UCA could be altered or revoked by unanimous consent.

## Procedural Change

The 1914 reform of Rule 12 provides an interesting glimpse at procedural development in the Senate, a process that scholars are only beginning to understand. Often, procedures in Congress begin as informal practices, gradually are incorporated into precedent, and eventually are codified into a chamber's standing rules.[16] For instance, the Legislative Reorganization Act of 1946, which appeared to overhaul committee jurisdictions in Congress, is said to have codified precedent that had been in place for decades.[17] As a result, some argue, students of congressional change should focus on the formation of precedent, rather than episodic attempts at congressional reform.

It should be stressed, however, that complex relationships can exist between precedents and rules in Congress. Consider the linkages between UCA practice, precedent, and the 1914 reform of Senate Rule 12. In the Senate, a point of order is an objection raised by a member about how a chamber rule is being implemented. Such motions are either sustained or overruled by the chair. If sustained, the ruling becomes a precedent and is used for guidance when similar situations arise in the future. From 1884 to 1927, fifty-five points of order were raised about the unanimous consent process: twenty-nine before the rule change and twenty-six afterward.[18] As figure 5-2 demonstrates, the level of procedural dispute was low until the years immediately preceding the rule change, at which point it increased sharply, peaking in 1913–14. From the content of the reformed Rule 12, it is clear that the rule change did constitute a break from prior precedent.

Thus the 1914 change did not codify past precedent. Instead, it was an attempt to clarify and compensate for the inadequacies of precedent and the accompanying procedural unrest. Indeed, a number of new points of order were raised subsequent to the rule change, as members ironed out implementation of the reformed Rule 12.

Figure 5-2. *UCA Points of Order, 1885–1930*

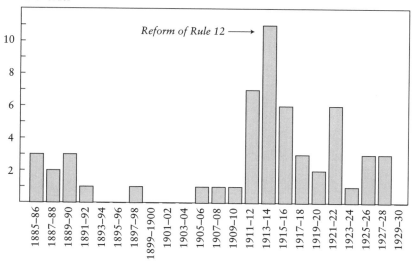

Some changes in congressional rules do serve to codify prior precedent. But the 1914 UCA reform suggests that rules can also make up for the limitations of precedent. In addition, there are still other potential relationships between precedent and rule. In some cases, precedent is created to fill gaps that exist in a standing rule. Following the 1946 overhaul of committee jurisdictions, there was a flurry of new jurisdictional precedent in the Senate, as the institution dealt with legislation that did not mesh cleanly with the new jurisdictions. Occasionally, precedent is used to overturn a standing rule. In 1995 Senator Kay Bailey Hutchison (R-Tex.) offered a legislative rider to an appropriations bill, which the chair ruled out of order because of the Rule 16 provision against attaching authorizing language to spending bills. But the Senate voted to overturn the chair's ruling, creating a precedent that essentially nullified the rule. (On July 26, 1999, the chamber voted to reinstate enforcement of Rule 16.) Clearly, the sources of procedural change in Congress are complex and will depend in part on the area of procedure under focus.

Following the 1914 change in Senate Rule 12, the chamber's reliance on UCAs further increased, with the accords gradually becoming important tools for the centralized party leadership. From the debate surrounding the pre-1914 UCAs for which points of order were raised, it is clear that the role of party leaders was fairly limited.[19] For the twenty-nine pre-rule change UCAs, the chair of the majority caucus participated in the floor debate on just eight of the disputes.[20] The minority caucus chair was active in just three of the debates. The relevant committee chair was somewhat more likely to play a role in the floor discussion about these matters (by our count, participating in eleven of the disputes), while informal Senate leaders such as Nelson Aldrich (R-R.I.) and Henry Cabot Lodge (R-Mass.) were more routinely involved.[21]

After the rule change, the presence of party leaders during floor disputes about UCAs increased markedly, especially among Republicans. For the twenty-six points of order raised between 1914 and 1927, the GOP floor leader participated in sixteen of the discussions. Democratic leader John Kern (D-Ind., 1913–17) preferred to manage the Senate's business in a "behind-the-scenes" fashion. He seldom appeared on the floor at all and left these debates to party lieutenants. But after Kern's electoral defeat in 1916, the Democratic floor leader was actively involved in most of the procedural disputes concerning the unanimous consent process.

By most accounts, the Senate's reliance on UCAs further increased following the March 1917 adoption of Rule 22, which provided members with a way to end filibusters. The new rule apparently facilitated the use of unanimous consent. One prominent historian wrote that "since the adoption of the Cloture Rule in 1917, it has been repeatedly evident that senators much prefer to end debate and get to a final vote by way of a unanimous-consent agreement with its appeal to senatorial courtesy, rather than under the compulsion of cloture, which may prove a precedent of evil omen."[22]

By the 1930s, the majority leader was regularly requesting unanimous consent to limit debate or bring matters to a vote. According to one count, there were 120 motions to limit or close debate on the floor by unanimous consent between February 2, 1937, and July 26, 1947. Fully 75 percent of these motions were made by the majority leader, Alben Barkley (D-Ky.). Between 1947 and 1952, 102 additional unanimous consent requests were accepted by the Senate. More than 90 of them included provisions to divide time, and 49 included a germaneness requirement for amendments.[23] In July 1952 Senator Wayne Morse (R-Oreg.) took to the floor to complain that "under the modern, postwar practice, unanimous-consent agreements are made to close debate on almost every major bill."[24]

## Scope and Restrictiveness Revisited

Along with the rise in incidence, UCAs also increased in scope and restrictiveness. Compare, for example, the UCA devised when Senator Ashurst tormented his colleagues about the Indian appropriations bill in February 1917 (box 5-2) and the July 1999 UCA that ended the procedural dispute over managed health care. For their respective eras, both accords were more complex than the typical UCA. Still, the 1917 agreement primarily served to schedule three measures, with just one time certain, and it included few restrictions on the amendment process. By contrast, the 1999 UCA is more detailed. It includes a time certain for the final passage vote; but also general time limits on amendments, restrictions on second-degree amendments, a relevance requirement, and guidelines on the order for taking up amendments. Overall, the scope and restrictiveness of UCAs increased substantially throughout the twentieth century, with qualitative shifts occurring in the 1960s and 1970s, especially under the majority leadership of Senator Robert C. Byrd (D-W.Va.).

The greatest transformation took place from 1955 to 1979.[25] The old communitarian norms of apprenticeship and specialization in the chamber broke down, and the legislative activities of members expanded accordingly.[26] The power of committee chairs and the old Southern oligarchy declined, the number of floor amendments exploded, and obstructionism became rampant. For Senate leaders, managing the floor became increasingly difficult. A consequence, asserts one study, was "innovations in the use and content of unanimous consent agreements."[27]

During the 1950s–70s, UCAs grew in number, increasingly included amendment-specific time limitations and deadlines, and became more likely to have provisions affecting individual senators. UCAs that adjusted the course of deliberations "mid-bill" also became more common: "As the Senate evolved from a communitarian to an individualistic legislative body, unanimous consent agreements became more tactical, complex, individualized, and ad hoc. Leadership strategy in managing the floor became more flexible and creative."[28]

The high-water mark for UCA complexity clearly occurred during Byrd's years as majority whip (1971–76) and during his first stint as majority leader (1977–81). Byrd assumed formal leadership at a time when the Washington interest group community was mushrooming in size and diversity, vastly expanding the array of political demands confronting the

Box 5-2. *UCAs, Then and Now*

**The Iron Hand: A 1917 UCA for Indian Appropriations**

It is agreed by unanimous consent that at 8 o'clock p.m. on Wednesday, February 28, 1917, the Senate will proceed to vote, without further debate, upon any amendment that may be pending, any amendment that may be offered, and upon the bill H.R. 20573, an act to provide increased revenue, etc., through the regular parliamentary stages to its final disposition; that the bill shall remain the unfinished business until finally disposed of, and no motion that would displace it shall be in order. If temporarily laid aside by unanimous consent, any Senator shall have the right to bring it immediately before the Senate, either to speak upon it or to propose an amendment to it. No motion to lay any amendment on the table shall be entertained by the Chair: provided, That it shall be in order on Monday, February 26, at 3 o'clock p.m., to make a motion to proceed for a period of not more than five hours to the consideration of H.R. 14777, the flood-control bill, so called; and, further, that immediately following the conclusion of the consideration of the flood-control bill, H.R. 14777, the Senate will consider and dispose of the conference report upon H.R. 18453, the Indian appropriation bill.

**Trent's Tractors: A 1999 UCA for Managed Care**

I ask unanimous consent that the majority leader or his designee, introduce the underlying health care bill and it be placed on the calendar by 12 noon on Thursday, July 8, and the bill become the pending business at 1 p.m. on Monday, July 12, 1999, with a vote occurring on final passage at the close

chamber and further complicating life for Senate leaders. Managing such forces required more intricate procedural devices. These practical exigencies dovetailed with Byrd's special strength: unparalleled mastery of the Senate rules and procedures to control the agenda and a keen desire to keep the legislative trains running on time. Especially in the late 1970s, Byrd routinely fashioned detailed and innovative UCAs to end parliamentary entanglements and facilitate the Senate agenda or the Democratic program.

of business on Thursday, July 15, and the bill be subject to the following agreement:

> That the bill be limited to 3 hours of debate, to be equally divided in the usual form, that all amendments in order to the bill be relevant to the subject of amendment Nos. 702, 703, the introduced bill or health care tax cuts, and all first degree amendments be offered in an alternating fashion with Senator Daschle to offer the initial first degree amendment and all first- and second-degree amendments be limited to 100 minutes each, to be equally divided in the usual form. I further ask consent that second-degree amendments be limited to one second-degree amendment per side, per party, with no motions to commit or recommit in order, or any other act with regard to the amendments in order, and that just prior to third reading of the bill, it be in order for the majority leader, or his designee to offer a final amendment, with no second-degree amendments in order.

> I further ask consent that following passage of the bill, should the bill, upon passage, contain any revenue blue slip matter, the bill remain at the desk and that when the Senate receives the House companion bill, the Senate proceed to its immediate consideration, all after the enacting clause be stricken, and the text of the Senate bill that was passed be inserted in lieu thereof, the bill as amended be passed, the Senate insist on its amendment and request a conference with the House, all without any intervening action or debate.

A classic Byrd UCA, relating to a controversial Alaskan lands bill, was accepted by the Senate in February 1980. This multipage agreement was so convoluted that parliamentary staff actually gave it a name: they called it "Fred." The underlying bill set aside an area equivalent in size to California and Maine as a wildlife region and natural parkland. The two Alaska Senators—Republican Ted Stevens and Democrat Mike Gravel—adamantly opposed the measure but went along with the UCA. A product of protracted and painstaking negotiations, it limited general debate on the measure to twenty hours and permitted a total of fourteen amendments (each with its own specific time limit) to be offered only by four principal senators who were party to the procedural deal. Among a multitude of other provisions, the UCA stipulated that the four members would have to file their amendment proposals over three months in advance of floor action; the parliamentarian would then determine if a proposal met the germaneness requirement included in the agreement. Even with the UCA, Gravel attempted to filibuster the measure by making repeated quorum calls and raising other procedural questions. The chamber adopted cloture in August 1980, the only time in Senate history that cloture has been invoked on a bill governed by a UCA.

Interestingly, over the years there has been a substantial *reduction* in the use of formal germaneness provisions. In the early 1950s, roughly half of complex UCAs stipulated germaneness requirements for possible amendments; for major bills considered in 1955–56, the percentage was 72.2.[29] Such restrictions have steadily become less prevalent, with the largest drops occurring in the mid-1960s and after 1980. In 1983–84, no major measures were debated subject to a germaneness requirement. One possible explanation (especially for the decrease in the mid-1960s) is "the increasing assertiveness of rank-and-file senators in protecting their prerogatives."[30] The drop in the 1980s, however, has more to do with the emergence of the "relevance standard" as an important component of UCAs.

Until recently, the terms "germane" and "relevant" have been treated as synonymous. Rule 16, for example, declares that no "amendment not germane or relevant to the subject matter contained in the bill [shall] be received." In the 1980s, senators and parliamentary staff began drawing a distinction between the two words, and relevance largely replaced germaneness as the standard nomenclature for UCAs.

What apparently triggered the distinction between the two words was the infamous post-cloture filibuster launched in 1977 by Senators James Abourezk (D-S.Dak.) and Howard Metzenbaum (D-Ohio), a fight Byrd considered among "the most vicious . . . that ever occurred in the history of the Senate."[31] The two senators were vehemently opposed to a natural gas bill and had the foresight to introduce hundreds of amendments in anticipation of cloture being invoked. At the time, Senate rules allowed Abourezk and Metzenbaum to prolong debate indefinitely, even post-cloture, by offering piles of potentially germane amendments that had been filed before cloture was invoked. An angry and frustrated Byrd eventually worked out a behind-the-scenes agreement with Vice President Walter

Mondale, in which the presiding officer recognized Byrd to make a motion aimed at ruling the amendments out of order. Mondale then sustained Byrd's point of order. It was upheld on appeal, the majority leader called up scores of amendments sponsored by Abourezk or Metzenbaum, and Mondale ruled them out of order. After nine heated days, the post-cloture filibuster was ended.

Under heightened time pressures to sort through the hundreds upon hundreds of amendments pre-filed by Abourezk and Metzenbaum, however, some easy-to-use criteria were needed to distinguish between germane and nongermane amendments. Here is where "germane" and "relevant" assumed distinct parliamentary meanings on Capitol Hill. In effect, the bar for germaneness was raised via a "technical amendment test," in which, for instance, amendments would be considered germane only if they restrict the scope of the bill, strike dates and numbers, or are nonbinding "sense-of-the-Senate" proposals. As a result, it was logistically possible to deal with the plethora of Abourezk-Metzenbaum proposals.

Before long, senators realized that the stricter construction of germaneness was going to be highly difficult to live with. It was not uncommon for amendments that had clear substantive linkages to a bill to be deemed nongermane according to the technical test. Senators wanted broader criteria that would enable them to offer their policy-related amendments to legislation on the floor; thus the term "relevant" began to surface regularly in UCAs in the early to mid-1980s. Party leaders also supported the change because they were concerned that senators might refuse to invoke cloture on the grounds that their pre-filed amendments would automatically be ruled out of order under the strict germaneness test. By the 1990s, the term "germane" almost never appeared in UCAs. In contrast, the looser relevance standard is now a regular component of these agreements.[32]

## Byrd and Lott

The emergence of the relevance standard marks an important difference in the UCAs used by Majority Leaders Byrd and Lott.[33] To facilitate further comparisons between the Byrd and Lott UCAs, we conducted a computer search of the *Congressional Record* during Byrd's second stint as majority leader (1987–88) and Lott's first full Congress in the position (1997–98). This search produced a representative sample of the UCAs used by each leader.[34] The sample includes 229 UCAs from the Byrd Congress and 71 UCAs from the Lott Congress. Each accord was personally proposed by the relevant majority leader and accepted by the chamber. We analyzed the content of these agreements, and the surrounding discussion in the *Record*, and tabulated certain information relating to the scope and restrictiveness of each accord.

In addition to the shift from germaneness to relevance, the most striking difference was the much larger number of agreements we found for Byrd. This change captures an important difference in the leadership styles of the two senators. As leader, Byrd was constantly on the floor, personally managing the flow of legislation, and regularly participating in the nitty-gritty of parliamentary procedure. Our search of the *Record* indicates that Byrd was an active participant in more than 90 percent of the floor discussions concerning unanimous consent agreements that occurred in 1987–88. In contrast, Lott appeared to be less personally involved in the intricate details of floor procedure and the unanimous consent process. Compared with Byrd, he appeared much more willing to delegate such responsibilities to other leaders, the relevant bill manager, and to key staff aides. On the UCA for managed health care, for instance, Majority Whip Don Nickles (R-Okla.) played a key role in the protracted negotiations with Daschle, Edward Kennedy (D-Mass.), and other Democrats. Before signing off on the accord, Lott briefed the entire Senate GOP conference about the bargaining process.[35]

It is possible to exaggerate the importance of formal participation in procedural discussions and of personally introducing, explaining, and defending proposed unanimous consent agreements. Much of the work of floor management is conducted through private conversations on the floor, in the cloakrooms, over the telephone, and via office meetings. Lott often delegated formal responsibility for devising UCAs to other members, even when he clearly played some role in outlining the procedural accord. However, the Senate staff with whom we spoke routinely commented that Majority Leader Lott seemed less personally involved in the day-to-day procedural business of the floor. In part, this change reflected the expanded public role that Senate party leaders now play, helping to craft, orchestrate, and publicize the party's public "message." We will return to this topic shortly. In part, the change also reflects the unique parliamentary interests and inclinations of Robert C. Byrd.

Interestingly, for all the differences in leadership style, here the similarities are much more striking than any differences (see table 5-2). For both Congresses, most UCAs are relatively narrow agreements that pertain to a

Table 5-2. *UCAs under Byrd and Lott*
Number (percent)[a]

| UCA | Byrd (1987–88) | | Lott (1997–98) | |
|---|---|---|---|---|
| Sample size | 229 | | 71 | |
| Provide for final passage, time certain for final vote, or time limits on overall amendments and debate | 82 | (35.8) | 35 | (49.3) |
| No amendments permitted | 26 | (11.4) | 3 | (4.2) |
| Reference specific amendment(s) | 144 | (75.8) | 46 | (78.0) |
| Reference just one amendment | 75 | (39.5) | 22 | (37.3) |
| Reference more than one amendment | 69 | (36.3) | 24 | (40.7) |
| Time limits or deadlines on one or more specific amendments | 90 | (47.4) | 36 | (50.7) |

a. The percentages for "no amendments permitted" exclude all matters that are basically unamendable, such as conference reports. The percentages for UCAs that reference specific amendment(s) and/or include amendment time limits or deadlines exclude the inherently unamendable matters, and also those items for which no amendments were permitted.

small portion of floor debate. For the agreements that refer to specific amendment proposals, about half mention just one. General time limits on the amendment process were rare, but approximately 50 percent of the accords (for which amendments were permitted) in both Congresses provided amendment-specific limitations. Regarding the number of discrete amendments mentioned in a UCA, the similarities across the Byrd and Lott Congresses are again prominent. For UCAs mentioning specific amendments, about 80 percent of the agreements in each Congress referenced five or fewer amendments (table 5-3). UCAs with extremely long amendment lists are not typical.

In short, tables 5-1 to 5-3 reinforce our earlier assertions about the ad hoc, piecemeal nature of the unanimous consent process. Mega-UCAs, which are occasionally and erroneously compared to House special rules, are highly unusual. If there is a modal process for major legislation (that is not being filibustered), the process probably begins with a narrow UCA aimed at bringing a bill before the Senate and starting the amendment process. As amendments are considered, senators seek unanimous consent to limit debate on one or a few items, perhaps agreeing to deadlines for votes. As deliberations continue, the floor leader or bill manager may attempt to devise a list of the remaining amendments to be in order. As the chamber works through this list, members will seek to arrive at a provision or time certain for the final passage vote.

Table 5-3. *Number of Amendments Referenced in a UCA*
*under Byrd and Lott*
Number (percent)[a]

| Number of amendments | Byrd (1987–88) | Lott (1997–98) |
|---|---|---|
| 1 | 75  (52.1) | 22  (47.8) |
| 2–5 | 45  (31.3) | 15  (32.6) |
| 6–10 | 14  (9.7) | 4  (8.7) |
| 11–20 | 3  (2.1) | 3  (6.5) |
| 21–50 | 2  (1.4) | 2  (4.3) |
| 51 or more | 5  (3.5) | 0 |

a. Figures in parentheses are the percentages of total UCAs for which individual amendments were referenced.

## Managing the Message

When Trent Lott accused Senate Democrats of engaging in a "Molotov minuet" over the floor procedure for managed care, he also suggested that the minority party was primarily interested in position taking and publicity on the matter, rather than in setting the stage for a legislative compromise with Republicans. "I began to wonder," Lott said, "do we want to address this issue or do we just want the issue? I have been through that before."[36]

Lott's remarks highlight a central feature of procedural politics in the contemporary Senate. Often the controversies over UCAs and other parliamentary devices are not rooted primarily in internal Senate politics and the legislative coalition-building process. Rather, the two political parties have attempted to use the House and Senate floors to publicize their issue agendas, frame policy disputes in a manner that puts them at an advantage electorally, and maximize the rhetorical distance between their positions and those of the other party.[37] Increasingly, both parties have used floor debate as a public stage for communicating party "messages" to core constituencies and the citizenry as a whole. Speaking from the other side of Capitol Hill, Representative David Obey (D-Wis.) recently observed that "more and more, the Congress is not passing real legislation, it is passing institutional press releases aimed far more at sending political messages than they are at solving problems."[38]

Of course, senators have long used floor debate as a vehicle for position taking. And prior Senate leaders have attempted to choreograph and stage-manage the legislative process. But over the past decade, the national political parties have become far more assertive and sophisticated at using the House and Senate floors to articulate and publicize their policy agendas.

Leading the Senate has been appropriately compared to "herding cats," and efforts to orchestrate distinct party messages in the upper body have been less intensive and less successful than in the House. Still, the more sophisticated communications strategies pioneered in the House have influenced the Senate parties. According to the legislative director to one Democrat, "Daschle doesn't push his colleagues, doesn't twist arms. . . . Where we look to his leadership is on the issues that are defining for Democrats. His job is to coordinate the party message. . . . When he does that, we're with him 100 percent."[39]

In the 106th Congress, Majority Leader Lott's ability to use the floor for message purposes—and to counteract Democratic message strategies—was severely hampered by the nature of Senate rules, especially the absence of a germaneness requirement. In addition, a number of issues important to the public (education, health care, the minimum wage) were matters upon which Democrats polled very well. During this period, conflict between the Senate parties centered on Democratic efforts to place such items on the floor agenda and to maximize their opportunities to offer politically popular amendments. Lott and other GOP leaders attempted to keep these issues off the floor, or to structure floor action in a manner that gave the advantage to the Republican program and message. Each party accused the other of using floor procedure to play partisan electoral games.

In March 1999, for instance, the Senate considered the so-called Ed-Flex bill, a bipartisan measure intended to give states additional flexibility in how they spend federal education dollars. GOP leaders hoped the bill would strengthen the party's record and public image on education issues. According to public opinion polls, improving education was the top priority for voters nationally. On Ed-Flex, Republicans sought to keep floor action focused on rolling back federal restrictions, which in their view framed the educational debate in terms favorable to the GOP. In contrast, congressional Democrats wanted to introduce amendments that would broaden the debate and focus it more on their education message. Chief among these initiatives was a popular Clinton administration proposal to hire one hundred thousand new teachers. Five days of intense procedural wrangling ensued before senators were able to agree on a UCA for the measure. Complained Robert C. Byrd, "I wish to express my dismay with the procedural battle evoked by this legislation. . . . [T]he Senate has expended most of its time and energy on procedural tactics intended to preclude one party or the other from debating the topics of utmost importance to them."[40]

Among other bills considered during the 106th Congress, similar dynamics were at work during procedural fights on gun control, the juvenile justice bill, the Social Security "lockbox" proposal, legislation to deal with the Y2K computer problem, and, of course, managed health care reform. Lott has attempted to use procedure to define these issues in terms favorable to Republicans, and unfavorable to Democrats. Armed with nongermane amendments and filibuster threats, minority party members likewise have sharpened and publicized their message via the floor legislative process.

One implication of message politics is that UCAs become more difficult to devise. There is typically middle ground in disputes over policy. Bargaining that centers on legislative outcomes usually is a positive-sum game, which allows for a degree of cooperation, as well as conflict. However, the national electoral game between the two political parties is strictly zero-sum. One party is the winner and the other is the loser. On the Senate floor, if an issue is framed in terms advantageous to Democrats nationally at the polls, then by implication this process hurts the Republican party. When issues touch on the message agenda of one or both parties, it becomes extremely difficult to devise an acceptable procedure for floor action, with gridlock a likely result.

In addition, the heightened electoral stakes associated with many recent UCAs, combined with Lott's penchant for including a broader circle of GOP senators in the negotiation process, complicated the sheer logistics of UCA bargaining. On managed health care, for instance, Senate Republicans believed they had devised an effective strategy to keep the issue off the floor for weeks, if not months. Dianne Feinstein (D-Calif.) intended to offer the Democratic plan as a legislative rider to the agriculture appropriations bill when the measure hit the floor in late June 1999. The Republican strategy was to get her to accept a time agreement on the rider, wait until all time had elapsed, and then raise a Rule 16 point of order against adding legislative language (which the health care plan clearly was) to a spending bill. The chair would have ruled the parliamentary objection out of order, and Republicans then would vote to overturn the point of order, effectively reinstating Rule 16's prohibition against attaching legislative language to appropriations bills, and blocking Democrats from forcing votes on managed care until after the year's spending bills had been processed. Apparently, during negotiations over the managed care UCA, Lott accidentally tipped the Republican hand to Daschle, who in turn warned Feinstein not to accept a time agreement on her amendment. The result was a minirevolt among exasperated GOP conservatives and a weeklong standstill on the Senate floor.[41]

There were other interesting procedural manifestations to message politics during Senate consideration of managed care reform. After railing against the Democratic plan for months, GOP leaders chose to make the Kennedy bill the base text for floor action. The Democratic proposal would serve as the vehicle open for amendment. Essentially, Lott and Nickles sought to complicate the Democrats' amendment strategy—they would have to modify their own bill—and also reduce the number of politically difficult votes for GOP senators. Then Lott would offer the Republican plan as the final amendment and attempt to hold his Republican troops in line on the vote. The Democrats countered the GOP's move by offering the Republican health plan as an amendment to the Kennedy health bill. Again, on both sides of the aisle, the procedural tactics used on managed care were largely aimed at shaping the broader public message emanating from floor action.

On other highly partisan measures considered in 1999, Lott's inability to restrict Democratic amendments via unanimous consent led him to make strategic use of cloture and the leader's floor recognition rights. By precedent, the majority leader has the right of priority recognition, and thus first dibs on offering floor amendments. On five major bills in 1999— Y2K, Social Security lockbox, Ed-Flex, Africa trade, and campaign finance reform—Lott "filled the amendment tree" to keep Democrats from offering nongermane amendments relating to the party message. He then attempted to close off further amendment opportunities by filing a cloture motion on each measure. At another point, Lott tried to organize a rump group of GOP senators, who he hoped would help decide which amendment proposals to make in order on the floor.

Perhaps Lott's approach to procedure in the 106th Congress reflected in part his long service as a member of the House Committee on Rules. Minority Leader Tom Daschle—himself a former House Member—remarked, "I have a great deal of affection for the majority leader, but I must say, I think he should have run for speaker because I really believe that he would be more comfortable as speaker."[42] But we believe that

Lott's behavior is better viewed as a strategic adaptation to the formidable political and electoral challenges confronting GOP leaders in the 106th Congress, that is, as an attempt to deal with the procedural context of Senate deliberation.

Of course, most legislation considered on the Senate floor is not central to the political message of either party. On these measures, the bargaining process for UCAs is less partisan, protracted, and difficult. As we have shown, the history and modern usage of unanimous consent provides a valuable window for exploring how Senate procedure develops, changes, and shapes legislative work within the chamber. In the contemporary Senate, UCAs remain a critical device for facilitating floor action while guarding the prerogatives of individual members. Absent a properly functioning process of unanimous consent, life within the Senate would quickly become (our apologies to Hobbes) nasty, brutish, and forever mired in morning business.

## Notes

1. *Congressional Record,* June 24, 1999, p. S7575.

2. Ibid., p. S7576.

3. "Senate in Gridlock over Managed Care; Tempers Flare," *National Journal's Congress Daily,* June 25, 1999, on-line version.

4. *Congressional Record,* December 18, 1876, p. 266.

5. *Congressional Record,* September 25, 1990, p. S13803.

6. The categorizations in table 5-1 are based on an informal poll and follow-up badgering of four good friends and prominent parliamentary experts, none of whom especially wanted to be associated by name with this project. In the few instances where they disagreed, we simply did our best to reconcile the different viewpoints.

7. Walter J. Oleszek, *Congressional Procedures and the Policy Process,* 4th ed. (Washington, D.C.: CQ Press, 1996), p. 209.

8. *Congressional Record,* May 14, 1999, p. S5329.

9. We thank Colton Campbell for providing us with the contents and timing of these messages.

10. *Congressional Record,* August 6, 1992, p. S11692.

11. Robert Keith, "The Use of Unanimous Consent in the Senate," in U.S. Senate, *Committees and Senate Procedures,* 94 Cong. 2 sess.; Gerald Gamm and Steven S. Smith, "Last among Equals: The Senate's Presiding Officer," paper presented at the Annual Meeting of the American Political Science Association, 1999.

12. *Congressional Record,* February 24, 1917, pp. 4148–50.

13. Frank Bruni, "Democrats Stall Senate to Force Debate on Health Care," *New York Times,* June 24, 1999, p. A24.

14. Krehbiel models the decision calculus behind choices to accept or object to a unanimous consent request. Keith Krehbiel, "Unanimous Consent Agreements: Going Along in the Senate," *Journal of Politics*, vol. 48 (August 1986), pp. 541–64.

15. *Congressional Record*, April 7, 1884, p. 2698.

16. For an overview, see C. Lawrence Evans, "Legislative Structure: Rules, Precedents, and Jurisdictions," *Legislative Studies Quarterly*, vol. 24 (1999), pp. 605–42.

17. David King, *Turf Wars: How Congressional Committees Claim Jurisdiction* (University of Chicago Press, 1997).

18. *Congressional Record*, July 2, 1952, p. 8829. These data are included in a remarkable floor statement about UCAs by Senator Wayne Morse (R-Ore.).

19. A complete and accurate list of majority and minority party caucus chairs, as well as floor leaders, has been compiled by Gerald Gamm and Steven S. Smith, "The Emergence of Senate Leadership," paper presented at the annual meeting of the Midwest Political Science Association, 1997. We rely on their list here.

20. On two more of the UCAs, Senator Gallinger was a participant. Although not formally the GOP conference chair, he was just one month short of assuming the position. The counts of who participated in the point of order debates should be viewed as careful estimates, because of the difficulty of discerning when the debates began and ended, the identity of the key actors, and so on.

21. In identifying the informal Senate leaders, we received valuable guidance from Don Ritchie of the Senate Historical Office.

22. George H. Haynes, *The Senate of the United States: Its History and Tradition*, vol. 1 (Boston: Houghton Mifflin, 1938), p. 396.

23. *Congressional Record*, July 2 , 1952, pp. 8828–32.

24. Ibid., p. 8828.

25. See especially Barbara Sinclair, *The Transformation of the U.S. Senate* (Johns Hopkins University Press, 1989); Steven S. Smith, *Call to Order* (Brookings, 1989); C. Lawrence Evans, *Leadership in Committee* (University of Michigan, 1991).

26. Norman J. Ornstein, Robert L. Peabody, and David W. Rohde, "The U.S. Senate: Toward the Twenty-First Century," in Lawrence C. Dodd and Bruce Oppenheimer, eds., *Congress Reconsidered*, 6th ed. (Washington, D.C.: CQ Press, 1997), pp. 1–28.

27. Steven S. Smith and Marcus Flathman, "Managing the Senate Floor: Complex Unanimous Consent Agreements since the 1950s," *Legislative Studies Quarterly*, vol. 14 (1989), p. 349.

28. Ibid.

29. Ibid., p. 359.

30. Ibid., p. 361.

31. *Congressional Record,* May 27, 1982, p. 12218.

32. Some close Senate watchers suggest that the chamber is gradually merging the two terms and informally returning to the pre-1977 period, when "relevant" and "germane" were coterminous words.

33. Unfortunately, there is no easy way to gather systematic data about UCAs. Many important accords are printed in the Daily Calendar, but only if they carry over from one day to another. Most UCAs do not extend beyond a single calendar

day. As orders of the Senate, UCAs are referenced in the *Senate Journal*. But the *Journal* for a typical year runs a thousand pages. Also, UCAs often are not clearly identified in the *Journal*, and it can be difficult to get a feel for the politics of an agreement from the *Journal* summary. Although the richest source of information about UCAs is the *Congressional Record*, these agreements are not fully indexed in the *Record* and can be difficult to find.

34. More concretely, we used LEXIS-NEXIS to search all issues of the *Congressional Record* during the 100th and 105th Congresses for key words and phrases that are commonly associated with UCAs. We focused on sections of the record where the relevant majority leader was an active participant; that is, he played a speaking role. After experimenting with a large number of phrases and words, we settled on "unanimous consent agreement" and "without objection, it is so ordered," which is the standard response of the presiding officer when a UCA is accepted. The goal here was not to produce a comprehensive list of UCAs, but to gather a representative sample of agreements across the two Congresses. Extensive conversations with LEXIS-NEXIS staff make us confident that the search process did not result in any significant distortions. UCAs that deal solely with motions to proceed on a measure are not included.

35. John Bresnahan, "Lott, Nickles Deny Friction over Health Care," *Roll Call*, July 5, 1999, p. 3.

36. *Congressional Record*, June 24, 1999, p. S7575.

37. C. Lawrence Evans, "Committees, Leaders, and Message Politics," in Lawrence C. Dodd and Bruce Oppenheimer, eds., *Congress Reconsidered*, 7th ed. (Washington, D.C.: CQ Press, 2001); and C. Lawrence Evans and Walter Oleszek, "Message Politics and Senate Procedure," paper presented at the conference on Partisanship in the Senate, Florida International University, January 2000.

38. *Congressional Record*, June 18, 1999, p. H4643.

39. Confidential interview with C. Lawrence Evans, July 7, 1999.

40. *Congressional Record*, March 9, 1999, p. S2460.

41. "GOP Conservatives Incensed by Lott-Daschle Agreement," *National Journal's Congress Daily AM*, July 1, 1999, p. 1.

42. Michelle Cottle, "Losing It," *New Republic*, July 12, 1999, p. 8.

# CHAPTER SIX

# Last among Equals:
# The Senate's Presiding Officer

### GERALD GAMM
### STEVEN S. SMITH

IN THE FINAL DAYS OF THE Constitutional Convention, the Framers placed the vice president at the head of the Senate. The Framers had given little thought to the creation of the vice presidency; the office itself was a by-product of the process for choosing a president. They gave even less attention to the consequences of naming the vice president the Senate's presiding officer. "If the vice-President were not to be President of the Senate, he would be without employment," Roger Sherman (Conn.) explained. Following such reasoning and by a vote of eight states to two, delegates adopted the provision.[1] Within a few days, and apparently without discussion, the delegates adopted the additional provision that "the Senate shall choose their other officers, and also a President pro tempore, in the absence of the Vice-President, or when he shall exercise the office of President of the United States."[2] The Framers' hasty decision—and the corresponding constitutional clause that "the House of Representatives shall chuse their Speaker"—is a critical reason that the House and Senate are radically different in their internal organization, their leadership structures, and their rules.

The history of the Senate's presiding officer did not end with the ratification of the Constitution. In fact, until the 1840s, granting powers to the president pro tempore was a principal vehicle for solving a variety of collective-action problems in the Senate. Understanding the failure of the president pro tempore to sustain these powers means reckoning with the

extent to which institutional change is a consequence of short-term political calculations. It means reckoning, too, with the difficulties that senators confront in solving collective-action problems while refusing to impose
constraining rules. Not until senators devised alternative methods for solving these problems could they permanently turn away from the president
pro tempore as a potential solution.

The failure of the vice president as a Senate leader was nearly preor-
dained by the inability of senators to hold him accountable, but the failure
of the president pro tempore presents a more intriguing puzzle. Chosen by
the Senate—selected, like the Speaker of the House, by the majority party's
caucus and ratified by the full chamber—the president pro tempore might
have emerged as a powerful leader. Indeed, in the late 1830s and early
1840s, a full half-century after the first Congress, the president pro tempore, like the Speaker, was routinely exercising the power to name the
chairmen and members of all standing committees. Elections for president
pro tempore were contested and closely watched. No seniority rule existed. But the influence of the president pro tempore over the Senate's
affairs reached its zenith in the early 1840s. Although senators continued
to refine the office's responsibilities for maintaining order and enforcing
rules, the president pro tempore never fulfilled its early promise.

This chapter focuses on the attempts by senators to create centralized
authority in the president pro tempore, the short-term factors that frustrated those attempts, and the evolution of the presiding officer into a
neutral enforcer of order, rules, and unanimous consent agreements. While
the weakness of the presiding officer's formal power is a leading feature of
the modern chamber, the presiding officer's role was not settled until the
early twentieth century. The withering of that office was intimately connected to the creation of party organs, particularly party leadership.

## The Selection of Presidents Pro Tempore

In March 1890, senators resolved to place the office of president pro tempore on a permanent footing. Until then, the rules and practice of the
Senate stated that the position of president pro tempore existed only in the
absence of the vice president. Not only had a senator ceased to exercise
the duties of presiding officer when the vice president reappeared in the
chamber, but the office itself was dissolved. As recently as 1876, senators
had even questioned their own ability to remove a president pro tempore
from office, with many of them arguing that only the vice president's ar-

rival could end the term of a president pro tempore. With the 1890 resolution, the Senate declared that the president pro tempore held his office at the pleasure of the Senate and that the office existed without regard to the presence or absence of the vice president. Four years before, in 1886, Congress had removed the president pro tempore and Speaker from the line of presidential succession.

In explaining the failure of the president pro tempore to become the leader of the Senate, scholars have called attention to the pre-1886 succession act, which placed the president pro tempore immediately after the vice president in line for the presidency.[3] This law generated various maneuvers by the vice president and the Senate majority that were unrelated to the business of leading the Senate. The usual and least pernicious effect of the old succession act was to encourage vice presidents to leave the Senate before a session ended, so that senators could elect a president pro tempore for the ensuing recess. But when vice presidents did not enjoy the support of the Senate majority, vice presidents refused to leave their posts, which created anxiety and occasional conflict.

More significant than the succession act for the presiding officer's weakness was the pre-1890 understanding that presidents pro tempore did not exist when the vice president was in the Senate chamber.[4] However, the effect of the noncontinuous term of the office is easily exaggerated. Although nineteenth-century senators understood that official "terms" ended with the appearance of the vice president, a presumptive president pro tempore existed throughout a Congress. Solomon Foot (R-Vt.) was chosen twelve consecutive times in 1861–64, Lafayette Foster (R-Conn.) served continuously from 1865 to 1867, Benjamin Wade (R-Ohio) served continuously from 1867 to 1869, and Henry B. Anthony (R-R.I.) was chosen fifteen consecutive times between 1869 and 1873. Discussing possible successors to Anthony in March 1873, the *New York Times* described Anthony's tenure as a continuous four-year term, rather than as fifteen terms interrupted by the vice president. "Senator Anthony, after having been unanimously chosen for four years to fill the office of President pro tempore of the Senate, has declined re-election, and Senator Carpenter was designated by the caucus to succeed him," the *Times* reported. "It has been usual for the same Senator to hold this position only through one Congress. Mr. Foote [sic] was President two [sic] years, and Foster, of Connecticut, two years. Mr. Anthony was paid the unusual compliment of an election for four years, and would have been chosen for two years more if he had not himself declined."[5]

From the vantage point of 1890—one century into the Senate's history—the position of president pro tempore had already been reduced to an honorific position. The term of office had been made continuous, and the post had been removed from the line of presidential succession. But in 1890 it bore no comparison to the extraordinary office that the House Speakership had become under Thomas B. Reed. There was no seniority system; of thirteen senators elected president pro tempore between 1870 and 1900, just two ranked first in their party. Senators instead tended to elect men who were distinguished, popular, and familiar with parliamentary law. According to the *New York Times*, John J. Ingalls (R-Kans.) was elected in 1887 because he was "one of the best parliamentarians in the Senate, and he [had] the ability to put business through with neatness and dispatch." Moreover, the *Times* noted, Ingalls had "the not unimportant advantage of a voice that can be heard in every nook and cranny of the chamber."[6] Charles F. Manderson (R-Nebr.), chosen four years later, possessed similar gifts. As the *Times* reported, "He is a gentleman of attractive manners, a good orator, is familiar with the rules of the Senate, and is popular among his associates."[7] Geographical considerations also mattered, at least at the margins, as senators attempted to balance the regions of the president pro tempore with both the majority caucus chairman and the vice president.[8]

Presidents pro tempore in the late nineteenth century recognized that the office was an honor that carried with it more burdens than responsibility. "It has one or two places in its gift more than ordinary Senators have, and the salary is $8,000 a year, against $5,000 for an ordinary Senator," the *New York Times* observed in 1887. "These and the supposed honor of the office are all the advantages of the Senate Presidency."[9] William Allison (R-Iowa) indicated in 1883 that he had no interest in serving as president pro tempore, since the office would take him away from the far more interesting work of chairing the Appropriations Committee.[10] That same year, because of his seniority and popularity, Henry B. Anthony was the obvious candidate for president pro tempore. His age and poor health made it unlikely that Anthony could actively preside, but this was no impediment to the honor: "He may receive the title out of the consideration and esteem in which he is held by both sides of the Chamber," according to the *Times*, "but younger men will have to hold the gavel through the long hours of droning debate."[11]

Until the 1850s, the right of presidents pro tempore to designate temporary presiding officers was not generally recognized. When Vice President George M. Dallas notified the Senate in December 1845 that he would be absent and that he had asked Ambrose Sevier (D-Ark.) to preside in his place for the day, John J. Crittenden (Whig-Ky.) immediately challenged the vice president's authority: "He had no kind of personal objection to the honorable Senator who was in the chair—very far from it," Crittenden declared. "But it occurred to him that the Vice President had no right to commission any one to preside over the body. It was a matter for the Senate itself to determine, in the absence of the presiding officer."[12] Although Crittenden agreed to withdraw his motion, he objected again in January 1847, the next time that Dallas attempted to appoint a presiding officer for a day. This time, a majority of the Senate supported Crittenden's position and firmly rejected Dallas's right to name David R. Atchison (D-Mo.) to the chair. In a series of votes, senators first refused to pass a resolution appointing Atchison president pro tempore, then approved a resolution to hold an election for president pro tempore, then finally chose Atchison themselves in the election.[13] Senators defending the vice president's right to name a temporary presiding officer cited Samuel Southard (W-N.J.), who as president pro tempore had exercised this right several times in the early 1840s. But George Badger (W-N.C.) rejected this as precedent, arguing that the status of the vice president, who was not a member of the Senate, differed fundamentally from that of the president pro tempore.[14] Other senators, however, rejected Badger's distinction between the two offices. "They are regarded as the same in the rule," William Allen (D-Ohio) observed. "They are treated precisely alike."[15]

Although presidents pro tempore occasionally appointed temporary presiding officers in the early and middle 1850s, their right to do so remained unsettled. On three different days in June 1856, Jesse D. Bright (D-Ind.), the president pro tempore, asked Charles E. Stuart (D-Mich.) to preside in his absence. On the first two occasions, senators offered no objection. But on the third day Crittenden rose in protest: "I deny that the President of the Senate has any right, by letter, to delegate his power to preside over this body," Crittenden stated. "It is a small affair now, but I think the Senate ought to have a little care of its own rights."[16] After a brief discussion, in which only the temporary chair himself attempted to justify Bright's action, the Senate rejected the appointment, then immediately elected Stuart president pro tempore. When Bright returned to the Senate two days later, he expressed his surprise at the dispute. "In requesting the honorable Senator from Michigan [Mr. Stuart] to preside during my absence," Bright explained from the chair, "I but followed precedent after precedent to be found in the Journal of the Senate's proceedings."[17]

Bright's explanation in June 1856 seems to have satisfied senators. Beginning that year, the *Congressional Globe* began regularly identifying the "presiding officers" who temporarily occupied the chair during a daily session. But presidents pro tempore and vice presidents appear to have used this right sparingly until the late 1870s. Not until 1879 does there appear to have been another instance of a president pro tempore naming a presiding officer to serve an entire day.[18] In 1882, when the practice was challenged again, the Senate considered amending its rules to authorize the president pro tempore to "designate, in writing, a Senator to perform the duties of the Chair."[19] The Senate adopted the change two years later. Increased reliance on this practice probably reflected the widespread understanding that the work of the presiding officer had grown tiresome. Distinguished senators accepted the honor with gratitude, but, beginning in the 1840s—when the president pro tempore declined in importance—they began asking others to perform the actual work.

To analyze changing patterns in the occupancy of the chair, we examined a full week in every fourth Congress. From the 1850s through the 1940s, either the vice president or the president pro tempore personally occupied the chair at the start of nearly every daily session; on average, they named one or two temporary presiding officers to relieve them in the course of a typical day. From the 1950s until the 1970s, both the president pro tempore and vice president continued to sit in the chair at least once or twice in a week, but "acting presidents pro tempore" began to appear on a frequent basis in the place of the two constitutional officers. An average of five temporary presiding officers served each day. In the sample weeks since the 1980s, the vice president does not sit in the chair, presidents pro tempore and "acting presidents pro tempore" open daily sessions, and an average of eight other senators sit in the chair each day.

The growing reliance on temporary presiding officers since the 1940s reflects not only the weakness of the office but the development of a seniority system. Seniority did not become a determining consideration until the 1940s, with the election of Kenneth McKellar (D-Tenn.). Since then, presidents pro tempore have been selected on a strict seniority basis. Senators adopted a seniority system for the president pro tempore two decades after the Senate Republican conference had abandoned seniority as its rule for selecting a caucus chairman and floor leader. In electing Charles Curtis (R-Kans.) as majority leader in 1924, Republicans had broken with a half-century of precedent, recognizing the need for vigor and ability in the office.[20] The caucus chairman—now also the floor leader—was no longer an elderly, distinguished gentleman who quietly presided over the boisterous, powerful caucus. The caucus chairman had real work to do, and the distinguished gentleman now presided over the Senate.

## Collective-Action Problems and Chair Leadership, 1816–56

From the start, senators struggled to balance their individual prerogatives against the need for chamber-wide coordination. They kept agenda-setting power on the Senate floor. But they gave their presiding officer—above all, the president pro tempore, whom they elected—significant powers in the first half of the nineteenth century. During three different periods, they entrusted the presiding officer with the power to appoint senators to standing committees. They also initially empowered their presiding officer to enforce order, decorum, and relevancy in debate. Presiding officers themselves abdicated their role in judging relevancy and diminished their ability to maintain order. And, responding to short-term concerns, senators on three occasions reclaimed the power to make committee assignments. The third occasion proved decisive, as senators of both parties transferred the power to their caucuses.

More than any deficiency inherent in the office of president pro tempore, the rise of party organizations and the ability of these new structures to coordinate the Senate's business precluded the restoration of these powers to the president pro tempore. "Caucuses with their chairmen and their committee machinery," Lauros G. McConachie observed in 1898, "have been [the Senate's] only escape from dire confusion and weakness of leadership due to Constitutional difficulties."[21] Wilson, writing a decade later, also recognized that caucuses, caucus committees, and caucus chairmen had become the real leaders of the Senate. The president pro tempore "is not in fact in command in debate or in the direction of party tactics," Wilson contended. "The leader of the Senate is the chairman of the majority caucus. Each party in the Senate finds its real, its permanent, its effective organization in its caucus, and follows the leadership, in all important parliamentary battles, of the chairman of that caucus, its organization and its leadership alike resting upon arrangements quite outside the Constitution."[22]

Although Wilson exaggerated the influence of the caucus chairman[23]—not until the 1910s did both parties begin recognizing their caucus chairmen as their floor leaders—he understood that the Senate's collective-action problems were resolved in caucus and not by the presiding officer. What neither McConachie nor Wilson explored, though, was the extent to which party organization was both a consequence and a cause of the weakness of the presiding officer: a consequence, because the instability of the president pro tempore's office in 1845 laid the groundwork for the modern caucus; a cause, because the modern caucus, once created, proved more reliable than the presiding officer for solving collective-action problems of any political importance.

### Committee Assignments

The Senate system of standing committees was born in December 1816, at the start of the second session of the 14th Congress.[24] James Barbour (R-Va.) proposed that the Senate adopt a rule "to appoint at each session certain standing Committees"—"the same as are now appointed by the House of Representatives," the *New York Evening Post* explained in an aside—and the resolution was adopted.[25] After approving the resolution, senators elected the committees, balloting separately for each member. After that the Senate named its standing committees at the start of every session. Table 6-1—based on the *Senate Journal* for each session, as well as the *Annals*, the *Register of Debates*, the *Congressional Globe*, and newspaper accounts—identifies the method of making committee assignment for each regular session of Congress between 1816, when committees were first named, and 1864, by which time the modern system of assignment was well established.

As table 6-1 shows, the Senate delegated committee-assignment power to its presiding officer at three different times (not including 1850): 1823–25, 1829–32, and 1837–44. With the exception of John C. Calhoun in 1825 and Richard M. Johnson in 1837, all the assignments in regular sessions were made by presidents pro tempore. Calhoun's behavior prompted senators to remove the power from the chair for the next four sessions. And, as the only vice president in American history who was elected by the Senate, Johnson was no typical vice president. (Indeed, in the case of Johnson, senators specifically noted in debate "that the arrangement should not be considered as a precedent.")[26] At the start of the 18th Congress in 1823, senators had grown accustomed to their presidents pro tempore occupying the chair at the start of Congress and with regularity throughout every session (see table 6-1, figure 6-1). This had been the experience of four full Congresses. The message of the Senate was unmistakable: when senators gave the power of committee appointments to the chair, they intended to give it only to an officer of their choos-

Table 6-1. *Methods for Senate Committee Assignments, 1815–64*[a]

| Congress | Date | Vice president | Vice president opens session | Method for committee assignment |
|---|---|---|---|---|
| 14 | Dec. 1815 | None | | No major committees |
| | Dec. 1816 | None | | Ballot |
| 15 | Dec. 1817 | Daniel D. Tompkins | | Ballot |
| | Nov. 1818 | Daniel D. Tompkins | | Ballot |
| 16 | Dec. 1819 | Daniel D. Tompkins | | Ballot |
| | Nov. 1820 | Daniel D. Tompkins | | Ballot |
| 17 | Dec. 1821 | Daniel D. Tompkins | | Ballot |
| | Dec. 1822 | Daniel D. Tompkins | | Ballot |
| 18 | Dec. 1823 | Daniel D. Tompkins | | President pro tempore |
| | Dec. 1824 | Daniel D. Tompkins | | President pro tempore |
| 19 | Dec. 1825 | John Calhoun | ✔ | Vice president |
| | Dec. 1826 | John Calhoun | ✔ | Ballot |
| 20 | Dec. 1827 | John Calhoun | ✔ | Ballot |
| | Dec. 1828 | John Calhoun | | Ballot |
| 21 | Dec. 1829 | John Calhoun | | President pro tempore |
| | Dec. 1830 | John Calhoun | | President pro tempore |
| 22 | Dec. 1831 | John Calhoun | | President pro tempore |
| | Dec. 1832 | John Calhoun | | President pro tempore |
| 23 | Dec. 1833 | Martin Van Buren | | Ballot |
| | Dec. 1834 | Martin Van Buren | ✔ | Ballot |
| 24 | Dec. 1835 | Martin Van Buren | ✔ | Ballot |
| | Dec. 1836 | Martin Van Buren | ✔ | Ballot |
| 25 | Sept. 1837 | Richard M. Johnson[b] | ✔ | Ballot; vice president |
| | Dec. 1837 | Richard M. Johnson | ✔ | Vice president |
| | Dec. 1838 | Richard M. Johnson | | President pro tempore |
| 26 | Dec. 1839 | Richard M. Johnson | | President pro tempore |
| | Dec. 1840 | Richard M. Johnson | | President pro tempore |
| 27 | June 1841 | None | | Ballot; president pro tempore |
| | Dec. 1841 | None | | President pro tempore |
| | Dec. 1842 | None | | President pro tempore |
| 28 | Dec. 1843 | None | | President pro tempore |
| | Dec. 1844 | None | | President pro tempore |
| 29 | Dec. 1845 | George M. Dallas | ✔ | Ballot; resolution |
| | Dec. 1846 | George M. Dallas | ✔ | Ballot; resolution |
| 30 | Dec. 1847 | George M. Dallas | ✔ | Resolution |
| | Dec. 1848 | George M. Dallas | | Resolution |
| 31 | Dec. 1849 | Millard Fillmore | ✔ | Ballot; resolution |
| | Dec. 1850 | None | | President pro tempore |
| 32 | Dec. 1851 | None | | Resolution |
| | Dec. 1852 | None | | Resolution |
| 33 | Dec. 1853 | None | | Resolution |
| | Dec. 1854 | None | | Resolution |
| 34 | Dec. 1855 | None | | Ballot; resolution |
| | Aug. 1856 | None | | Resolution |
| | Dec. 1856 | None | | Resolution |

(continued)

Table 6-1. *(continued)*

| Congress | Date | Vice president | Vice president opens session | Method for committee assignment |
|---|---|---|---|---|
| 35 | Dec. 1857 | John C. Breckinridge | | Resolution |
| | Dec. 1858 | John C. Breckinridge | ✔ | Resolution |
| 36 | Dec. 1859 | John C. Breckinridge | ✔ | Resolution |
| | Dec. 1860 | John C. Breckinridge | ✔ | Resolution |
| 37 | July 1861 | Hannibal Hamlin | ✔ | Resolution |
| | Dec. 1861 | Hannibal Hamlin | ✔ | Resolution |
| | Dec. 1862 | Hannibal Hamlin | | Resolution |
| 38 | Dec. 1863 | Hannibal Hamlin | ✔ | Resolution |
| | Dec. 1864 | Hannibal Hamlin | | Resolution |

*Source:* The *Senate Journal*, the *Annals of Congress*, the *Register of Debates*, and the *Congressional Globe*; and for the 1810s and 1820s, when official sources did not specify the method of assignment, the *New York Evening Post*.

a. The table reports the method used for naming the chairmen and basic membership of the standing committees. In many cases, the Senate used a different method for filling vacancies. The table does not include the special sessions of the Senate, which were usually very brief.

b. No vice presidential candidate received a majority of electoral votes in the 1836 election. The U.S. Senate elected Richard M. Johnson vice president on February 8, 1837, the only time since the adoption of the Twelfth Amendment that the Senate has exercised this power and chosen its own president. See Hatfield, *Vice Presidents of the United States*, pp. 121, 127.

ing. Most vice presidents understood that they were not welcome on the opening days of a new session. They left their chair before the previous session adjourned to permit the Senate to elect a president pro tempore. This practice, the *New York Post* explained in 1833, was designed not only to protect the succession to the presidency during the recess, but also to permit the president pro tempore to assume "the Chair at the beginning of the session, for the purpose of organizing the body, and to appoint Committees."[27]

Senators often assigned this power to their presidents pro tempore in these years because the only alternative method—balloting—was time-consuming and produced outcomes that accorded with no one's preferences. In aggregating votes one committee position at a time, senators annually rediscovered the perverse consequences of collective action. Each time the Senate turned to the presiding officer—in 1823, 1829, and 1837—senators understood the collective-action problem and expressed the hope that empowering the president pro tempore to name committees would solve it. Barbour, proposing the new method in 1823, suggested that the Senate "adopt the practice of the House of Representatives, and give the selection of its Standing Committees to the presiding officer."[28] Felix Grundy

Figure 6-1. *Length of Service of Presidents pro Tempore, 1789–1889*[a]

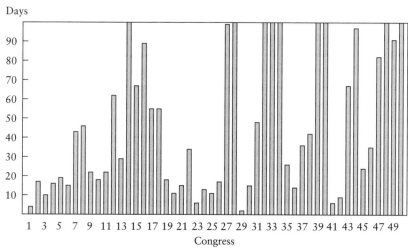

Days

Congress

Source: This figure is based on the dates of service listed in table 6-1.

a. In measuring the length of a president pro tempore's term, we count the total number of days that elapse between the beginning and end of each term, excluding recesses. This is similar to the method used by the *Congressional Directory* to measure the "length in days" of each session of Congress. The *Congressional Directory,* though, counts all elapsed days, including recesses. Consequently, we subtracted recesses from the total "length in days" reported in the *Congressional Directory;* in early Congresses for which recesses are not listed in the *Directory,* we subtracted Christmas recesses of at least four days.

(D-Tenn.), who offered the resolution in December 1837, "explained his object to be to save time and trouble."[29] Four years before, when partisan considerations led the Senate's anti-Jackson majority to debate a return to balloting, William R. King (Jackson-Ala.) reminded his colleagues that the decision to abandon balloting and transfer the power to the president pro tempore had been wise:

> They had placed the matter in the hands of an individual well calculated to fulfil the important duty which devolved upon him; one who knew the separate capabilities of each member—some gentlemen had talents for one description of business, others for another; one who would be able to parcel out the labor in a proper manner; one who was of, and amenable to, their own body; and one who had hitherto, in every respect, fulfilled his duties to their satisfaction. The matter is at present, he (Mr. K.) believed, settled in the manner most conducive to the general good; he saw no necessity for change.[30]

Grundy, for reasons of partisanship as much as logic, agreed with King's assessment that the president pro tempore had successfully resolved this collective-action problem for the Senate. "Since the alteration of the rule to its present form, Mr. G. had been sensible of no inconvenience, and he doubted whether there had been any sufficient to authorize a change, because it had been the instrument of harmony and despatch in their proceedings."[31]

Three times, however—one instance was in 1833—the Senate removed this power from the presiding officer and returned it to the floor. For a Senate majority, the horrors of balloting were preferable to delegating this power to a presiding officer they had not chosen. In December 1833, Hugh L. White (J-Tenn.) resumed his chair as president. Elected in the preceding Congress by a Jacksonian majority, White continued in his office at the opening of the 23d Congress, in which the Senate was controlled by an anti-Jackson majority. Because senators believed that the terms of presidents pro tempore could end only with the appearance of the vice president, anti-Jackson senators could not depose White until Vice President Martin Van Buren had arrived.

Anti-Jackson senators, who planned to ballot for committees once Van Buren assumed the chair, vigorously attacked Van Buren for not attending the Senate for the first two weeks of the session. They regarded Van Buren's absence as strategic: "It was generally supposed," the *Columbian Centinel* reported, "that the Vice President held back a few days, to secure the organization of the committees by the acting President, conformably to the views of the Administration."[32] Rather than permit the president pro tempore to name committees in Van Buren's absence—which, as Jacksonian senators correctly but disingenuously insisted, had been standard practice for the previous four sessions—the anti-Jackson majority returned to balloting in 1833. "The resolution had no reference to the present presiding officer," George Poindexter (Anti-Jackson-Miss.) argued. "A single consideration ought to govern the vote; the committees should represent the Senate. It was of great importance that their reports should express to the public the sense of the Senate on all important measures."[33]

The Senate's decision to resume balloting in 1826, like that in 1833, reflected short-term considerations and the inability of a Senate majority to control its presiding officer. In that year, however, the problem was straightforward: the vice president sat in the chair, preventing a president pro tempore from exercising the power to name committees. "Calhoun, taking the Chair contrary to precedent on the opening day of the Nineteenth Congress, assumed this power, and appointed the committees with such obvious bias that the session was only four months old when, with hardly a dissenting vote, the Senate took the appointment of committees away" from its presiding officer.[34]

A new alternative to balloting emerged in December 1845, when the Senate caucuses assumed full control of the standing committees. That month, senators refused to permit Vice President George M. Dallas to appoint the committees, though they had permitted him to do so during the brief special session in March.[35] At a time when the two parties were again closely balanced, four Democrats voted with the Whig minority to force the election of committees by ballot.[36] "The present case was different from that where the appointment of the standing committees is devolved on a President *pro tempore*, who is an officer selected from our own body, and responsible to the Senate," Willie Mangum (W-N.C.) asserted. "The Senate, by conferring this power upon an officer who is not responsible to the body for his acts, would be, on our part, an abdication of our legislative powers."[37] Thomas Hart Benton (D-Mo.), one of the four Democrats who refused to allow the vice president to name committees, defended his decision as a matter of principle, or, in the language of the 1826 debate, which he quoted at length, "on the score of its abstract propriety."[38]

That decision stimulated senators to employ the party caucus.[39] Within a few days, establishing another lasting precedent, members of the Senate adopted committee lists as resolutions by unanimous consent, with senators ranked on these prearranged lists according to party.[40] The Whig claim that their vote had been based on principle rather than politics had merit. Freed of any pretense of impartiality, which might have constrained the vice president's assignments, the Democratic caucus made assignments and established committee rankings to secure the greatest possible partisan advantage.

With the caucus now responsible for assembling committee lists, senators increased the coordination capacity of the caucus. In December 1847, the Democratic caucus created its first committee on committees, charging it to recommend committee assignments to the full caucus.[41] Because of its ability to coordinate the caucus's decision and floor strategy, the committee on committees quickly became a powerful organ of the party. Abruptly, in 1845, the window to a new institutional world had opened in the Senate. No longer would senators rely only on their presiding officer to bring order to their collective chaos.

*Maintaining Order*

While senators never seriously entertained the idea of granting agenda-setting authority to presiding officers, at times in the nineteenth century they confronted serious challenges to order and decorum on the floor and evolved rules intended to give the presiding officer responsibility for maintaining order and making parliamentary rulings.[42] Early vice presidents and presidents pro tempore appeared quite willing to enforce the rules of the Senate, call senators to order when they offered intemperate remarks, and, at times, to insist that debate be germane to the question pending before the Senate. They did so under the 1789 Senate rule and general parliamentary law, encapsulated in Jefferson's *Manual*.[43]

In fact, the 1789 rule left some doubt as to whether the presiding officer should take the initiative to call a senator to order if the senator's remarks violated the Senate's rules. The ambiguity was exploited by Vice President John Calhoun in 1826, who presided during a tirade by John Randolph (J-Va.) against President John Quincy Adams and Henry Clay. Calhoun, a political foe of the president and Clay, conveniently let Randolph proceed even after demands were heard that he be stopped. Sharp criticism of the vice president followed this incident, which led Calhoun to respond with a carefully worded statement in which he asserted that the chair may intervene only upon the demand of a senator.[44] Calhoun's action, or inaction, and subsequent statement set a precedent that other presiding officers cited for decades.

Not all senators agreed with Calhoun's ruling. To the contrary, a lengthy debate over a rule to eliminate ambiguity about the duty of the presiding officer followed two years later. A proponent of the new rule, David Barton (Adams Republican-Mo.), offered some historical perspective by contrasting Calhoun to John Gaillard (Jackson Republican-S.C.), who had served as president pro tempore during most of the preceding decade. Gaillard, noted Barton, was placed in a situation that gave him "decided advantage over the present presiding officer. . . . He presided in a time when the present rancor of party strife was unknown." From Gaillard's example, Barton concluded that "he considered the law of the Senate clearly settled, that the Vice President possessed, and ought to have exercised, the power of restraining the wholly irrelevant latitude of debate of that period."[45]

Most senators agreed with Barton on the question of calling a senator to order for uncivil language, but a few supporters of the new rule indicated that they had no intention of insisting that senators be held to a standard of relevancy. The new rule explicitly recognized the presiding officer's ability to call a senator to order for transgressing the rules of the Senate. It also clearly established the right of any senator to appeal the chair's ruling, unlike the previous rule, which allowed the chair to let the Senate decide whether a senator was out of order.[46]

Opponents of the new rule insisted that the Senate should not hand power to the vice president. Thomas Hart Benton (J-Mo.) argued that the vice president could not be trusted. It is not "safe to vest the power of restraining debates in an officer like him, not concerned in the debate, and not responsible to us for the exercise of his power," Benton stated. "He may abuse his power and we are without remedy."[47] Proponents countered that the provision guaranteeing to each senator the right to appeal the chair's ruling to the full Senate was adequate protection against abuse.

The Senate adopted the new rule, but maintaining order continued to be a problem. "Unparliamentary" language, nongermane argument, and physical confrontation became everyday occurrences in the late 1840s in debates over slavery and states' rights.[48] Following one highly charged debate over California statehood—between Henry Foote (D-Miss.) and Benton—Vice President Millard Fillmore warned the Senate that he would henceforth use his power to call a senator to order to maintain the "dignity and comfort of the body."[49] No one challenged Fillmore's promise, but it proved vacuous. Two weeks later, Foote lashed into Benton again. Benton became so outraged that he rushed toward Foote down the center aisle. As Benton approached, Foote drew a pistol and had to be restrained by colleagues.[50] A special committee absolved Foote of intent to assassinate Benton and managed only to recommend that senators not bring pistols into the Senate chamber.

The obligation of the chair to maintain order became the subject of lengthy debate, however, following the infamous caning of Charles Sumner (R-Mass.) by Representative Preston Brooks (D-S.C.) in 1856. Brooks had attacked Sumner in retaliation for Sumner's characterization of Senator Andrew Butler (D-S.C.) as "a modern Don Quixote" who had chosen for his "polluted" mistress "the harlot, Slavery."[51] Some senators and observers believed that the presiding officer's failure to call Sumner to order for unparliamentary language precipitated the brutal beating. Jesse Bright (D-Ind.), who as president pro tempore was in the chair, later noted that he was following Calhoun's precedent in not calling Sumner to order.[52]

A committee investigating the episode recommended several rules changes, including a requirement that senators confine themselves to the subject under debate. The rule eventually adopted provided that "if any member in speaking, or otherwise, transgress the rules of the Senate, the Presiding Officer shall, or any member may, call to order." The use of "shall" established the affirmative obligation of the chair to maintain order in debate; the phrase "or otherwise" extended the reach beyond the words spoken.[53]

In the 1856 debate, opponents to the new rule argued that it represented an overreaction to the caning and that the proposed power was already implied in parliamentary law. Proponents replied that senators could not be expected to call a colleague to order without an explicit rule. This debate was the last major controversy over the role of the presiding officer in enforcing decorum and relevancy. Although the Senate in 1856 had explicitly authorized its presiding officer to maintain order, it had decisively rejected a role for its presiding officer in maintaining the relevancy of debate. In the future, presiding officers varied in their aggressiveness in maintaining order. Experienced legislators in the late nineteenth century, such as Henry B. Anthony (R-R.I.), George F. Edmunds (R-Vt.), and John Sherman (R-Ohio), retained firm procedural control but understood the limits of their authority.

## Party Organization and the Neutrality of the Chair, 1845–1925

The president pro tempore, once an obvious solution to the Senate's collective-action problems, faced new competitors in the 1840s and 1850s. Short-term considerations—in 1826, in 1833, then finally in 1845—had caused senators to remove from their presiding officer the power to name the standing committees. In 1845 both parties turned to their caucuses to assemble committee lists. Once caucuses assumed this power—and began articulating new institutions, such as committees on committees—they did not relinquish it. Similarly, by the 1850s, when senators had grown accustomed to unlimited debate on irrelevant subjects, they were no longer willing to return to their chair the authority to define relevancy. The diminution of the Senate's presiding officer came ultimately not from deficiencies in the position of president pro tempore but in the construction of alternative institutions and practices. As a result, the principal task of the presiding officer became the enforcement of the Senate's rules and orders.

### Scheduling and Recognition

In the 1870s and 1880s, the Senate's workload burgeoned. Since parties lacked effective agenda-setting mechanisms until the early 1890s and the presiding officer possessed no authority over the agenda, senators fended for themselves much of the time, as they struggled to gain consideration of measures put in their charge. Consequently, presiding officers were left helpless to deal with a backlogged calendar of measures waiting for floor action. In the second half of the nineteenth century, morning hour was filled with squabbles among members, often all of the majority party, seeking action on their bills. As the mandatory March 3 adjournment date approached, conflict became particularly intense. As a general rule, vice presidents and presidents pro tempore presided over these turbulent proceedings in a neutral fashion.

To ease the burden on morning-hour consideration of routine and sometimes not-so-routine legislation, the Senate adopted the so-called Anthony rule at the start of each Congress in the 1870s and early 1880s. Named after Henry B. Anthony—who authored the rule and served simultaneously as president pro tempore and Republican caucus chairman during the 1869–75 period—the rule provided that a senator could speak only once, and for only five minutes on any question, during the call of the calendar following routine morning business. In the early 1880s, the Senate incorporated the Anthony rule in its standing rules. Other rules were adopted to try to handle the Senate's workload more efficiently.

In 1882 George Edmunds argued that the Senate was still unable to manage routine scheduling problems because

> the business [of the Senate] has so increased and accumulated, with the increasing number of Senators as well, that it has become a matter of more labor, difficulty, and time, to take it month in and month out, to find out what bill we are willing to consider than to consider and dispose of it; and the thing goes just by a kind of sporadic impulse if I may so speak. A Senator today from Vermont gets up and appeals to the Senate out of consideration to him to let him call up a bill that is at the very bottom of the calendar, the last one reported. I say, "it will not take a minute; it is a hard case, poor man," or whatever it may be. That occupies on average ten minutes probably. Then another Senator, a Senator who is more modest than we are, who has had his constituents' bill reported four weeks before, is squeezed out. And so we are in a continuous struggle, of good temper and good nature generally, but a continual struggle that takes up time, to see what it is we will do rather than in spending our time doing it.[54]

Edmunds hoped, in vain, that the Senate would tighten its procedures to allow bills to be considered during morning hour in the order in which they were placed on the calendar.

Responding to the problem identified by Edmunds, presiding officers by the late 1880s maintained a list of senators who sought recognition during morning hour to move consideration of a bill. John Ingalls (R-Kans.), the president pro tempere in 1888, explained:

> The Chair has been subject to great embarrassment by importunitites, natural and reasonable, from members of the Senate for action upon bills in which they are concerned. The rules require the presiding officer to recognize the first Senator who rises in his place and addresses the Chair. When several [senators] rise simultaneously and address the Chair, it is obviously impossible for that rule to be literally executed, and therefore, to avoid embarrassment, by the exercise of arbitrary authority and apparent partiality, the Chair has followed the practice of setting down upon a list alternately those who desire to be recognized, first upon one side of the Chamber and then upon the other, in the order in which they have applied, as being the only equitable and practicable method of escaping from the difficulties which the Chair experiences in consequence of the applications that are made for recognition.[55]

In short, the Senate's rule, dating to 1788, requiring the presiding officer to call on the senator first seeking recognition proved inadequate. If the list were discontinued, however, a mad scramble for recognition would be the result. When a senator challenged the list, another senator noted that Ingalls's predecessors had followed the same procedure.[56] No one suggested another mechanism, and complaints by a senator that he had a right to be recognized—as no doubt he did according to a strict interpretation of the rule—went unanswered. The presiding officer's reliance on such a list appears to have persisted for decades. In the 1910s and 1920s, the chair maintained a list of senators seeking recognition when a measure was debated under a time-limit agreement.[57]

Beyond adopting the Anthony rule and relying on a list of senators to be recognized, senators in the late nineteenth century more frequently employed other parliamentary devices—special orders, and, as we discuss below, unanimous consent agreements—to secure Senate action on bills, often quite important bills. A special order required a two-thirds majority, but if approved, the special order guaranteed that the bill would be taken up at a specified time or immediately after the Senate disposed of a pending bill. Routine unanimous consent requests were used to call up measures or ask that a measure be considered next in order. Individuals' repetitive and conflicting efforts to use these techniques, all without the coordination of floor leaders, further cluttered floor sessions and created animosities among members of the same party.

Throughout the 1880s and 1890s, the majority caucus was itself paying more attention to scheduling priorities. Although most of the caucus's attention was initially devoted to major legislation, by the early 1890s steering committees had begun managing the floor agenda.[58] These developments helped coordinate the efforts of members to gain Senate action on their bills and relieved some of the pressure on the presiding officer to manage the process of considering routine legislation. But they did not immediately reduce the use of special orders and certainly did not slow down unanimous consent requests, which became an everyday feature of floor activity in these years.

### Unanimous Consent Agreements

The modern responsibilities of the presiding officer are closely connected with the rise of unanimous consent agreements (UCAs), which are now critical to managing the business of the modern Senate. On a daily basis, the majority leader takes the lead in arranging agreements that expedite consideration of legislation by limiting or structuring debate and amending activity. Usually distinguished from routine motions that take the form of unanimous consent requests, UCAs supplement or supplant the standing rules of the Senate to organize floor debate. The term "complex" has sometimes been applied to this more important class of unanimous consent agreements.[59]

UCAs did not exist in the early Senate. Though the Senate has always been less formal and more leisurely than the House in its handling of legislation, unanimous agreements to limit debate or amendments do not appear to have been utilized until 1846.[60] In the late nineteenth century, UCAs became a standard feature of bill managers' strategies and raised significant questions about how the Senate governed itself that were not answered until the Senate amended Rule XII in 1914. The evolution in unanimous consent practices, largely untold in existing literature, is closely connected to the authority of the modern presiding officer and his relationship to party leaders.

Since UCAs are not reliably indexed in any source, we reconstructed the emergence of UCAs in Senate procedure by searching the *Globe* and the *Record* for UCAs associated with bills that were considered on the Senate floor for more than one day, as indicated in the bill index of the *Journal*.

Consequently, we do not have a systematic count of all UCAs and miss many UCAs that concern floor action on bills considered on a single day.

The 1846 agreement appears to have happened by accident.[61] A senator observed that the debate on the Oregon resolutions seemed to be winding down (after more than two months) and that "it would be an accommodation to many Senators to have an understanding as to the exact day" the Senate would vote. The agreement was quite informal, merely to vote on the resolutions in three days. A senator noted that the chamber could not be sure that debate on amendments would end by then; another assured him that debate would be short. Notably, one senator said that he "had not the slightest objection to fixing upon some day for terminating the debate, provided it was not to be regarded as establishing a precedent." On the appointed day, the debate lasted longer than some senators expected, but they brought the resolutions to a vote.

By 1870, UCAs were being used with some frequency. These early UCAs were, as they are today, time-limitation agreements that provided for disposal of a measure by a specified time. The typical UCA provided for a vote on a bill by time certain (usually 4 or 5 o'clock) and a certain day (usually a day or two in the future). By that time, the presiding officer, who was invisible in the process of reaching an agreement in 1846, usually repeated the agreement once offered so that senators could hear and understand it.

As UCAs became more common and as violations of agreements reached by unanimous consent occurred, the Senate found itself bound by an interpretation of the parliamentary status of UCAs that made them difficult to enforce. On Saturday, July 4, 1870, with many senators losing patience with their extended stay in Washington, the hour for a final vote on a naturalization bill under a UCA passed with opponents continuing to press amendments and debate the bill. Senators observed that the debate continued in violation of the UCA. John Sherman, in fact, complained that it was the first violation of a UCA in the history of the practice.[62] When a point of order was raised by another senator, the president pro tempore, Henry Anthony, stated that the chair did not have the power to enforce the agreement. "The agreement under which the Senate came to an understanding to vote at five o'clock on Saturday was by unanimous consent," Anthony declared. "It was not an order entered on the Journal, but merely an understanding among Senators. The Chair has no power and no right to enforce an agreement of that kind."[63] Anthony's repeated rulings established a precedent that led to much confusion over the next four decades.

Anthony's interpretation appeared to be based on the casual nature of UCAs in the years before the Civil War, when they were viewed as "gentlemen's agreements." The argument was based on two premises: that UCAs were not recognized in the Senate's rules and that the presiding officer had no authority except that granted explicitly by the rules. After Anthony left the Senate, Henry Cabot Lodge (R-Mass.) became the Senate's parliamentarian-in-residence and frequently articulated this rationale.

Presiding officers were not entirely consistent in their approach to UCAs in the late nineteenth century. From time to time, presiding officers suggested a UCA as a way out of a sticky scheduling problem. At other times, they restated UCAs and encouraged clarification and approval of unanimous consent requests.[64] Most presiding officers contributed to the implementation of UCAs by noting that the time had arrived to call up or vote on a measure subject to a UCA. But senators varied in their understanding of the role of the presiding officer. John Ingalls, Ambrose Burnside (R-R.I.), and Thomas Ferry (R-Mich.), who had just served as president pro tempore for four years, had this exchange in 1880:

> *Ingalls.* It has always been the case when that hour has been reached which has been agreed upon that the presiding officer rapped with his gavel upon the table and announced that the hour had arrived. He failed to do it in this case. I say that that agreement was abrogated by unanimous consent, and it is entirely competent now to make another agreement.
>
> *Ferry.* I restate the fact that the Senator from Alabama was making a speech and had not concluded when the hour of four o'clock arrived. The Senate has always in such instances yielded to the condition of things and allowed the Senator to continue when objection was not made.
>
> *Ingalls.* Never.
>
> *Burnside.* I do not think there ever has been a vote since I have been in the Senate that was taken at the hour it was agreed to be taken.[65]

Ingalls was probably right about some presiding officers, but Ferry and Burnside seem to have been right about the general practice. In fact, when limits on individual speeches became common features of UCAs in the 1880s, the presiding officer kept time.

While presiding officers routinely refused to enforce UCAs, some chose to go their own way, at least at times when it seemed convenient to do so. In 1888 Ingalls, then president pro tempore, interrupted a senator who exceeded the five-minute limit for a speech under a UCA and asked if there was objection to allowing the senator to continue.[66] President pro tempore William Frye (R-Maine) once took the initiative to note that debate was not in order under a UCA and ruled on a point of order raised against amendments based on provisions of the same UCA.[67] And Vice Presidents Charles Fairbanks and James Sherman were not timid about enforcing UCAs at times.[68]

Responsibility for negotiating UCAs appears to have rested with bill managers until the second decade of the twentieth century. The long exchanges on the Senate floor concerning unanimous consent requests reflected a great deal of confusion about the provisions of UCAs. As Stephen White (D-Calif.) observed:

> So an hour and a half or two hours' discussion of the rules may not be amiss. Their lucidity is daily becoming more apparent, and the remarkably clear statement of the position which we are in which has been had from a large number of Senators, no one of whom agree with another, demonstrates that the American Republic cannot exist without the present rules. [Laughter.][69]

Senators sometimes complained that they were not present when unanimous consent was granted.

Further complicating the use of UCAs after the turn of the century was the understanding that UCAs could not be modified, even by unanimous consent. Lodge made this argument in 1907 and consistently maintained the position, along with the view that the presiding officer could not enforce UCAs.[70] Lodge's theory was that UCAs, as gentlemen's agreements, created an obligation that could not be violated by senators who happened to be on the floor and were seeking a modification at a later time. Lodge argued, as Sherman had in 1870, that modifications in UCAs, even by unanimous consent, would eventually undermine confidence in them. Although presiding officers were not consistent on this matter, the Lodge view appears to have prevailed during the first decade of the twentieth century.

Agreements that provided for a vote on a bill and pending amendments at a time certain were a regular part of floor management practice at the turn of the century. Although compliance with UCAs was generally good, critical features of modern floor practice were not in place. No formal party floor leaders were present to orchestrate agreements and oversee their implementation. Holding to the view that UCAs could not be modified by unanimous consent, senators found them inflexible tools for scheduling. Presiding officers enforced agreements sporadically, whether because of the ignorance of precedent or the forbearance of senators.

In the first years of the twentieth century, the Senate adopted practices that reduced confusion about UCAs. Senators began to submit unanimous consent requests in writing to the desk, where they often were read by the secretary at the request of the presiding officer. UCAs that were intended to govern the conduct of business on subsequent days were printed on the title page of the daily calendar of business as long as they were operative. And the secretary appears to have reworded numerous agreements so that they would conform with what had become the "usual form," as some senators noted on the floor.

An event in early 1913 exposed the problems inherent in the mix of accumulated precedents concerning UCAs.[71] After having failed in previous days to gain unanimous consent for consideration and a vote on a prohibition bill, Newell Sanders (R-Tenn.) asked for unanimous consent once again and, probably much to his surprise, received it. In a moment, Reed Smoot (R-Utah) inquired, "Was there a unanimous consent agreement just entered?" When the substitute presiding officer indicated that there was, Smoot immediately asked that it be reconsidered, to which the presiding officer responded that "it is beyond the power of the Senate to change or interfere with a unanimous consent agreement after it is made." Several senators insisted that they had not heard the request and that previous practice in such cases was to have the request submitted to the Senate again. Others, including Lodge, had to confess that a UCA must be observed. Joseph Bristow (R-Kans.) proclaimed that he was free to violate the UCA. The next day, Smoot suggested that the request be resubmitted to the Senate. Over the strong protest of Jacob Gallinger (R-N.H.), President Pro Tempore Augustus Bacon (D-Ga.), now back in the chair, indicated that he had no power to rule on the matter and allowed the issue to be decided by the Senate. A large majority voted to have the request resubmitted, which it was, and Smoot promptly objected to the request. Gallinger then restated the request—with a different date for action on the measure—and it was accepted.

Arguments about the twisted logic in Senate precedents on UCAs came to a head on those two January days. By the beginning of the next session, a committee recommended the adoption of a new rule, a third paragraph for Rule XII. The proposed rule provided that no request by a Senator for unanimous consent for the taking of a final vote on a specified date upon the passage of a bill or joint resolution shall be submitted to the Senate for agreement thereto until, upon a roll call ordered for the purpose by the presiding officer, it shall be disclosed that a quorum of the Senate is present; and when unanimous consent is thus given, the same shall operate as the order of the Senate, but any unanimous consent may be revoked by another unanimous consent granted in the prescribed manner.[72]

The requirement for a quorum call was not controversial. Even the provision that UCAs be considered orders of the Senate, enabling the presiding officer to enforce them, received little discussion. Lodge and Smoot complained about the ability to modify UCAs by unanimous consent but appeared to accept the logic once the proponents of the rule accepted an amendment that required one day's notice of a request to modify such a UCA (one providing for a final vote). A bipartisan majority supported the proposal, as amended.[73]

With the new rule, the Senate adopted a formal procedure for approving an important class of UCAs and, also for the first time, granted the presiding officer the authority to enforce them. Presiding officers began to exhibit consistency in their interpretation of the parliamentary status of UCAs and their power to implement them.[74] In practice, as far as we have been able to determine, all UCAs were thenceforth treated as orders of the Senate.

By the late 1910s, central features of modern Senate floor practice were in place. Not only was the modern interpretation of UCAs finally established, but modern party floor leadership posts were created.[75] It took a few years for floor leaders to assume primary responsibility for negotiating UCAs and managing their approval on the floor. By 1921, however, party leaders were actively engaged in the process.[76] In the 1910s and 1920s, as party leaders assumed control of the Senate floor, the presiding officer's role as neutral arbiter was settled.

Practices surrounding unanimous consent agreements were still not entirely settled in the mid-twentieth century. In the last half of the century, the majority leader became more inventive in designing agreements to limit debate and amendments.[77] Presiding officers, under the guidance of the parliamentarian, found themselves enforcing ever more complicated agreements. Among the issues raised but not resolved was whether the Senate should, by majority vote, overturn rulings of the presiding officer based on unanimous consent agreements. For example, should the Senate overturn a ruling that an amendment is out of order because it violates a UCA that requires amendments to be germane? In these circumstances, the power to appeal a ruling to the Senate may undermine senators' confidence that a UCA will be observed and threaten the entire practice of operating by unanimous consent.[78] But to back away from appeals when proceeding under a UCA hands to the presiding officer a source of influence over outcomes that the Senate had not explicitly granted.

## Conclusion

To the casual observer, the Senate does not appear to have changed significantly since it was first organized. Indeed, political scientists have tended to treat the Senate as if there were few important developments deserving systematic study and theory. In our view, it is important to recognize that the institutional development of the Senate was not settled in the first Congresses. The need for order, a detailed order of business, complex unanimous consent agreements, committee assignments, effective presiding officers, and party organization and floor leaders did not arise until decades after the Senate first organized and adopted rules. Senators' struggles with, and solutions to, these problems warrant more attention.

Senators often sought solutions to collective-action problems by experimenting with enhanced authority for their presiding officer. Maintaining order on the floor and assigning senators to committees proved difficult at times before the Civil War, while managing the floor agenda and implementing unanimous consent agreements were vexing problems in the last decades of the century. In most cases, the arrangement of dual presiding officers—the vice president and the president pro tempore—reduced the viability of turning to a strong presiding officer for a solution. Vice presidents, who were not chosen by the Senate and were often political opponents of the Senate majority, proved untrustworthy; presidents pro tempore were only temporary officeholders. On matters concerning basic features of Senate floor procedure, such as maintaining order and enforcing unanimous consent agreements, the presiding officer was eventually granted clear authority. But the authority was nondiscretionary. And, on other matters, such as setting the agenda and making committee assignments, senators and their parties eventually invented other means for managing collective-action problems.

Senators proved remarkably tolerant of inconvenience and uncertainty, sometimes for decades, until a plainly unacceptable event generated a consensus for a new rule or practice. Particularly destructive behavior on the floor, perverse outcomes in committee assignment balloting, genuine confusion in setting the daily schedule, and eventually a truly convoluted interpretation of a unanimous consent agreement persuaded most senators of the need for a change in the inherited practice. A common response of senators was to propose a new rule or set of rules. In some cases, new rules were adopted; in other cases, rules were put off in hope that the events would not recur. But in all cases, many senators initially turned to the presiding officer for a solution.

Circumstantial evidence and senatorial commentary have long suggested that the weakness of the Senate's presiding officers merely reflects the tradition of informal governance preferred by senators. An important point to remember, however, is that senators who were frustrated under informal practices or ambiguous rules found their efforts to change the rules easily blocked by others. Only when extraordinary events forced nearly all senators to recognize the severity of a festering collective-action problem was a new rule tried.

By understanding more fully what did not happen in the Senate—a powerful presiding officer did not emerge—we can better approach the study of those solutions to collective action that have lasted through the twentieth century. Senators of the nineteenth century saw nothing inevitable about the emergence of modern party caucuses, scheduling routines, unanimous consent practices, or party leadership. These features of the modern Senate developed only after failed experiments with other approaches, often involving the chamber's presiding officer. Some of these developments, such as the emergence of modern unanimous consent procedures and party floor leadership, appear to have been closely connected to each other and to the role of the presiding officer. Not until party leadership emerged—first in the caucus, then in the caucus committees, ultimately in floor leaders—could senators abandon their attempts to place critical powers in the hands of their presiding officer.

## Notes

We are grateful to Scott Amrozowicz, Casey Clementson, Jeff Jackson, Daniel Stevens, and Jon Sustarich for superb research assistance. We are also grateful to the Senate Historical Office, the Center for Legislative Archives, the Congressional Research Service, and Rush Rhees Library at the University of Rochester. Stan Bach, Dick Baker, Catherine Hansen, and Elizabeth Rybicki have contributed critical assistance to this project. Gamm thanks the Woodrow Wilson Center for its support, and Smith thanks the Dirksen Congressional Center for its support.

1. Max Farrand, ed., *The Records of the Federal Convention of 1787,* 4 vols. (New Haven: Yale University Press, 1966), 2: p. 537.

2. Ibid., p. 592.

3. Lauros G. McConachie, *Congressional Committees* (New York: Thomas Y. Crowell, 1898), p. 332; Woodrow Wilson, *Constitutional Government in the United States* (Columbia University Press, 1908), p. 132; George H. Haynes, *The Senate of the United States: Its History and Practice,* 2 vols. (Boston: Houghton Mifflin, 1938), 1: pp. 256–59.

4. McConachie, *Congressional Committees,* pp. 332–38; Wilson, *Constitutional Government in the United States,* pp. 132–33; Walter Kravitz, "The United States Senate: An Interpretive History," unpublished manuscript, Senate Historical Office, 1966, 5: p. 49; Elaine K. Swift, *The Making of an American Senate: Reconstitutive Change in Congress, 1787–1841* (University of Michigan Press, 1996), pp. 76–77.

5. "Senator Anthony Declines Re-Election," *New York Times,* March 9, 1873, p. 1.

6. "Voting for Retaliation," *New York Times,* February 24, 1887, p. 1.

7. "The Expiring Congress," *New York Times,* March 2, 1891, p. 5.

8. Haynes, *The Senate of the United States,* 1: p. 255; "The President Pro Tem," *New York Times,* March 9, 1875, p. 1. In fact, there was a tendency for the caucus chairs and presidents pro tempore to come from different regions of the country, although explicit references by senators to this consideration have not been found.

9. "Voting for Retaliation," p. 1.

10. "Avoiding a Special Session," *New York Times,* February 28, 1883, p. 1.

11. "Senator Anthony," *New York Times,* October 30, 1883, p. 1.

12. *Congressional Globe,* December 27, 1845, pp. 95–96, as quoted in Henry H. Gilfry, *President of the Senate Pro Tempore,* S. Doc. 104, 62 Cong. 1 sess. (GPO, 1911), pp. 22–23.

13. *Senate Journal,* January 11, 1847, pp. 91–92, as cited in Gilfry, *President of the Senate Pro Tempore,* pp. 24–25.

14. *Congressional Globe,* January 11, 1847, pp. 161–64, as cited in Gilfry, *President of the Senate Pro Tempore,* p. 27.

15. Ibid.

16. *Congressional Globe,* June 9, 1856, p. 1368.

17. *Congressional Globe,* June 11, 1856, p. 1385.

18. Gilfry, *President of the Senate Pro Tempore,* p. 111.

19. George P. Furber, *Precedents Relating to the Privileges of the Senate of the United States,* S. Misc. Doc. 68, 52 Cong. 2 sess. (GPO, 1893), pp. 167, 188–89.

20. Gerald Gamm and Steven S. Smith, "Emergence of Senate Party Leadership," unpublished paper, 1998.

21. McConachie, *Congressional Committees,* p. 343.

22. Wilson, *Constitutional Government in the United States,* p. 133.

23. Gamm and Smith, "Emergence of Senate Party Leadership."

24. Gerald Gamm and Kenneth Shepsle, "Emergence of Legislative Institutions: Standing Committees in the House and Senate, 1810–1825," *Legislative Studies Quarterly,* vol. 14 (February 1989), pp. 53–57.

25. "Congress," *New York Evening Post,* December 9, 1816, p. 2.

26. "Twenty-Fifth Congress," *Columbian Centinel,* December 9, 1837, p. 2.

27. *New York Post,* December 12, 1833, p. 2.

28. *Annals of Congress,* 18 Cong. 1 sess., p. 26, as cited in Swift, *The Making of an American Senate,* p. 134.

29. *Congressional Globe,* December 6, 1837, p. 9.

30. *Register of Debates,* December 9, 1833, p. 21.

31. Ibid.

32. "Committees in the Senate," *Columbian Centinel,* December 25, 1833, p. 1. See also *Albany Argus,* December 13, 1833, p. 2.

33. *Register of Debates,* December 10, 1833, p. 24.

34. Haynes, *The Senate of the United States,* 1: p. 274.

35. McConachie, *Congressional Committees,* pp. 330–31; Haynes, *The Senate of the United States,* 1: p. 276.

36. Mark O. Hatfield, *Vice Presidents of the United States, 1789–1993,* S. Doc. 104-26, 104 Cong. 2 sess. (GPO, 1997), p. 156.

37. *Congressional Globe,* December 4, 1845, pp. 19–20.

38. Ibid., p. 21.

39. See Gamm and Smith, "Emergence of Senate Party Leadership."

40. *Congressional Globe,* December 10, 1845, p. 39, and December 17, 1845, p. 66; McConachie, *Congressional Committees,* pp. 282–83, 325–26.

41. "From the South," *New York Evening Post,* December 11, 1847, p. 3.

42. Haynes, *The Senate of the United States,* pp. 212–16. On the modern Senate practice on rulings of the chair, see Stanley Bach, "The Senate's Compliance with Its Legislative Rules: The Appeal of Order," *Congress and the Presidency,* vol. 18 (Spring 1991), pp. 77–92.

43. Rule XVI of the 1789 rules provided that "when a Member shall be called to order he shall sit down until the President shall have determined whether he is in order or not; and every question of order shall be decided by the President without debate; but if there be a doubt in his mind he may call the sense of the Senate."

44. *Register of Debates,* April 15, 1826, pp. 572–73; Richard R. Beeman, "Unlimited Debate in the Senate: The First Phase," *Political Science Quarterly,* vol. 83 (September 1968), pp. 421–25; Louis C. Hatch, *A History of the Vice-Presidency of the United States,* (New York: American Historical Society, 1934), pp. 71–76.

45. *Register of Debates,* February 12, 1828, pp. 305–06.

46. The 1828 rule referred to "when a member shall be called to order *by the President or a Senator*" (emphasis added), thus explicitly recognizing two ways to call a senator to order. The new rule also made the presiding officer's decision "subject to appeal to the Senate."

47. *Register of Debates,* February 11, 1828, p. 282.

48. Beeman, "Unlimited Debate in the Senate," pp. 428–31.

49. *Congressional Globe,* April 3, 1850, p. 632, and March 26, 1850, pp. 602–04.

50. Robert C. Byrd, *The Senate, 1789–1989,* 4 vols., S. Doc. 100-20, 100 Cong. 1 sess. (GPO, 1988–94), 1: pp. 195–96. See also Elbert Smith, *Magnificent Missourian: The Life of Thomas Hart Benton* (Philadelphia: Lippincott, 1958), pp. 265–72.

51. Byrd, *The Senate,* 1: p. 209. See also Robert Dole, *Historical Almanac of the United States Senate,* Doc. 100-35, 100 Cong. 2 sess. (GPO, 1989), pp. 106–07.

52. *Congressional Globe,* June 26, 1856, p. 1483.

53. Ibid., pp. 1477–78. The procedure for an appeal to the Senate was clarified in 1877 when the rule was modified to prohibit debate on a motion to allow a senator to proceed in order. Debate on such a motion would prevent the senator from continuing to address the Senate and undermine the point of appealing the decision of the chair.

54. *Congressional Record,* January 27, 1883, p. 675.

55. *Congressional Record,* August 1, 1888, p. 7110.

56. Ibid., pp. 7109–10.

57. *Congressional Record,* March 4, 1917, p. 5012, and February 9, 1924, p. 2185.

58. See Gamm and Smith, "Emergence of Senate Party Leadership."

59. Robert Keith, "The Use of Unanimous Consent in the Senate," in U.S. Senate, *Committees and Senate Procedures,* 94 Cong. 2 sess. (GPO, 1977); Steven S. Smith and Marcus Flathman, "Managing the Senate Floor: Complex Unanimous Consent Agreements since the 1950s," *Legislative Studies Quarterly,* vol. 24 (August 1989), pp. 349–73.

60. Keith, "The Use of Unanimous Consent in the Senate."

61. *Congressional Globe,* April 13, 1846, p. 659.

62. *Congressional Globe,* July 4, 1870, p. 5152.

63. Ibid., p. 5150.

64. *Congressional Record,* April 9, 1880, p. 2268.

65. *Congressional Record,* January 6, 1880, p. 193.

66. *Congressional Record,* March 8, 1888, p. 1848. For another example, see *Congressional Record,* March 19, 1908, p. 3615.

67. *Congressional Record,* March 1, 1900, pp. 2448–49.

68. *Congressional Record,* March 19, 1908, p. 3602; January 6, 1909, pp. 549–50; August 15, 1912, p. 10974; December 8, 1913, pp. 423–26.

69. *Congressional Record,* January 25, 1895, p. 1344.

70. *Congressional Record,* January 10, 1907, pp. 878–79, 1389–90.

71. *Congressional Record,* January 10–11, 1913, pp. 1324–29, 1354–56, 1388–95.

72. *Congressional Record,* January 16, 1914, p. 1756.

73. Ibid., pp. 1756–59.

74. See, for example, *Congressional Record,* March 1, 1916, p. 3347, and April 8, 1916, p. 5717.

75. See Gamm and Smith, "Emergence of Senate Party Leadership."

76. *Congressional Record,* July 20, 1921, p. 4115, and August 1, 1921, p. 4480.

77. See Smith and Flathman, "Managing the Senate Floor."

78. Stanley Bach, "Rules, Rulings, and the Rule of Law in Congress," paper presented at the annual meeting of the Midwest Political Science Association, Chicago, Ill., 1997.

# PART III
## *Senate Deliberation in Context*

# CHAPTER SEVEN

# Constituency Size and the Strategic Behavior of Senators

## BRUCE I. OPPENHEIMER

AMERICANS TAKE THE REPRESENTATIONAL basis of the U.S. Senate for granted. Although it was the issue of greatest contention at the Constitutional Convention, equal representation of states in the Senate has generated little concern since ratification. Yet the Senate's apportionment scheme has profound consequences for this legislative institution and for the operation of American democracy. In *Sizing Up the Senate: The Unequal Consequences of Equal Representation,* Frances Lee and I explore four areas where Senate apportionment has significant effects: the representational relationships of senators and constituents, the conduct of Senate elections, the strategic behavior of senators, and the design of public policy.[1]

Hence the implications of Senate representation may well provide an important key to the perceived civility problems of that institution.[2] Furthermore, any effort to address these concerns needs to be sensitive to the representational diversity of senators. Unlike House members, senators serve constituencies that range enormously in size. A central question posed in this chapter, then, is how do the population size differences of the states affect the jobs of senators—the incentive structures they face and their paths to success—and how in turn do these influence the institutional civility that has been historically valued?

To lay some groundwork, I should first mention that, from the perspective of the one-person, one-vote standard, the Senate is now the most malapportioned democratic legislature in the democratic world. The degree of malapportionment has increased fairly continuously over the nation's history. And the magnitude of the population differences among the states has grown markedly. The Senate comprises a relatively small number of members representing very populous states and a relatively large number of members representing small states. Second, the representational experiences of senators and their constituents in large states is very different from that of senators and constituents in small states. In this respect, senators from small states have more in common with House members than with senators from populous states. Accordingly, some of the tensions that naturally exist between the House and the Senate because of the different constituency bases of the members of each institution also exist within the Senate itself. Third, because of these representational differences, the goals of senators and their paths to political success differ with the population size of the states they represent. This affects what activities senators view as important, the committees on which they choose to serve, the time they spend on different activities, and how they behave strategically in the Senate.

Note, however, I do not claim that state size affects the issue positions of senators or that coalitions of small-state senators oppose coalitions of senators from populous states. One rationale that delegates to the Constitutional Convention offered for equal state representation in the Senate— namely, that without it the populous states would discriminate against the small states—was without foundation then and remains so now. James Madison and Alexander Hamilton, among others, argued without success that cleavages in the new government would not form around state size.[3] In fact, there has been no major issue in the nation's history that has pitted large states against small ones. Rather, party, ideology, and region have defined the major cleavages. By contrast, state population size affects how senators behave and their ordering of priorities, but not how they stand on issues.

## Senate Malapportionment

The degree of malapportionment in the Senate, though not great immediately after ratification of the Constitution, has grown steadily over time when measured against a population-based standard.[4] Wyoming, with fewer than a half million residents, enjoys the same level of representation as California, which has over 30 million. The seventeen least populous states—none of which have a population of more than 2 million and col-

Figure 7-1. *Minimum Percentage of the Nation's Population Able to Elect a Senate Majority*

Percent

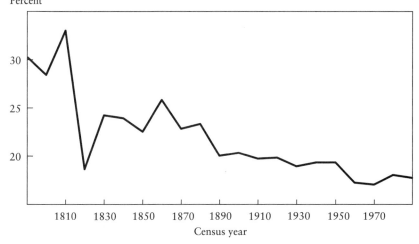

Census year

Source: This figure is taken from Lee and Oppenheimer, *Sizing Up the Senate*, p. 11.

lectively have only 7 percent of the entire national population—are represented by thirty-four senators. By contrast, only six senators represent the three faster-growing, populous states: California, Texas, and Florida, which are now home to more than a quarter of the nation's population.

Thus it is not enough to recognize that the Senate deviates from the one-person, one-vote standard; the magnitude to which those differences have grown must also be taken into account. The change can be seen in figure 7-1, which reports on different measures of legislative malapportionment; it plots the Dauer-Kelsay apportionment index as applied to the U.S. Senate.[5] The Dauer-Kelsay index is a measure of the minimum percentage of the population that would be required to elect a majority of the Senate. As can be seen, that percentage has declined fairly consistently over the nation's history and has been less than 20 percent for nearly a century.

A more sophisticated index developed by Schubert and Press provides further evidence that today's Senate is clearly more malapportioned than at any time in its history.[6] While the overall apportionment score of .48 is the same in the 1990s as in the 1970s, in terms of the standard deviation, skewness, and kurtosis of the distribution of state populations, the decade of the 1990s is the most extreme. The largest states have grown even larger, and the number of states overrepresented (compared with a one-person, one-vote standard) has increased.[7] Moreover, the trend is not likely to reverse in the foreseeable future. The fastest-growing states are composed heavily of the most populous ones, whereas many of the small states have low growth rates. Although Madison predicted that Senate malapportionment would increase over time, none of the Founders could have possibly anticipated the levels it would reach by 2000 or the magnitude of the differences in state populations.[8]

However, there is no reason to expect a groundswell of support for changing the base of Senate apportionment, nor would the Constitution likely be amended even if this were to occur. As Article 5 of the Constitution states, "No state, without its consent, shall be deprived of equal suffrage in the Senate." This provision makes it almost impossible to alter equal state representation because states that benefit from the scheme would not be likely to consent to a change.

If the Senate representation were without consequences, there might be little reason for concern, even as the institution increasingly deviates from the one-person, one-vote standard. But that is not the case.

## The Representational Experience

To illustrate the effect of state size on the representative experiences of senators and constituents, it is useful to examine one area of that experience, the levels of contact between senators and their constituents. If one thinks of representation as "acting in the interest of the represented in a manner responsive to them," then contact between senators and constituents is fundamental to responsive representation.[9] It is literally the ability to be "in touch" as opposed to being "out of touch" that is the foundation of legitimate representation. As will be demonstrated, staying in touch in populous states is a far more difficult undertaking than in small states.

One can assess the effects of state size on contact between senators and constituents from data collected in the NES's Senate Election Study conducted in 1988, 1990, and 1992.[10] This study was based on interviews with roughly equal numbers of respondents in each state about their senators. One battery of questions dealt with contact between senators and the respondents.

On all five contact items, there was a clear indication that the levels of reported contact decrease as population increases.[11] On some items the level of reported contact is four times as great in states with a single congressional district as in the most populous states (those with greater than nineteen districts). These findings are hardly surprising. There are limits on how many constituents a senator can meet or how many engagements at which a senator can speak. A senator from California could personally meet fifty times as many constituents as one from Wyoming but would still have a lower contact rate. But differences exist even in reports about receiving mail, an activity on which populous-state senators would not seemingly be limited.

Regressions on these data provide more accurate estimates of the effects of state size on contact levels. When this exercise was done on the percentage of respondents who reported that they had personally met the senator, for example, for each increase of 1 million constituents in a state there is an estimated 1.2 percent decline in those reporting the contact. That means there will be an estimated difference of 33 percent between those reporting this contact in the smallest state and those in the largest.

What is even more striking is that respondents in small states (those with three or fewer congressional districts) actually report higher contact levels with their senators than with their House members. This finding undermines the generalization that House members have closer contact with their constituents than do senators. It may be true in populous states, but in that third of the states with three or fewer House districts the generalization does not hold.

The relationship between state size and senator-constituent contact holds for constituent-initiated contact as well as contact initiated by the senator. On the item that asked respondents if they or any member of their families had ever contacted the senator or the senator's office, the reported contact level in the smallest states (one district) was more than twice that in the largest states (more than nineteen districts). This makes sense. After all, when constituents decide whether and which elected official to contact, they are likely to consider the chances of getting access, the clout or potential influence of the official, and the likelihood that the official will act on the request. In populous states constituents may consider it so difficult to gain access to their senators that they will choose to contact other officials instead, such as their House members. As one senator put it, "The lines in large states are shorter to the congresswoman or congressman than to the senator." But as state population declines, constituents are likely to perceive little difference in ease of access to their senators as opposed to their House member. And the same is likely to be true when they calculate which official is more likely to act favorably on their request. With no difference in accessibility or responsiveness, constituents then have the option of going to the official who they perceive has more clout. Thus the contact differences between constituents and senators in small and large states is a two-way street. In small states it is not only easier for senators to reach a higher proportion of their constituents, but it is also easier for the constituents to reach their senators.

It is not merely the quantity of contact between senators and constituents that varies inversely with population size of the states. The quality of senator-constituent contact also is affected. Of those respondents who said that they had contacted their senator, a follow-up question was asked about the nature of that contact. Respondents were asked whether the contact was to express an opinion on an issue, to seek information, or to seek help with a problem. In small states (three or fewer congressional districts) respondents were more than twice as likely to say that their contact was for the purpose of seeking help with a problem as was the case in the largest states (nineteen or more congressional districts). In the largest states nearly two-thirds of the respondents said that they contacted their senator to express an opinion. It may not be very difficult for a constituent to contact a public official whom she has never met and never expects to meet simply to express her opinion on an issue. But asking for help with a problem seems to call for a greater level of interpersonal comfort, just as people may be reluctant to ask a stranger for assistance. It is only in smaller states where constituents have these comfort levels with their senators.[12]

Again, the mix of reasons respondents reported for contacting their senators in small states looks very similar to the reasons they reported for contacting their House members. It is not just on the quantity of contact that the representational experiences of senators and constituents in small states look more like those of House members than of large state senators. The same holds for the quality of contact. In large states it is far more impersonal.

In sum, in small states constituents and senators have contacts that look very much more like the contacts that exist nationally between constituents and House members than they do like the relationships between constituents and senators in populous states. In large states the contact levels are far lower and less intimate. This suggests that for constituents in small states having two senators, the situation is like having two additional House members. These different representational experiences that senators have in small and large states are the key to understanding why state size is linked to behavior differences of senators in the institution and the potential for conflict.

Two additional points deserve a brief mention here.[13] First, it is not just individual constituents who find it easier to gain access to their senators in small states than in large ones. The same also applies to interest groups. The number and range of interests that exist in populous states is so large that gaining access to senators from California, Texas, and New York is a major task. By contrast, with fewer home state interests, groups find it far easier to reach small-state senators both directly and indirectly.

Second, the closer ties that small-state senators are able to develop with their constituents have payoffs in the job approval ratings they receive. There is a strong negative relationship between state size and a range of job approval ratings of senators.[14] Small-state senators have the capacity to build trust relationships with their constituents that are not within the reach of their colleagues from populous states.

It is in these differing types of representational experiences that some of the seeds of tension among senators are planted, germinate, and begin to flourish. Their paths to successful Senate careers are necessarily differing ones that often have them pursuing goals that engender a certain level of interpersonal conflict.

## State Size and Senate Campaign Fund-Raising

Although campaign fund-raising is not directly linked to the differing representational experiences of senators in large and small states, it is affected by state size in and of itself and hence merits a comment as well. This effect has increased since the early 1970s, when campaign finance reforms eliminated the ability of senators to rely on a relatively small number of large donors. Over that period, political campaigns have also become more expensive. The obvious way that state population affects Senate campaigns is that they become more costly as the size of the state increases. Most clearly, beyond certain fixed costs, campaign advertising expenses (television, radio, and direct mail) increase with the number of people a campaign has to reach. Senators from the most populous states simply have to raise much more money to fund their reelection campaigns than do senators from the smallest states. The data in table 7-1 on campaign fund-raising by incumbent senators running for reelection from 1992

Table 7-1. *State Population and Fund-Raising of Incumbent Senators, 1992–98 Campaigns*

| Number of congressional districts in the state | First 4 years of term | | Last 2 years of term | | |
|---|---|---|---|---|---|
| | Funds raised[a] (dollars) | Percentage of funds raised | Funds raised (dollars) | Percentage of funds raised | Total funds raised (dollars) |
| 1 | 501,340 (15) | 18.5 | 2,393,951 | 81.5 | 2,895,291 |
| 2–3 | 722,484 (17) | 23.6 | 2,458,500 | 77.4 | 3,180,984 |
| 4–6 | 760,810 (21) | 17.0 | 3,239,736 | 83.0 | 4,000,546 |
| 7–10 | 1,044,697 (19) | 18.5 | 4,791,013 | 81.4 | 5,835,710 |
| 11–20 | 1,888,503 (11) | 21.6 | 6,045,524 | 78.4 | 7,934,027 |
| 21–25 | 1,876,485 (5) | 25.7 | 4,975,865 | 74.3 | 6,852,350 |
| 26–52 | 5,485,798 (5) | 35.5 | 9,974,005 | 64.5 | 15,459,803 |

Source: Author's calculations, based on Federal Election Commission data.
a. Numbers in parentheses are the number of races in each grouping.

to 1998 illustrate this point. Senators in states with only a single congressional district raised on average less than $3 million over their six-year terms for their reelection campaigns. By contrast, senators in the most populous states raised an average of more than $15 million. And there is a steady increase as population size increases. (The seeming anomaly is that senators in states with eleven to twenty congressional districts raised more money than those in states with twenty-one to twenty-five districts. But that is due to the fact that nearly all the races in the former grouping were close, while most of those in the latter were not highly competitive.)

These data lead to one fairly obvious conclusion: senators in more populous states must devote more effort to fund-raising than those in smaller states. But the differences in the amounts being raised tell only part of the story. The amounts that senators have to raise also affect when they raise the money and where they raise it. And differences in the when and where make the task of populous-state senators even more arduous than one would assume from the dollar differences alone.

Regarding when the money is raised, senators from populous states must raise campaign funds on a fairly continuous basis throughout their terms, while those in smaller states can concentrate their fund-raising in the final two years of their terms. As for the percentage of funds raised in the final two years, the differences do not appear that great among senators from states with twenty or fewer congressional districts: the figures range from a low of 77.4 percent to a high of 83 percent. Only in the two groupings of senators from the largest states does the amount raised in the final two years drop off more noticeably, with those in the most populous states raising less than two-thirds of their funds in the last part of the cycle. But this understates the effect, because as state size increases, senators have to raise more money. So in the first four years of their terms senators from states with a single district raised an average of about $125,000 a year, while incumbents from the most populous states raised over $1.4 million per year.[15] As state population increases, then, fund-raising for incumbent senators goes from an activity that is primarily focused in the final two years of a term to a constant activity.

Sources of the funds represent a second complicating factor. These can be divided into two groups: investors and consumers. Investors are those who contribute to campaigns to obtain "private benefits in return for their money."[16] Such benefits may include, but are certainly not limited to, access to the senator, assistance with government agencies, or efforts to influence the senator's behavior in some way. Consumers, however, contribute to candidates as a means of helping them get elected rather than for private benefit. They offer their support because they share party identification, ideology, or some other affiliation with the candidate.

All senators rely on a mix of investors and consumers to finance their campaigns. But the mix is not the same for all senators. Although some senators are more influential than others, Senate power is distributed fairly broadly among the members in a highly individualistic institution. Senators derive power first from being senators and then from who they are in the Senate. True, investors may well consider a number of factors in deciding whose campaigns they will contribute to. Indeed, some senators may be better positioned and be able to attract more campaign funds from investors. However, because senators are relatively equal in power, they will be able to raise similar amounts of money from investors. By contrast, the amount of money senators can raise from consumers varies with the total number of supporters a senator has. Senators from large states will, in general, have more supporters than those from less populous states. (Of

Table 7-2. *State Population and the Funds Raised by Incumbent Senators for Their Campaigns, Controlling for Other Factors, 1992–98*[a]

| Variable | Amount from PACs (dollars) | Amount from non-PAC sources (dollars) | Percentage of funds from PACs |
|---|---|---|---|
| Constant | 1,440,760*** | 564,142 | 43.58*** |
| | (10.52) | (0.92) | (14.7) |
| State population (millions) | 23,112** | 478,179*** | -1.26*** |
| | (2.35) | (10.78) | (-5.90) |
| Competitive race (dummy) | 317,292*** | 1,691,415*** | -2.76 |
| | (2.80) | (3.32) | (-1.13) |
| Seniority | -130,180** | 206,920 | -2.08* |
| | (-2,387) | (0.84) | (-1.76) |
| Accepts limited or does not accept PAC dollars | -1,304,421*** | -1,304,421*** | -31.02*** |
| | (-5.39) | (3.39) | (-5.92) |
| *Summary statistic* | | | |
| Adj. $R^2$ | 0.34 | 0.61 | 0.42 |
| F | 13.7*** | 39.4*** | 18.6*** |
| Mean of dependent variable | 1,356,924 | 4,165,404 | 30.71 |
| N | 100 | 100 | 100 |

Source: Compiled from Federal Election Commission data.
*$p < .10$ (2-tailed test); **$p < .05$ (2-tailed test); ***$p < .01$ (2-tailed test).
a. $t$ statistics in parentheses.

course, there may be senators with broad national followings who raise substantial campaign funds from consumers outside their home states.) It follows from these distinctions that state population will affect the mix of contributions that senators receive when they campaign for reelection. Senators from small states will find that investors contribute a higher proportion of their campaign funds than will senators from large states. And populous-state senators will have to rely more heavily on contributions from consumers. The data in table 7-2 support this conclusion. Using political action committee (PAC) and non-PAC contributions as surrogates (albeit imperfect ones) for funds raised from "investors" and "consumers," respectively, one can see that "investor" contributions to Senate incumbents do not vary much with state population, whereas "consumer" contributions are strongly related to state population. Controlling for other factors that may be related to the source and amount of campaign funds (whether the race is a competitive one, the seniority level of the senator, and whether the senator accepts PAC money), it appears that for each million increase in state population PAC contributions increase by $23,112.

From that information I project that a senator from California would raise about $700,000 more in PAC money than a senator from Wyoming. Given the base of nearly $1.5 million (the constant), that means a California senator would be predicted to raise one and a half times that of her colleague from Wyoming. The difference is not all that great given that California's population is sixty times as large.

The effect of population on funds raised from "consumers" is much larger. For each increase of 1 million in population, the projected amount increases by $478,179. Thus, going from the smallest to the largest state, there would be a difference of nearly $14 million raised from non-PAC sources, around twenty-five times the base of $564,142 (the constant).

Taken together, these results mean that senators from small states can rely much more heavily on PAC dollars to finance their reelection campaigns than can senators from large states. The regression model predicting the percentage of funds raised from PACs shows that for each increase of 1 million in population, senators will raise 1.26 percent less of their funds from PACs. That projects to a 38 percent difference going from the least to the most populous state. Senators from the smallest states may raise nearly half of their money from PACs, while those from the largest states receive only 10–15 percent from them.

That senators from large states must raise not only more campaign funds but must raise a greater percentage of them from "consumers" has added implications for the time senators need to devote to fund-raising. It is simply easier to raise money from investors than from consumers. The former are organized for the purpose of contributing money to campaigns. They have incentives to contribute, and senators can exert pressure to encourage those contributions. But contributions from consumers are less certain and take more time to obtain.[17] With little leverage over consumers, senators must actively court their support, especially from consumers making larger donations who are unlikely to respond to direct mail solicitations.[18]

In sum, senators from populous states must devote considerably greater time and resources to campaign fund-raising than do their small-state colleagues. They have to raise more money. They have to raise money on a continuing basis. And because they have to raise proportionately more money from less predictable sources, they have to commit more time to the activity. With the already great demands on senators' time, the extra time large-state senators spend on fund-raising means less time for other senatorial activities. Hence they must inevitably develop behavioral strategies to deal with these demands.

## State Size and the Strategic Behavior of Senators

Because the representational experiences of senators vary considerably with state size and because state size has enormous impact on funding of their reelection campaigns, these differences will be reflected in the ways senators act in office. The representational contexts and campaign finance situations they face will create different incentive structures as they use their work in the Senate as a vehicle to justify their reelections. The effects of these differences will encourage, but not limit, small-state senators to pursue particularized benefits on behalf of their constituents as a strategy for success, while restricting their colleagues from populous states to a strategy of policy activism on a range of national issues as a path to reelection.[19]

Small-state senators will have greater incentive to work for particularized benefits for their constituents for a number of reasons. First, because they have the same close relationships with constituents that House members do, small-state senators will find that their constituents expect more personalized attention. Second, any project in a small state will affect a greater proportion of a senator's constituents and will have greater "advertising" and "credit-claiming" value than a similar project in a large state.[20] A new bridge in Austin has little meaning to voters in Dallas or Houston and is unlikely to get much media attention there. But a project of similar size in Cheyenne or Montpelier or Pierre will affect a high percentage of the state's constituents and receive statewide media coverage. Third, to get similar credit, a large-state senator would have to deliver a much larger project. And a larger project will be more difficult to procure. Moreover, senators may be reluctant to fund an expensive project in a single large state when the same money could be of equal political benefit for multiple senators in smaller states. As one senator observed, "The smaller the state, the more important the projects." Thus there are both incentives for small-state senators to pursue particularized benefits and disincentives for populous-state senators to do so.

This does not mean that all small-state senators will necessarily choose a particularized benefit strategy. Just as some House members decide to focus on broader public policy concerns rather than to be single-minded tenders to constituency concerns, there are small-state senators whose personal preferences for a policy-focused career may outweigh the incentives of a particularized benefit strategy. Because they have potentially close representational ties to their constituents, small-state senators have a certain level of strategic flexibility. Nevertheless, the incentive structure is such that many, if not most, will place high priority on serving the particularized interests of their states.[21]

Large-state senators are likely to travel a different path to success. Not possessing the close ties to constituents that their small-state colleagues do (and, in fact, being unable to develop them), senators representing populous states need to find alternative ways to reach their constituents and convince them that they are worthy of continued support and reelection. They will of necessity become more media dependent.[22] And devoting the lion's share of their efforts to a particularized benefits strategy will not produce the extensive media coverage they need. To build broad support in such populous constituencies and to attract the necessary funds for a reelection campaign, large-state senators will instead become policy activists or, as more cynically described, "position takers."[23] They will devote their efforts to the work of policy committees, getting appearances on national television, establishing a reputation for policy expertise on national issues. In sum, they need to be more highly visible as senators than their small-state colleagues.

Of course, all senators pursue some mix of strategies. Even the most policy-oriented senators pay some attention to particularized benefits for their states, and highly constituency-focused senators do not ignore national issues. But the overall pattern should reflect the influence of constituency size. Small-state senators have some flexibility. Especially if they have goals beyond reelection, such as presidential ambitions, they may pursue policy activism more aggressively. But for most small-state senators a particularized benefit strategy may be considerably less risky than one of proposing policy initiatives on potentially divisive national issues. Large-state senators do not have the same flexibility. In a populous state the choice of a strategy mix that is weighted in the particularized benefits direction is an inefficient use of the scarce resources they have available. These suggestions linking state population to the strategic behavior of senators can be tested in two areas where senators make choices about how to spend their time: committee assignments and appearance on the national media.

## Committee Assignments

A number of factors influence the committee assignment choices of senators. If the theory described above is correct, however, one would expect senators to seek assignments that further their goals. Accordingly, small-state senators will tend to prefer membership on committees that foster

their pursuit of particularized benefits for their states, and they will dispro-
portionately serve on those referred to as "constituency" or "reelection"
committees. By contrast, large-state senators will find their strategy of national policy visibility more effectively achieved through membership on
"policy" committees. Those are the committees that are more likely to attract the attention of the national media and to serve as vehicles that attract
the support of consumers they need to finance their expensive campaigns.

Using Smith and Deering's classification of Senate committees,[24] Lee
and I conducted two tests of the link between state population and committee membership.[25] Smith and Deering designate Senate committees according to the member goals that those committees foster: constituency,
policy, or mixed constituency-policy. The first test examined the membership on three most preferred Senate committees—Appropriations, Finance,
and Foreign Relations—from the 80th to the 105th Congress. Smith and
Deering classify Appropriations as a constituency committee, Finance as a
mixed committee, and Foreign Relations as a policy committee. In addition, senators must normally choose among the three because they are
rarely allowed to serve on more than one of them at the same time. In
both the 104th and 105th Congresses, for example, sixty-six senators filled
the slots on these committees. Taking an average of the median state size
(in terms of number of congressional districts) of states represented by
senators on these committees during the time period revealed a clear link
between state population and committee membership. For the constituency committee, Appropriations, the average was 5.29 congressional districts. For Finance, the mixed committee, it was 6.35. And for the policy
committee, Foreign Relations, it was 7.63. As expected, large-state senators gravitate to policy committees, while those from small states prefer
the constituency committee.[26]

To see whether this relationship holds for all Senate committees, we
also calculated the mean for the median number of congressional districts
in states represented on the other committees for the same time period.
None of the eight committees with the largest mean median state size is a
constituency committee while the five smallest all are. The results from
the first test must be qualified, however, because there was little difference
between policy and mixed committees. (It may be that either type allows
large-state senators to pursue broad policy interests.) Nevertheless, the
general finding still holds. Small-state senators tend to choose those committees that help them service their constituencies, whereas large-state senators select committees that give them national policy outlets.[27] Constituency

committee membership fits with the particularized benefits strategy of small-state senators. It allows them to "bring home the bacon" and advances their reelection goal. Because that strategy is an inefficient one for their populous state colleagues, they prefer policy committees that, as we shall see, better serve their strategy for getting the media attention they need to reach far larger constituencies.

## Media Coverage

Policy committee membership is attractive to large-state senators because, among other things, those committees "supply good platforms for position-taking."[28] They are the committees that receive more media attention.[29] And the national prominence senators acquire as a result of policy activism and media coverage affects their visibility among their constituents.[30]

Not all senators desire or need national media coverage to achieve their goals. Senators who serve the particularized needs of their constituents as a strategy for reelection have little interest in pursuing national media coverage.[31] Similarly, the national media have no interest in covering those senators. However, for large-state senators for whom serving constituents' local needs is neither an effective or efficient strategy, national media coverage may be necessary in order to get reelected. It is their vehicle for communicating their effectiveness with their constituents and for developing the large base of consumers they will need to finance a reelection campaign. And service on policy committees allows the senators to develop the reputation for policy activism that will attract national media coverage.

If this line of argument is correct, then one should expect large-state senators to receive more media coverage than small-state senators, other things being equal. The data in appendix 7A show the number of times each senator was mentioned or quoted on one of the nightly news broadcasts during the 103d, 104th, and 105th Congresses (on ABC, CBS, CNN, and NBC).[32] To test the relationship between mentions on the nightly news and state size, I ran regressions that controlled for other factors that have previously been found to affect coverage levels.[33] Thus variables were included for party floor leaders, committee chairs, ranking minority members, senators actively running for president (104th Congress only), whether the senator was in a reelection campaign, and whether the senator was the subject of special notoriety. The results of the regressions for the three

Table 7-3. *Effect of State Population on Senators' Network News Coverage, Controlling for Other Factors, 103d–105th Congresses, 1993–98*[a]

| Variable | 103d Congress | 104th Congress | 105th Congress |
|---|---|---|---|
| Constant | 8.57* | 6.06* | 5.47* |
|  | (2.67) | (1.95) | (2.02) |
| Number of congressional | 1.00** | 0.51* | 0.33 |
| districts in the state | (4.75) | (2.55) | (1.92) |
| Party leader | 183.95** | 81.01** | 114.09** |
|  | (13.09) | (7.16) | (9.79) |
| Committee chair | 21.02** | 12.53* | 19.17** |
|  | (3.69) | (2.36) | (4.27) |
| Ranking minority member | 11.89* | 4.21 | 3.14 |
|  | (2.05) | (0.81) | (0.64) |
| Running in upcoming election | –0.155 | 5.25 | –3.13 |
|  | (~0.03) | (1.09) | (–0.87) |
| Scandal or fame | 29.52* | . . . | 86.06** |
|  | (2.09) |  | (5.10) |
| Running for president in 1996 | . . . | 78.66** | . . . |
|  |  | (7.97) |  |
| *Summary statistic* |  |  |  |
| F | 32.49** | 29.49** | 23.13** |
| Adj. $R^2$ | 0.66 | 0.64 | 0.57 |
| N | 100 | 99[b] | 100 |
| Median number news stories | 17.00 | 11.00 | 6.50 |

Source: The Vanderbilt Television News Archive Index. Data for the 103d and 104th Congresses are from Lee and Oppenheimer, *Sizing Up the Senate*, p. 137.

*$p < .05$; **$p < .01$.

a. *t* statistics in parentheses.

b. The missing case is the Oregon seat that Senator Bob Packwood resigned in late 1995 and to which Senator Ron Wyden was elected in early 1996.

congresses appear in table 7-3. In all three regressions, state population has the expected effect. For each additional congressional district in a state, senators received one additional mention on network evening news in the 103d Congress, slightly more than one-half an additional mention in the 104th, and about one-third of an additional mention in the 105th. The seemingly smaller effect across the three Congresses is largely explained by the decline in the overall number of times senators were mentioned in each Congress, declining from over 2,606 in the 103d to 1,947 in the 104th, to only 1,411 in the 105th. Even with this declining effect, however, the projected difference between the senators from the smallest and largest states in the 105th Congress was about seventeen mentions on the evening news. And these differences in evening news coverage are likely to be symptomatic of coverage in other national sources. One would expect the senators who are mentioned more frequently on the evening news to be more likely to be guests on the Sunday morning interview shows, to be quoted in the weekly news magazines, and to receive coverage in the major national newspapers. Thus, compared with their small-state colleagues, senators from large states achieve far more national media coverage than just the differences in evening news coverage.

Moreover, national media coverage of a senator in most instances does not just happen. Unless one is a party leader or a committee chair, a senator must consciously decide to pursue the coverage. This is an option for senators from smaller states, but it is close to being a required part of the strategy of large-state senators who do not have close personal ties with their constituents, for whom a particularized benefits strategy is inefficient, and who anticipate competitive contests for reelection.[34]

In sum, I have painted two different portraits of senators. One is of the senator from the small state. This senator is able to establish and retain person-to-person relationships with a sizable portion of his constituents. He is able to contact many of them through retail politics, not just through the mass media, and they feel that they can contact him. When constituents need help, they view their senator as someone to whom they have access, who will be responsive to their requests, and who has the clout necessary to be helpful. Their senator is not all that different from their House member, except that the senator may be considered more influential.

For the small-state senator, the cost of running for reelection, although not insubstantial, is manageable. Fund-raising activity can be limited mainly to the final two years of a senator's term, and nearly half the money can be raised from PACs that are seeking campaigns in which to invest. Although the small-state senator has alternative paths to a successful career in the Senate, he has strong incentives to pursue a particularized benefits approach. In pursuing this strategy, the senator focuses on serving the needs of his state and its residents through membership on constituency-oriented committees that have jurisdiction over matters of importance to a high percentage of his constituents and using opportunities that arise to ensure his state gets more than its fair share of the federal largess. An alternative course some small-state senators pursue is to seek national policy influence, but that strategy is potentially dangerous. The small-state senator must avoid being seen as being out of touch with those back home. Thus he or she may even go so far as to shun national media attention.

The other portrait is of the populous-state senator. This senator represents such a large number of constituents that it is impossible to establish an intimate relationship with them. The relationship therefore is far more impersonal than senators from small states have. And the constituents have no expectation that they will have easy access to their senator. When they do communicate, it will be about issues, not about assistance. For help with problems, constituents in large states will contact their House members, not their senators.

The large-state senator is also faced with a very different electoral environment. Because of its size, the constituency will include a heterogeneous range of interests and a highly competitive electoral situation. Reelection campaigns are so expensive and must rely more heavily on the support of individual contributors that fund-raising is continuous throughout the term and competes for the senator's time and attention with governing activities.

A large-state senator does not have the option of a particularized benefits strategy. Instead the incentive structure leads her to pursue a national policy or position-taking strategy. This involves membership on policy committees and the pursuit of national media attention. These are the vehicles for communicating with her constituents about her effectiveness as a senator and for attracting sufficient funds for a reelection campaign.

These sketches are necessarily incomplete. Other ways exist in which state size affects the strategic behavior of senators.[35] The analysis of campaign fund-raising, committee assignment, and national media coverage presented here only illustrates the degree of influence of state size. Nor would I suggest that all senators fit neatly into one of these two patterns. What the portraits do demonstrate, however, is that the magnitude of the differences in state populations has serious and systematic implications for the behavior of senators. Two questions remain: Do these differences affect the civility level in the Senate? and Why are these state size differences of particular concern in the transformed Senate?

## Variation in Constituency Size as a Catalyst to Declining Senate Civility?

If there is a civility problem in the contemporary Senate, it is certainly not the first time this has occurred. Throughout its institutional history, the Senate has had episodes when civility levels among senators have been put to the test. Indeed, there is every reason to expect such breakdowns in institutions that try to resolve issues so conflictual that they have been brought into the public arena. Perhaps the surprise is that such break-downs are not more frequent. Although the institutional setting is sup-portive of norms that are designed to foster civility, there are contexts in which the goals of senators are so intense and in such great conflict that institutional constraints prove an insufficient countervailing force. Thus one needs to ask what it is about the contemporary context of the "trans-formed" Senate that has eroded institutional civility.

Although the growth of partisan and ideological polarization in the Senate has been rightly blamed for a large proportion of perceived civility problems, other incentives, too, drive the individualized behavior of sena-tors in competing directions. If, in fact, there has been a decline in the level of civility in the U.S. Senate in recent years, the enormous range in the size of constituencies that senators represent and the effect of those size differ-ences on the behavior of senators might be considered a source of this erosion. Furthermore, efforts to bolster civility will not succeed unless they take the effects of state size into account.

The effect of constituency size on senators' behavior was not always as great as it is today, and in earlier eras the Senate as an institution was better able to adapt to the competing priorities of its members. After all, until the 1970s the Senate did not generally operate from January to De-cember. Its workload was more manageable. There were fewer bills intro-duced, fewer committee meetings, fewer floor amendments offered, fewer filibusters and threats to filibuster, and fewer roll call votes. Until the en-actment of the Great Society programs, the range of federal government policy activity in civil rights, education, health care, economic manage-ment, and environmental matters was far more limited. And not until the 1970s did Congress make major commitments to reassert itself in dealing with the executive branch. The Reorganization Act of 1970, War Powers Act, the Budget Process, and the extensive use of legislative veto provi-sions all contributed to a much heavier workload. In addition to the mush-rooming legislative agenda, senators were also faced with an enormous growth in interest group activity and in communications from constitu-ents. Finally, the professionalization of campaigns and the changes in cam-paign finance laws and regulations increased the cost and means of financing reelection efforts.[36]

Before the 1970s senators from states of differing sizes no doubt had some competing individual goals. But there was enough slack in the de-mands on the institution and on its members that conflict could be minimized. Not only was there time to nourish more personal interaction among senators, but there was also time to address their differing policy concerns, whether particularized benefits for constituencies or broader issues of national policy. This is not the case in the transformed Senate.

Although the changes that have occurred in the Senate since the early 1970s have placed a disproportionate burden on senators from larger states, especially in terms of financing campaigns and interest group activity, all senators must now cope with a more stressful work environment in which achieving their individual goals is more competitive. With a more packed agenda, not all senators are able to get what they want. Determining the priority of issues has become as important a part of the legislative struggle as mobilizing the necessary votes for passage. The situation is akin to the struggle of driving home in rush-hour traffic on a crowded freeway as opposed to being able to drive on a busy, but uncongested, highway. In the latter situation, one may have to observe the speed limit but should be able to move along smoothly with the other cars and trucks. On the crowded freeway, one must compete with the other vehicles, all of whose drivers are also in a rush to get home. Cutting in front, breakdowns, and accidents lead to horn-honking, confusion, frustration, and, on occasion, rage.

If the Senate of today is more like the crowded freeway, then it is easy to see why ideological and partisan polarization may affect the level of civility. But differences in state size may well contribute independently to the civility problem. Even if one were able to soften the ideological and partisan rancor, tensions among the goals of individual senators would remain threats to institutional civility. Though many small-state senators would still want to ensure that the Senate completes its work in a timely fashion on the constituency-serving, distributive legislation that has considerable political payoff for them, senators from populous states would continue to prefer that attention to such legislation not delay or prevent consideration of issues of broader national policy. Those are the issues that fall in the jurisdictions of the committees on which they sit and are the ones on which they garner national media attention and reach their constituents. Even within pieces of broad national policy legislation, the priorities of senators from small and large states will differ. The small-state senator may use a budget resolution, for example, to protect a small program of particular interest to his state, or may focus on getting added incentives for rural health maintenance organizations in a Medicare bill, or may withhold support for a $500 billion economic program over a 1¢ difference in a fuel tax. Populous-state colleagues may react to this behavior with emotions ranging from mild frustration to outrage to apoplexy.

There is no easy cure for the tensions arising from the Senate's representational base in the transformed Senate. Every indication is that the level of Senate malapportionment continues to increase. The fastest-growing states tend to be the most populous ones. Easing perceived civility problems accordingly may depend on making the day-to-day lives of senators more manageable. But one needs to recognize that changes that would ameliorate the lives of large-state senators may be of little value to those from small states. Thus, for example, large-state senators might gain from campaign finance reform that would ease the time commitment that fundraising necessitates for them. But the same reform might work to the detriment of other senators who find the current system of campaign financing not particularly burdensome and who have been successful under the current rules.

As various solutions to problems of the Senate are proposed, it is critical to keep in mind how much of the Senate's diversity results from the range in the sizes of the constituencies that senators represent. Plans based on some concept of the average senator from an average-size state are unlikely to work. The Senate, unlike some other legislative institutions, is not one where one size fits all.

Appendix 7A. *Senators Mentioned on Television during National Nightly News Broadcasts*[a]

Number of times mentioned

| Senator | Party and state | 103d Congress | 104th Congress | 105th Congress |
|---|---|---|---|---|
| Abraham | R-Mich. | ... | 4 | 2 |
| Akaka | D-Hawaii | 0 | 0 | 0 |
| Allard | R-Colo. | ... | ... | 1 |
| Ashcroft | R-Mo. | ... | 2 | 20 |
| Baucus | D-Mont. | 18 | 6 | 2 |
| Bennett | R-Utah | 0 | 2 | 6 |
| Biden | D-Del. | 52 | 14 | 12 |
| Bingaman | D-N.Mex. | 3 | 1 | 3 |
| Bond | R-Mo. | 15 | 4 | 7 |
| Boren | D-Okla. | 52 | ... | ... |
| Boxer | D-Calif. | 26 | 16 | 22 |
| Bradley | D-N.J. | 32 | 28 | ... |
| Breaux | D-La. | 70 | 18 | 6 |
| Brown | R-Colo. | 9 | 5 | ... |
| Brownback | R-Kans. | ... | ... | 8 |
| Bryan | D-Nev. | 17 | 7 | 1 |
| Bumpers | D-Ark. | 8 | 5 | 5 |
| Burns | R-Mont. | 3 | 1 | 0 |
| Byrd | D-W.Va. | 37 | 22 | 18 |
| Campbell[a] | D-R-Colo.[b] | 2 | 8 | 11 |
| Chafee | R-R.I. | 53 | 17 | 1 |
| Cleland | D-Ga. | ... | ... | 4 |
| Coats | R-Ind. | 2 | 14 | 11 |
| Cochran | R-Miss. | 8 | 7 | 14 |
| Cohen | R-Maine | 30 | 34 | ... |
| Collins | R-Maine | ... | ... | 14 |
| Conrad | D-N.Dak. | 9 | 12 | 5 |
| Coverdell | R-Ga. | 1 | 1 | 4 |
| Craig | R-Idaho | 1 | 11 | 3 |
| D'Amato | R-N.Y. | 69 | 105 | 21 |
| Danforth | R-Mo. | 14 | ... | ... |
| Daschle | D-S.Dak. | 22 | 79 | 48 |
| DeConcini | D-Ariz. | 50 | ... | ... |
| Dewine | R-Ohio | ... | 5 | 4 |
| Dodd | D-Conn. | 31 | 46 | 11 |
| Dole | R-Kans. | 200 | 200 | ... |
| Domenici | R-N.Mex. | 26 | 49 | 21 |
| Dorgan | D-N.Dak. | 17 | 14 | 5 |
| Durbin | D-Ill. | ... | ... | 11 |
| Durenberger | R-Minn. | 20 | ... | ... |
| Enzi | R-Wyo. | ... | ... | 1 |
| Exon | D-Nebr. | 16 | 19 | ... |
| Faircloth | R-N.C. | 5 | 12 | 5 |
| Feingold | D-Wis. | 2 | 9 | 7 |
| Feinstein | D-Calif. | 66 | 21 | 17 |

*(continued)*

Appendix 7A. *(continued)*

| Senator | Party and state | 103d Congress | 104th Congress | 105th Congress |
|---|---|---|---|---|
| Ford | D-Ky. | 2 | 3 | 2 |
| Frist | R-Tenn. | . . . | 7 | 5 |
| Glenn | D-Ohio | 42 | 18 | 101 |
| Gorton | R-Wash. | 2 | 2 | 7 |
| Graham | D-Fla. | 25 | 2 | 6 |
| Gramm | R-Tex. | 95 | 163 | 19 |
| Grams | R-Minn. | . . . | 3 | 1 |
| Grassley | R-Iowa | 9 | 22 | 10 |
| Gregg | R-N.H. | 3 | 10 | 0 |
| Hagel | R-Nebr. | . . . | . . . | 5 |
| Harkin | D-Iowa | 17 | 6 | 15 |
| Hatch | R-Utah | 46 | 38 | 81 |
| Hatfield | R-Oreg. | 5 | 18 | . . . |
| Heflin | D-Ala. | 7 | 3 | . . . |
| Helms | R-N.C. | 32 | 35 | 51 |
| Hollings | D-S.C. | 20 | 6 | 3 |
| Hutchinson | R-Ark. | . . . | . . . | 1 |
| Hutchison | R-Tex. | 31 | 16 | 11 |
| Inhofe | R-Okla. | . . . | 3 | 4 |
| Inouye | D-Hawaii | 10 | 2 | 3 |
| Jeffords | R-Vt. | 1 | 4 | 4 |
| Johnson | D-S.Dak. | . . . | . . . | 2 |
| Johnston | D-La. | 15 | 7 | . . . |
| Kassebaum | R-Kans. | 22 | 30 | . . . |
| Kempthorne | R-Idaho | 2 | 3 | 5 |
| Kennedy | D-Mass. | 57 | 31 | 23 |
| Kerrey | D-Nebr. | 45 | 26 | 20 |
| Kerry | D-Mass. | 29 | 29 | 21 |
| Kohl | D-Wis. | 7 | 6 | 0 |
| Kyl | R-Ariz. | . . . | 5 | 5 |
| Landrieu | D-La. | . . . | . . . | 4 |
| Lautenberg | D-N.J. | 21 | 11 | 11 |
| Leahy | D-Vt. | 33 | 15 | 12 |
| Levin | D-Mich. | 12 | 2 | 8 |
| Lieberman | D-Conn. | 0 | 8 | 31 |
| Lott | R-Miss. | 19 | 66 | 190 |
| Lugar | R-Ind. | 33 | 50 | 20 |
| Mack | R-Fla. | 15 | 17 | 1 |
| Mathews | D-Tenn. | 0 | . . . | . . . |
| McCain | R-Ariz. | 71 | 87 | 75 |
| McConnell | R-Ky. | 7 | 17 | 14 |
| Metzenbaum | D-Ohio | 31 | . . . | . . . |
| Mikulski | D-Md. | 18 | 8 | 1 |
| Mitchell | D-Maine | 191 | . . . | . . . |
| Moseley-Braun | D-Ill. | 14 | 4 | 14 |

*(continued)*

## Appendix 7A. *(continued)*

| Senator | Party and state | 103d Congress | 104th Congress | 105th Congress |
|---|---|---|---|---|
| Moynihan | D-N.Y. | 90 | 22 | 23 |
| Murkowski | R-Alaska | 3 | 9 | 2 |
| Murray | D-Wash. | 9 | 1 | 5 |
| Nickles | R-Okla. | 15 | 25 | 20 |
| Nunn | D-Ga. | 108 | 45 | . . . |
| Packwood | R-Oreg. | 81 | . . . | . . . |
| Pell | D-R.I. | 1 | 2 | . . . |
| Pressler | R-S.Dak. | 8 | 10 | . . . |
| Pryor | D-Ark. | 20 | 5 | . . . |
| Reed | D-R.I. | . . . | . . . | 0 |
| Reid | D-Nev. | 7 | 3 | 2 |
| Riegle | D-Mich. | 20 | . . . | . . . |
| Robb | D-Va. | 11 | 5 | 1 |
| Roberts | R-Kans. | . . . | . . . | 5 |
| Rockefeller | D-W.Va. | 35 | 2 | 5 |
| Roth | R-Del. | 6 | 15 | 14 |
| Santorum | R-Pa. | . . . | 4 | 11 |
| Sarbanes | D-Md. | 8 | 7 | 1 |
| Sasser | D-Tenn. | 15 | . . . | . . . |
| Sessions | R-Ala. | . . . | . . . | 1 |
| Shelby[a] | D-R-Ala.[b] | 14 | 14 | 21 |
| Simon | D-Ill. | 37 | 20 | . . . |
| Simpson | R-Wyo. | 27 | 26 | . . . |
| Smith | R-Oreg. | . . . | . . . | 0 |
| Smith | R-N.H. | 4 | 10 | 3 |
| Snowe | R-Maine | . . . | 11 | 13 |
| Specter | R-Pa. | 29 | 58 | 31 |
| Stevens | R-Alaska | 3 | 6 | 3 |
| Thomas | R-Wyo. | . . . | 2 | 1 |
| Thompson | R-Tenn. | . . . | 14 | 69 |
| Thurmond | R-S.C. | 9 | 18 | 12 |
| Torricelli | D-N.J. | . . . | . . . | 19 |
| Wallop | R-Wyo. | 7 | . . . | . . . |
| Warner | R-Va. | 24 | 19 | 9 |
| Wellstone | D-Minn. | 17 | 13 | 13 |
| Wofford | D-Pa. | 8 | . . . | . . . |
| Wyden | D-Ore. | . . . | . . . | 10 |

Source: Vanderbilt Television News Archive Index.

a. Number of mentions on the ABC, CBS, CNN, and NBC national nightly news broadcasts.

b. Senators Campbell and Shelby switched party in the 103d Congress.

# Notes

1. See Frances E. Lee and Bruce I. Oppenheimer, *Sizing Up the Senate: The Unequal Consequences of Equal Representation* (University of Chicago Press, 1999).

2. Barbara Sinclair, *The Transformation of the U.S. Senate* (Johns Hopkins University Press, 1989).

3. Max Farrand, ed., *The Records of the Federal Constitution of 1787*, vol. 1 (Yale University Press, 1966), p. 476.

4. Arend Lijphart, *Democracies: Patterns of Majoritarian and Consensus Government in Twenty-One Countries* (Yale University Press, 1984).

5. Manning J. Dauer and Robert G. Kelsay, "Unrepresentative States," *National Municipal Review*, vol. 45 (1955), pp. 571–75.

6. Glendon Schubert and Charles Press, "Measuring Malapportionment," *American Political Science Review*, vol. 58 (June 1964), pp. 302–27.

7. Lee and Oppenheimer, *Sizing Up the Senate*, pp. 237–38.

8. Max Farrand, ed., *The Records of the Federal Constitution of 1787*, vol. 2 (Yale University Press, 1937), p. 10.

9. Hannah Pitkin, *The Concept of Representation* (University of California Press, 1967), p. 209.

10. Bruce I. Oppenheimer, "The Representational Experience: The Effect of State Population on Senator-Constituency Linkages," *American Journal of Political Science*, vol. 40 (November 1996), pp. 1280–99.

11. The five items asked whether the respondent had personally met the incumbent senator, had attended a meeting where the incumbent spoke, had spoken to a member of the senator's staff, had received mail from the senator, and had contacted the senator or the senator's office.

12. Lee and Oppenheimer, *Sizing Up the Senate*, p. 63.

13. Ibid., pp. 73–79.

14. Sarah Binder, Forrest Maltzman, and Lee Sigelman, "Accounting for Senators' Home-State Reputations: Why Do Constituents Love a Bill Cohen So Much More Than an Al D'Amato?" *Legislative Studies Quarterly*, vol. 23 (November 1998), pp. 545–60.

15. The first four years can be combined because an incumbent senator may adjust fund-raising efforts in years when the other Senate seat in the state is being contested. This may be especially true if the other senator is of the same party. When these years are combined, each senator's fund-raising includes two years when there was no Senate contest and two years when a campaign was going on for the other Senate seat.

16. James M. Snyder Jr., "The Market for Campaign Contributions: Evidence for the U.S. Senate, 1980–1986," *Economics and Politics*, vol. 5 (1993), p. 219.

17. For a fuller elaboration on this point, see Lee and Oppenheimer, *Sizing Up the Senate*, p. 110.

18. Herbert E. Alexander, *Financing Politics: Money, Elections, and Political Reform* (Washington, D.C.: CQ Press, 1992), p. 50.

19. Lee and Oppenheimer, *Sizing Up the Senate*.

20. David R. Mayhew, *Congress: The Electoral Connection* (Yale University Press, 1984), p. 52.

21. In addition, senators from small states may have to compensate for the limited jurisdictional coverage their state has in the House of Representatives. Large states are likely to have House members on every standing committee, but a state with a single member will likely be represented on only two committees. Although in a populous state there is bound to be a House member(s) also trying to claim credit for some particularized benefit, in a small state the Senate may be in a position to take full credit.

22. Barbara Sinclair, "Washington Behavior and Home-State Reputation: The Impact of National Prominence on Senators' Images," *Legislative Studies Quarterly*, vol. 15 (November 1990), pp. 484–85.

23. Mayhew, *Congress: The Electoral Connection*, p. 61.

24. Steven S. Smith and Christopher J. Deering, *Committees in Congress*, 2d ed. (Washington, D.C.: CQ Press, 1990), p. 101.

25. Lee and Oppenheimer, *Sizing Up the Senate*, pp. 127–33.

26. The reason for using the mean of the medians here is straightforward. In any given Congress the presence of one or more senators from very large states on a given committee will have an exaggerated impact as a measure of central tendency. Using the median avoids the effect of outliers and is therefore a better measure. However, this eliminates the outlier problem so the mean can be taken of these medians to get a comparison over time among the three committees. A difference of means tests revealed that the differences among these committees in terms of state size represented by their members are statistically significant ($p < .05$).

27. The results of running a regression of state size on committee type, for which a value of 1 was assigned to policy and mixed committees and a value of 0 was assigned to constituency committees, estimated that the mean median state size on policy and mixed committees was 2.5 congressional districts greater than on constituency committees.

28. Mayhew, *Congress: The Electoral Connection*, p. 85.

29. Stephen Hess, *The Ultimate Insiders: U.S. Senators in the National Media* (Brookings, 1986), p. 34; and Smith and Deering, *Committees in Congress*, p. 100.

30. Sinclair, "Washington Behavior and Home-State Reputation." In addition, see Wendy J. Schiller, "Senators as Political Entrepreneurs: Using Bill Sponsorship to Shape Legislative Agendas," *American Journal of Political Science*, vol. 39 (February 1995), pp. 186–203. Schiller finds another indicator that suggests greater policy activism of large-state senators. They cosponsor more bills than do small-state senators.

31. Hess, *The Ultimate Insiders*, p. 7.

32. The data were collected from the Vanderbilt Television News Archive Index.

33. See Sinclair, "Washington Behavior and Home-State Reputation." The analysis here extends the data that Lee and I reported in *Sizing Up the Senate*, p. 137, by adding the 105th Congress to the analysis.

34. It might be argued that the Senate career of Al D'Amato is an exception to this rule, and that his reelection success hinged on his reputation for delivering

particularized benefits to New York. Only 17.1 percent or less of respondents to the Senate Election Study survey thought D'Amato would be very helpful with a problem, and only 19.2 percent could recall something he had done for the state. Percentages for small-state senators were about twice those for D'Amato. Even with D'Amato's efforts to get media attention for minding the particularized needs of New York constituents, the payoff from this strategy may have been limited because of the state's size, or a policy activist strategy may not have been a reasonable alternative given D'Amato's conservative policy stance in a politically liberal state. Clearly, some of the other variables—such as being a party leader or a committee chair or being in the public eye (in the case of John Glenn, on one hand, or Bob Packwood, on the other)—have very large effects on levels of national media coverage that senators receive. There are also some exceptions to the general tendency, especially among some small-state senators who receive a good deal of national media coverage, such as Senators Orrin Hatch and Pete Domenici, both of whom are senior committee chairs.

35. In our book, Lee and I examine how state size influences other choices senators make. We find, for example, small-state senators are much more likely to engage in "holdout" behavior on close votes in the Senate as a means of obtaining particularized benefits for their states.

36. Many of these and other changes are discussed in Sinclair, *The Transformation of the U.S. Senate.*

# CHAPTER EIGHT

# Senators and
# Reporters Revisited

TIMOTHY E. COOK

THE STATE OF CIVILITY AND deliberation in today's Senate cannot escape comparison with the Senate of the 1950s.[1] Donald Matthews's *U.S. Senators and Their World* constitutes the finest and fullest account of that era. His portrait is well remembered: an insular, clubby, efficient institution with its own "folkways" of hard work, specialization, devotion to the institution, courtesy, reciprocity, and mutual accommodation.[2] But what is less familiar is how Matthews documented aspects of the Senate that militated against those folkways. Indeed, well before most political scientists of his time, he was to devote an entire chapter, called "Senators and Reporters," to one such threat to the apparent "intra-Senate harmony." Matthews noted how newsmaking often stemmed not just from hard work on important legislation, but also from "grandstanding" or investigations. What is more,

> If enough senators do not voluntarily engage in such activities, the reporters, especially those from the wire services, try to stimulate conflict. "They often call up my boss," one legislative assistant explained, "and say, 'Senator so-and-so just made this statement. Do you want to attack it?' If he makes a tough enough statement they print it. Their attitude is 'Want to fight? I'll hold your coat.'" The reporters' desire for controversy-laden national news and the relatively uninfluential senator's desire to make it are highly subversive to the Senate folkways.[3]

Changes in the Senate since the 1950s can be attributed to a number of factors: the altered nature of campaigning and elections, the resurgence of partisanship, the explosion in the number of participants in Washington both on and off Capitol Hill, and the more inclusive (and more complete) political agenda from the mid-1960s on. But as Matthews deftly noted, the news media had become another force interacting with and helping to shape the processes, activities, and outputs of senators and the Senate. These and other factors help explain why the Senate has evolved as it has in recent decades, from an insular, hierarchical, specialized, highly regulated collective legislative body to a much more responsive, egalitarian, unpredictable, and individualistic institution where action can be obtained only by crafting complex unanimous consent agreements to avoid the filibusters and holds that can stop the process dead in its tracks.[4]

What is deliberation in the Senate like now that it is more open to reporters and the news media? What should one make of the fact that senators are turning more and more to the news not simply as a means for personal advancement or ego gratification but as a crucial way to deal with issues: to set them on the political agenda, raise their priority within Congress, frame them in such a way as to pressure opponents and protect allies, and to provoke the Senate as a whole to act?

## The Negotiation of Newsworthiness

To begin, news is not something that happens "to" senators. The process of newsmaking is not entirely or even largely controlled by journalists alone. They literally have ultimate control over the news: they assemble the final product. But prior and crucial stages invariably involve sources, usually officials, who provide information. This can be described as a "negotiation of newsworthiness" between official sources and reporters.[5] Each side controls key resources. Officials, on one hand, certify something as newsworthy by instigating governmental action, staging an event to be a timely "peg" for an underlying issue, and by speaking on given concerns and agenda items. Moreover, officials decide when and whether to answer questions, or more generally, whether and how to interact with reporters. Officials thus generally define importance. Reporters, on the other hand, have more power in deciding whether something is interesting enough to be in the news. They select items from what officials say and do to fit the story they would like to recount, whether or not they elicit quotations from other more critical sources. Each side prepares for the actual negotiation, trying to anticipate the other and gain advantage in that way. News is thus the result of a complex negotiation between journalists and sources that prevents anyone from attributing authorship of the news to any single actor or institution.

Sources and reporters alike stand to gain a great deal from making news. At its most cooperative, the negotiation approaches symbiosis if not collaboration, as officials trade the copy that reporters require for the publicity they need. Such an exchange is not entirely smooth for the simple reason that the needs of journalists and of politicians for news often diverge. Yet the news is still of high value for political actors such as senators. News does not simply reach the public who would reelect them or elevate them to higher office but communicates across institutional divides within Washington and within their own institution itself.[6] Even the "small town" Senate of the 1950s had this potential:

> Most important legislative events take place in the myriad committee and subcommittee meetings occurring all over the Hill. Senators have neither the time nor the energy to keep tab on this hundred-ring circus. The newspapers help immeasurably in the senators' never-ending struggle to keep track of what is going on in the Senate. It is ironic but still true that the members of so small a legislative body should find it necessary to communicate with each other via public print, but often they do.[7]

Now, if such advantages held for the Washington of the 1950s, imagine the use of the news media for senators in the 1990s, in a far less hierarchical, more individualistic Senate, and in a Washington populated by a huge number of participants in and out of government. If senators need the news, they are obliged to respond to and incorporate journalistic definitions of newsworthiness in order to gain the attention they desire. The institution of the Senate will end up following suit and being shaped accordingly.

## Senators and Reporters over Time

The relationship between senators and reporters, and between the Senate as a whole and the news media as a whole, is best understood by considering how these two political institutions evolved in tandem over time. The news media did not just emerge independently from the courageous attempts of journalists to hold elected officials accountable. Rather, the media's rise resembles other collective intermediary institutions such as the political party system and the interest group system, intimately influencing and being influenced by the resources provided by other political actors.[8]

Likewise, theories of congressional change stress both micro-factors (the goals and preferences of individual members) and macro-factors (the institutional contexts, including those outside of Congress, which provide differing resources and opportunities for particular approaches).[9] The news media have always constituted part of the context for political actors in Washington.

This is not to suggest that the media's impact consists of what they did *to* the Senate. Instead, every changed shape of the media provides resources for senators to act productively in a new way, though such shifts influence the Senate and senators only as the latter find these changes beneficial to the goals they pursue. Otherwise, rational-actor senators presumably would concentrate their attention on attaining their immediate goals within the current set of practices, norms, and rules.

This dynamic can be seen in operation at key turning points in the Senate's history: in the rise of the Senate as a coequal chamber with the House of Representatives into what is often deemed a "golden age" of senatorial debate and deliberation, in the Progressive Era's move toward a more careerist and parochial legislature, and in the shift in the 1960s and 1970s from a hierarchical, specialized, committee-centered chamber to an egalitarian, individualized, and floor-oriented body.

## The Party Press and Senatorial Alliances

Up until the turn of the twentieth century, Congress, not the presidency, was the most newsworthy branch of government in Washington, particularly in institutional rather than electoral coverage.[10] The reasons are not hard to find: presidents were reluctant to make public pronouncements on policy, Congress was more willing to accommodate reporters and allow them to hear deliberations, and the presumptions of newsworthiness (and of politics) focused on political debate and discussion, whether in electoral campaigns or in congressional deliberations.[11]

The House was the more prominent half of Congress for the first decades of the republic. One reason is the early Senate's aloofness from publicity. Any visitor to the two restored legislative chambers in Philadelphia is immediately struck by one key architectural detail: the Senate had no public gallery. The Founders designed the Senate not only to be an American version of the House of Lords, dealing with legislation only by revising what had been already passed by the House of Representatives, but also to attend to and protect the interests of the states, and to buttress the executive branch. This blueprint was faithfully carried out by the first senators, even to the point of being hidden from public view.[12]

News from the Senate was of little interest for other reasons, too. Whether or not reporters have easy access to newsmakers in and of itself will only facilitate coverage; it will not guarantee it. After all, officials still may not be interested in making news according to the canons of newsworthiness that reporters can reserve for themselves to decide what is important and interesting enough to print or broadcast. Note what happened when, under pressure from southern state legislatures suspicious of the power of the federal government, the Senate, after several defeated attempts, finally voted to build open public galleries in 1795.[13] Reporters were then granted access to the floor in 1802. Nevertheless, these actions had little immediate effect on the prominence of the Senate in the news or on its institutional operations.[14] Senators continued to follow the model of the House of Lords. The news canons of the time, particularly in the more egalitarian Jeffersonian era, still put more stress on the popularly elected House. One House member elected to the Senate in 1802 wrote to his wife, in an oft-cited phrase, "Henceforward you will read little of me in the Gazettes. Senators are less exposed to public view than Representatives. Nor have they near so much hard work and drudgery to perform."[15]

By the 1820s, however, the gap between the Senate and the House had narrowed. As of the mid-1830s, the amount of Senate and House coverage was about the same, and by 1841, the Senate was more prominent.[16] What happened? Several factors may have been involved: the collapse of parties in the "Era of Good Feelings" and the rise of individual political enterprises; a broader, more democratic electorate; and a transformed national political agenda.[17] In addition, the news media system in the nation as a whole, and in Washington in particular, had begun by the 1830s and 1840s to shift away from the heavily politically sponsored networks of partisan newspapers, focused in the official Washington press, that reached its heyday in Jacksonian America.

The initial news media system in the United States was organized by political factions, then by parties. As President George Washington's administration split into Hamiltonian and Jeffersonian wings, newspapers arose to represent each side, supported by patronage respectively from the Treasury and State Departments. When the federal government moved to Washington in 1800, Thomas Jefferson invited Samuel Harrison Smith to launch a newspaper, the *National Intelligencer*, to be affiliated with his party. After Jefferson's election, Smith received congressional printing contracts and other largesse to keep his precarious business afloat. At that time, Washington reporters were few and fleeting; none represented a newspaper outside the District of Columbia. Smith's one-person operation remained for years the official outlet for Washington news, widely excerpted by newspapers throughout the country, even those with a Federalist leaning.[18]

The *National Intelligencer* was published through extraordinary cooperation with presidents and members of Congress. President Jefferson leaked so much information that one journalism historian labeled Smith a virtual presidential press secretary.[19] Members of Congress, too, cooperated with Smith in reworking their spontaneous, ill-heard, and poorly transcribed remarks for public dissemination. Smith acted more as a stenographer than a reporter in the modern sense, as senators and representatives began the practice now known as "revising and extending their remarks."

Legislators, it seems, spoke first and edited later: "In the early republic political debate in each house was staged as an oral performance, not an exchange of texts."[20] The famed eloquence of "golden age" senators such as Henry Clay or Daniel Webster is due at least in part to the assistance of reporters in helping polish their sometimes broken prose. Reporters from Washington papers were more than willing to play this role; they were, after all, fellow mess-hall residents with members of Congress, were linked by partisan loyalty, and received impressive federal patronage to boot. This relationship worked well for senators, too: "Early in the nineteenth century political leaders had what they would never again enjoy: separate worlds for what they said and what they published. In the oral world they could be just as accountable and flexible as they chose to be."[21]

## The "Letter-Writers" and the Transformation of Senate Debate

The partisan press reached its zenith during the presidency of Andrew Jackson, when editors were party politicians as much as anything else. Much of the party-building leading up to Jackson's election in 1828 consisted of establishing newspapers around the country linked to the sponsored party organs in Washington.[22] Editors saw their tasks not as giving dispassionate, impartial coverage of both sides but as presenting the best, often highly opinionated case for their party, much as an attorney would do in a trial. In the workings of the early press, then, reporters and legislators—at least within the same party—were allies, protecting the operations of the chamber from intrusion.

Yet during this same era, new developments in journalism would arise that undercut these alliances. Newspapers outside of Washington began to contract with "correspondents," that is, "letter-writers," who communicated with their home newspapers from their bailiwick in Washington. Although the first identifiable Washington correspondent was a member of Congress, other newspapers began to send reporters and editors to contribute letters.[23] Most notably, James Gordon Bennett, first as a Washington correspondent for the *New York Enquirer* in 1827 and then as the founding editor of the *New York Herald* from 1835 on, launched a new style of Washington journalism. Bennett moved away from stenographic reports of debates toward lively, personalized, and often critical correspondence: "The arrival of letter writers . . . disturbed the understandings that Washington newspapers had fashioned with Congress. The *National Intelligencer* reported what congressmen said and permitted them to edit their remarks. The letter writers dared to critique, and often ridicule what members said, offering them no chance to correct the record."[24]

Such journalistic innovations became yet more crucial as the press shifted from partisan networks of newspapers toward a more varied group of newspapers that pledged its editorial support to a particular party but were "independent," that is, not financially reliant on partisan patronage. Starting with the first penny paper, the *New York Sun,* in 1833, these news outlets sought a wider mass audience. They began to neglect political issues and debates in favor of zippier topics, such as crime and society, and more dramatic, albeit fact-filled, narratives.[25] These papers also preferred to rely on their own staff for news instead of clipping and reprinting debates from the parties' Washington organs.

This shift, not surprisingly, went neither unnoticed nor unchallenged on Capitol Hill. Over several years, senators waged a battle against granting newspapers outside Washington access to the Senate's proceedings.[26] After admitting reporters in 1802, the next Senate decision of note took place in 1827, when the secretary of the Senate was directed to prepare seats to accommodate reporters, though it was unclear whether these would be on the acoustically preferable floor or in the eastern gallery. In 1835 the Senate passed a resolution to reserve seats on the floor, which conveniently paved the way for a decision in 1838 to limit such access to newspapers published in Washington.

Several correspondents for newspapers outside of Washington protested and asked that they be assigned seats on the floor or in the galleries. The committee considering the request recommended reserving the front seats of the eastern gallery. However, the debate that ensued showed considerable senatorial displeasure with the new forms of journalism. Senator John Niles (D-Conn.), himself an old-style partisan newspaper editor, moved to table the motion following his outburst against "these letter-writers":

> Who were these persons who styled themselves reporters? Why miserable slanderers, hirelings hanging on to the skirts of literature. . . . Perhaps no member of that body had been more misrepresented and caricatured than himself by those venal and profligate scribblers, who were sent here to earn a disreputable living by catering to the depraved appetite of the papers they work for. Shall we sanction such miserable caricatures of the proceedings of this body as are daily sent abroad by these hirelings, and thus give currency to them? For their vile trash goes out to the world in advance of the reports of the regular reporters! No. . . . Let them take their seats in the galleries and write what they pleased, without asking for the sanction of the Senate.[27]

When Niles's motion to table was passed, it expressed the Senate's majority preference for the deferential and stately journalism exemplified by the party-sponsored Washington newspapers above the more independent, critical, and dramatic approach of the letter-writers.[28] This precedent could then be used in 1841 when the Whigs came to power. Bennett's Democrat-leaning *New York Herald* promised "an efficient corps of the ablest reporters that this country can afford" to cover the special session of Congress called by President William Henry Harrison to consider the Whigs' agenda.[29] But the Senate's president pro tem, Samuel Southard (Whig-N.J.), apparently saw no reason to deviate from precedent, especially for a Jacksonian editor such as Bennett, and refused to admit the *Herald* to the reporters' desks in the chamber. Only after Bennett asked for Henry Clay's intercession did the Senate reconsider its previous decision and direct the secretary to "cause suitable accommodations to be prepared in the eastern gallery for such reporters as may be admitted by the rules of the Senate."[30]

As of 1841, then, commercial journalism had access to the Senate proceedings on equal footing with partisan Washington newspapers. Moreover, Southard's order implementing the vote basically got the Senate out of deciding journalists' credentials and delegated that power to the newspapers themselves: "None are to be admitted within the Reporters' rail, who are not really and *bona fide* Reporters, to be so certified by the *Editors* of the papers for which they report."[31] Yet this was not a surrender on the part of the Senate. This decision removed reporters from the floor and relegated them instead to the gallery, simultaneously accommodating and regulating their activities, as is common throughout the history of Congress and the news media.[32]

For present purposes, though, the victory of the letter-writers in the Senate is best understood as a decision in 1841 (just as it was a refusal in 1838) to "sanction" the new forms of journalism. The growing presence of out-of-town correspondents from commercial newspapers, furthered by the later creation of the Associated Press as a cooperative venture of newspapers in gathering news to be sent by the newly invented telegraph, provided new resources for senators to act in different ways. Commercial forms of journalism allowed senators such as Charles Sumner (R-Mass.) to reach larger audiences than his fellow senators alone with his carefully prepared and uncompromising language.[33] Whereas predecessors like Webster spoke spontaneously and revised remarks for publication, Sumner painstakingly prepared speeches that he read in the Senate: "More than any senator before him, Sumner turned discussion on vital issues into a performance that closed off exchanges of views."[34]

These mid-nineteenth-century examples, then, show a shift in the content and style of deliberation. Larger and physically absent audiences took priority over those present in the Senate chamber. Collective development of ideas and compromises in free-form discussion were displaced by hard-and-fast rhetoric aimed at newspaper publicity. As definitions of news changed, so too did the opportunities for and constraints on deliberation.

## The Progressive Era and the Decline of the Capitol Hill Newsbeat

Changes in news media systems could also contribute to institutional realignments. The transformation of the press from partisanship to commercialism was a gradual one, occurring in stages across the nineteenth century, with old and new forms of journalism often coexisting.[35] The news eventually moved away from the primacy of the editor and the editorial page to the centrality of the reporter and the front page; from dry accounts of debates to colorful, dramatic stories; and from prolix opinionated essays to terser, fact-filled "objective" accounts.

This wholesale redefinition of news did not work to the advantage of legislators. In particular, the shift away from issues and debates toward drama and storylines made legislative processes less useful for reporters. Nor did the multiple, shifting coalitions of political players facilitate the writing of continuing sagas with easily gauged day-to-day movement and familiar protagonists. Finally, the invention of new forms of gathering information—most notably, the interview—made the traditional locus of newsgathering, the House and Senate floors, less valuable to reporters.[36] In 1903 one *Baltimore Sun* reporter looked back to his arrival in the congressional press gallery in 1865 and commented: "Washington has become so fruitful in gossip and scandal, and intrigue, political and otherwise, that in contrast the ordinary debates can prove exceedingly dry reading. The gentlemen who declaim at the different ends of the Capitol are much aggrieved over this. I do not see how they can remedy it."[37]

Again, this redefinition of news helped redistribute political power. For one, it enabled the presidency to emerge as a public institution. Presidents, starting with William McKinley, welcomed reporters into the White House and inaugurated the White House newsbeat.[38] Their activities fit well with the redefinition of journalism in the Progressive Era, which emphasized heroic lone crusaders seeking to manage the industrial revolution through professionalism, expertise, and nonpartisan administration. Presidents could play a starring role in journalists' narratives in the early twentieth century in ways that members of Congress seemingly could not or would not, especially as progressive reforms weakened party machines and provoked increasingly career-minded legislators to emphasize parochialism and specialization on their committees.[39]

Consequently, House members and senators alike began generally to favor their hometown press above all else. Their local newspapers considered them newsworthy sources to an extent unmatched in the national news; such dependence produced regular and positive coverage. By contrast, national coverage was deemed dangerous to the behind-the-scenes coalition-building that prevailed in a Senate where parties were cross-pressured and weak, and where reciprocity and institutional patriotism were crucial norms. Some "outsiders" with different ideas of legislative accomplishment did woo the national news media, but they were in a distinct minority.[40] Senators and House members alike concentrated largely on their constituents, either directly or through local outlets, and neglected national news almost entirely.[41] The local-national split of the congressional press corps already apparent in the 1930s, later dubbed "the two levels of reporting," has tended to reinforce the parochialism and specialization of both houses of Congress for much of the twentieth century.[42]

## Television and the Reforms of the 1970s

The most recent "reconstitutive change" of Congress came with the reforms of the 1970s.[43] Perhaps not coincidentally, the changes included opening up congressional proceedings to the scrutiny of the public and the news media, and providing resources to individual members of Congress that better allowed them to pursue public strategies. The explosion of staff enabled almost all senators and the majority of House members to hire at least one full-time press secretary by the early 1980s.[44] The move to "subcommittee government" in the 1970s meant that "middle-management members" could also claim a base for being an authoritative source to the news.[45] And all of this could be easily rationalized as an attempt to catch up to the media-mindedness that characterized and seemingly empowered the presidency, particularly starting with John F. Kennedy.[46]

It is tempting to chalk up these equalizing reforms to television, as some political scientists did in the early 1980s.[47] Certainly, the news media in general, and television in particular, became much more evident on Capitol Hill in this time period. The number of newspaper reporters admitted to the congressional press galleries was eclipsed by the number of radio and television personnel (admittedly a more labor-intensive medium) for the first time in the mid-1980s.[48] Floor proceedings became televised— and thereby usable for excerpts in television news—in the House in 1979 and the Senate in 1986, following debates that revealed the legislators' own sense, at least, of the potentially large impact of these decisions.[49]

Yet television's greater presence on Capitol Hill does not mean that it single-handedly changed how Congress operates. The contrast of television news and newspaper news is more quantitative than qualitative. Though television is an audiovisual medium, its stories are assembled around a spoken text that is then matched with footage that illustrates that text.[50] Listening to a television story with one's eyes closed makes the story considerably more comprehensible than watching the same story with the sound turned off; it is little wonder that television news has been called "visual radio." Moreover, the subject matter of television is similar to that of newspapers.[51] After all, reporters consider themselves to be journalistic professionals following agreed-upon norms; they often have a "pack" mentality from interacting with each other at the newsbeat, and the ambiguity of newsworthiness favors the imitation of leading outlets such as the *New York Times*.

Television does work differently.[52] Its style of presentation produces more visual images, more personalized approaches, and an inclination to frame rather than analyze an occurrence. Audiences evaluate the stories consistently as more attention-grabbing, emotional, surprising, and vivid than is the case with print.

But television tends to magnify the preexisting tendencies of American newspapers that stem from the production values associated with quality journalism.[53] The individualism of newspaper accounts is heightened by the preference of television for anecdotal personal experience. The fragmentary, episodic quality of newspaper coverage, derived from its focus on a wide variety of topics over a length of time, is exacerbated by television's severe time constraints. The gravitation of newspapers toward the concrete over the abstract is reinforced by television's search for visual images that will help to explain the reporter's spoken words. Newspapers' preferences for narrative and spectacle are stronger still when audiences are supposed to be kept interested enough to maintain the "flow" from the television program preceding the news to the one after it. And so forth. But if television did not alter but simply magnified previous tendencies of the American news media, two things did change.

First, television benefits from an open process in ways that print media do not. It may have been a moot point for newspaper reporters whether or not the deliberations of the Senate during President Bill Clinton's impeachment trial were open or not, as long as senators provided statements recapping what they said behind closed doors. Indeed, the tendency up until 1926 of the Senate to work in private on nominations and treaties worked out well for both senators and reporters, given that the latter could receive leaks that ensured favorable coverage of the former.[54] Such arrangements do not work well for television, which has more trouble doing its job without on-the-record soundbites and direct access to the proceedings.

The second shift was due to the perceived reach and ubiquity of the new medium. In the 1950s, there was no national newspaper, and network news broadcasts were cursory fifteen-minute headline services illustrated with film. Under such circumstances, the information that Washington relied upon was relatively insulated from what the citizenry obtained. By the 1970s, the seemingly more omniscient "you-are-there" television broadcast had gained a huge mass audience, with Washingtonians tuning in, not for new information but to discover what the rest of the country was learning about.[55] The indicators that Washingtonians consult to assess reputations of each other are no longer so distinct from what the people themselves are exposed to.[56]

Yet the impact of television *on* the Senate in and of itself is limited without understanding how senators seek out television for help in their jobs. Television, like other news outlets, could reinforce standing power, inasmuch as it concentrates its attention on party and committee leaders and/or legislative activists.[57]

Instead, television helped to change the Senate in providing a resource to address an altered political environment following the increase in governmental responsibilities in the 1960s, the resultant growth in the size and complexity of the political agenda, and the explosion in the number and range of interest groups, middle managers in the executive branch, and congressional staffers:[58]

> The new system that began to emerge during the late 1960s and came to fruition in the 1970s is much more open, less bounded, and less stable; it is characterized by a much larger number and greater diversity of significant actors, by more fluid and less predictable lines of conflict, and, consequently, by a much more intense struggle to gain space on the agenda.[59]

When the agenda was easily set by presidents or by congressional leaders, then the help of the media was not crucial for most senators, excepting those whose issues or concerns were being overlooked and who therefore thought of legislative effectiveness in different ways. But when Congress faces, as it so often does, problems of collective action, the media as a whole—whether print or television, or both—become a useful tool to focus attention on given issues and solutions.

Prominence in any news, for one, tends to cause the public to view a problem as more serious, and as requiring a solution.[60] Moreover, merely enhancing the salience of an issue, whatever the public's response, often causes legislators to react differently, knowing they are being watched and that their actions are thus more "traceable" than would otherwise be the case.[61] Finally, the media are often taken as a surrogate for public opinion, among legislators concerned not with current snapshots of the public, but how their constituents might react down the road.[62]

Senators face a dispersed and confusing political environment where it is far from clear whom to bargain with, much less how to do so. Working with the media to raise the salience of an issue onto the political agenda— hopefully with one's chosen solution attached—and persuade en masse becomes a much more valuable tool. To be sure, legislators and their staffs are well aware that media attention is most useful at only certain stages in the legislative process. As one illustration, House top staffers perceive the media's role in the policy process as most powerful in "setting the agenda" and "framing the terms of debate," substantially more so than "influencing interest groups" or "generating floor support," let alone "moving bills in committees" or "generating support in the other chamber."[63]

All of these examples indicate, then, that it is not simply the media's different shape or presence, but senators' goal-oriented reasons for using the media that has helped to change the ways the Senate operates. But what difference does it make that senators now turn to reporters on a day-to-day basis to help them manage their jobs?

## Symbiosis and Adversarial Relations

Is the relationship between the Senate and the media symbiotic or adversarial? The answer depends on how willing reporters are to assist (consciously or not) senators' missions. Differences here between television and print are relatively minor. In both modalities, there are contradictory pressures, which lead to symbiosis and adversarial relations, often simultaneously. Some called the relationship "living in symbiosis."[64] Local reporters, of course, favor senators as key state-level politicians. But senators have a built-in boost on the national front, too. Newly elected senators must adjust not only to the Senate itself but to the new prominence and access they have to the national news media.[65] Reporters find Congress an ideal spot for newsgathering for any issues in Washington, to the point that the news easily takes on a congressional perspective, even when the stories are not about Congress itself.[66] Senators themselves are familiar protagonists and antagonists representing, unlike House members, known political jurisdictions, and they can be counted on to stage events on their own or comment on others. The evidence tends to say that the Senate as an institution receives more coverage than the House, and it is undeniable that the average senator is far likelier to be in the national news than the average House member.[67] From 1969 through 1986, for instance, only the rare senator went unmentioned on the networks in any year, whereas at least half of House members, and usually considerably more, received no reference on any of the networks for any year.[68] The greater prominence of senators tends to reinforce the newsworthiness of the chamber in which they serve: "It is easier and faster to build a coherent story with a smaller cast of characters. The House of Representatives is too much like *War and Peace*; the Senate is more on the scale of *Crime and Punishment*."[69]

To be sure, senators are not equal in the eyes of journalists. The national news gravitates toward party leaders, leaders of committees that are prestigious or that control newsworthy jurisdictions, senators from large states, and legislative activists. Yet does this mean that the "invisible senators" could not care less about the national news? Not necessarily, for a few simple reasons. First of all, the amount of coverage received is no indication of how hard senators try to get into the news; as with the House, legislators may work hard for those one or two media mentions.[70] Second, there is considerable randomness in deciding newsworthiness; senators must be on the alert for the possibility of making news (sometimes inadvertently). In the case of newly elected senators, they

> campaign in ways designed to attract free media. And media attentiveness follows them to Washington. For some, this means more attention than they have ever received before. For some, it may mean less attention than they have been accustomed to. But for virtually all of them, it means more *national* attention. And for all of them it means more national political attention.[71]

If senators are attractive to the national news media, they are attracted to the national news as well. It helps them reach state and national publics and, perhaps, nurtures presidential ambitions; it also helps in the legislative process through agenda-setting and framing issues. In other words, senators have few reasons nowadays to be "recalcitrant sources," unwilling to work with reporters.[72]

The conditions would thus seem present for symbiosis if not collaboration to occur in the Senate. Yet the news media's concentration on powerful newsmakers does not always or even usually work to the latter's benefit. The adversarial model of reporters holding officials accountable and "speaking truth to power" is impracticable when reporters must operate under the strictures of deadlines and thus constantly need defensible, even "authoritative" information on a continuing basis. An "exchange model" might appear to have more merit, but symbiosis is also an incomplete account. Although the adversarial model may be difficult in practice, it exists as a potent ideology for journalists who wish to maximize their professional autonomy and minimize the perception of them as mere "flacks."[73] As important, what officials want out of the news and what reporters want out of the news are often at odds with each other. I have listed a few of these differences in table 8-1. They are derived mainly from comparisons of news and candidate-controlled communications in cam-

Table 8-1. *Reporters' and Officials' Preferences for Communication*

| Journalists | Officeholders/politicians |
| --- | --- |
| Clear-cut | Nuanced/ambiguous |
| Concrete/personalized/anecdotal | Abstract/principled/programmatic |
| Terse | Expansive |
| Conflictual | One-sided |
| Narrative drama | Issues/policies |

paigns, but I would at least hypothesize that the same tension occurs in covering Congress as well.[74]

Journalists favor a certain kind of news, and therefore certain kinds of communications from officials, not because of ideology so much as agreed-upon "production values" for how the news should be reported and presented. In pursuit of a "good story," reporters glean tidbits from what officials provide them in order to assemble a compelling narrative with limited space and time. Thus "while governmental processes provide the stages, the actors and the lines for the accounts that journalists create, the latter cut and paste these elements together according to their own standards of quality and interest."[75]

Part of the problem for senators seeking publicity is the growing negativity, if not cynicism, of the news.[76] Although reporters may well be true believers in the American way, such values are revealed most when threatened most. Consequently, "the news defends democratic theory against an almost inevitably inferior democratic practice."[77] Compared with an idealized smooth process of how-a-bill-becomes-a-law, the convoluted, unpredictable, and "unorthodox" legislative processes of recent years simply seem like "squabbling," "bickering," or just a plain "mess."[78] Yet the absence of conflict does not guarantee good news. Even amidst consensus in Washington about a problem and the best solution to fix it, the news can easily critique the ineffectiveness of the methods used toward that agreed-upon end, as was the case in the Panama invasion of 1989.[79]

More important, the news is ill-prepared to encourage communication that would seem to be optimal for deliberation. Complexity gives way to simplicity; nuanced arguments get shrunk into soundbites; abstract programs are discussed in terms of individual personal anecdotes. Above all, it becomes difficult to focus on issues when reporters are most interested in following the game of politics from day to day, as has long been the case with campaigns and is increasingly so between elections in Washington as well.[80] Now that officials are enmeshed in what Sidney Blumenthal many years ago called "the permanent campaign," it is almost as if reporters too are on a permanent campaign footing, in the way they interpret what Congress does (or fails to do) and why.[81]

Yet senators and reporters, in spite of this basic disagreement about the forms and uses of political communication, must work with each other, because each depends on the other to do their job. The greater unpredictability of the American political system—and the Senate in particular—invites senators to turn to the news to help manage the governmental process. One indication of how much the Senate has changed over the last forty years is that whereas media-mindedness in the 1950s was a preoccupation largely of "outsiders," it is now the purview of the Senate's leaders. The senators who initiate the most news events on Capitol Hill are not backbenchers but the already powerful: senior senators, party leaders, members of the majority party in particular.[82] The rank and file now expect leaders to use the national news to articulate congressional actions and to shape public opinion to provide political protection for the legislation they will be asked to support.[83]

"Media effects" include not merely what the news media do either in shaping public opinion or in reworking the raw material that sources provide to them. The media's influence also encompasses how they provoke political actors to behave in ways they would not if the media were not there.[84] Senators seeking publicity must anticipate the news in deciding what to do, how, where, and when, with the unsettling prospect that the news media's production values will become central determinants of Senate decisionmaking.

## Conclusion

Turning to the news media to help make the process work can be a valuable short-term fix for senators. Such coverage provides a key and rare way to focus the Senate's attention on certain problems, issues, and solutions. Party leaders use the natural tendency of reporters to seek out those deemed most influential in making the process (and the storyline) move along, and they focus that attention on their agenda. Not only do members now expect that party leaders will do this, leaders are more aggressive in coordinating senators to frame the message that the media will broadcast.[85] In that way, Congress has picked up some tricks from the State Department and from the Clinton presidency, where the need to make news furnishes a good excuse for greater daily policy coordination and decisions.[86]

The long-term consequences of turning to the news media to help in governance are less positive. The irony is that the news media have become ever more useful to senators in governance just as Congress and its members have become less attractive to the news media. The move from coaxial cables to satellite, the increasing concern of news enterprises with the bottom line, the consequently tighter budgets and greater attention to the public's preference for matters closer to home have all caused Washington news in general and congressional news in particular to shrink dramatically.[87] The diminished corps of Capitol Hill reporters sees what Congress does as valuable, but their superiors are not convinced.[88] All these developments have reinforced the tendency to see congressional deliberations through the "game frame." As a result, to get the news that they need, senators must be even more sensitive to the criteria by which news is made and work hard to incorporate those into their day-to-day decisionmaking.

What, then, of deliberation? A recent definition calls attention to "an *idealized process* consisting of *fair procedures* within which political actors engage in *reasoned argument* for the *purpose of resolving political conflict.*"[89] To that, I would add that legislative deliberation should be aimed at the public good, not at narrow self-interest, and that legislators must be open to be persuaded by information and arguments rather than sheer bargaining and threats.[90]

There are certainly benefits for deliberation in opening up the Senate to the news media. Stated simply, the public interest may be well served by public (and well-publicized) proceedings. Indeed, legislators are less influenced by automatic cue-giving when they vote on matters that are more prominent in the news.[91] Raising the salience of an issue not only makes congressional inaction less likely, but pushes legislators to consider "extrinsic" standards of good public policy.[92] This idea has much in common with the notion of "traceability," whereby legislators reflect more intensively on their positions when they presume they will be held accountable for them.[93] At the very least, public deliberations may ensure that political decisions will be actuated by what can be stated in the public interest, not merely in the private interest.[94]

Yet having the news media decide whether, when, and why certain issues in Congress receive attention skews if not counteracts this benefit. The news media's widely agreed-upon production values pressure Congress in ways that do not match up well with focusing on substantive arguments, with listening to and considering alternative possibilities, and with attending to the public good. Consider the following points.

1. *Political agendas are increasingly reactive to news agendas, and policies have to be crafted with news values in mind.* If mere repetition of an issue in the news heightens the public's sense of its importance, as well as the public's tendency to judge political actors by their actions on that issue, then the news is a powerful political tool for agenda-setting in the Senate. This power might not be a problem if the news media merely reflected the Senate's notion of importance, yet that is far from the case, given how journalists cling to the final choice over newsworthiness, and as the "newshole" available for Capitol Hill shrinks. Not all policies equally fit the demands of the news outlined above. Those that do not must somehow be communicated through anecdotes, dramatic sound bites, sloganeering, props, and visual stunts, all of which tend to detract from focusing on substantive effect. To be sure, the Senate must consider recurring agenda items every year, notably budget, appropriations, and tax issues.[95] But "discretionary" agenda items, one might surmise, are further shaped with news values in mind, despite the fact that they bear little resemblance to political values and provide few clear criteria on the effectiveness of policies.

2. *Political processes are sped up under the media spotlight.* Slowness is only central for deliberation if it encourages the careful weighing of evidence. Page boldly suggests that deliberation can well be swift, when the news media try to reach a conclusion about the underlying causes of a particular event, and thus the problem that needs to be fixed.[96] However, once one gets to assessing a solution, speed tends not to work well for deliberation, since an answer to a problem takes more sifting and winnowing than is the case with deciding a cause.

Being in the media spotlight tends to accelerate the policymaking process, known as the "fast-forward effect."[97] An inventive series of studies by a team of Northwestern University researchers provides strong empirical substantiation.[98] The researchers were tipped off in advance to six forthcoming investigative reports and arranged before/after surveys for various combinations of mass and elite samples. Their working hypothesis was the "mobilization model": whistle-blowers give journalists a tip that becomes the basis for a story that provokes public opinion to pressure decisionmakers who comply with the public demand. They found that this mobilization model did not work. Powerful sources, not whistle-blowers, provided the information in the first place. And in all of these case studies, elites were at least as affected, and usually more so—and more quickly—by the reports than was the public. In four of the six cases, the priority the elites attached to the problem was higher; and in all six, the pace of addressing the problem stepped up.[99]

In other words, news coverage pushes for a quick elite response, whether or not the public is mobilized. Speed favors the most available alternative, whether or not it might address the problem very well. Matters are yet worse if the news media interpret the legislative process as a dramatic game, on who's ahead and who's behind, and on the strategies used by each side, rather than a crucial and sober process of decision. In short, the media's presence provides few incentives to engage in reasoned argument.

3. *The public, and the interests of the public, are not necessarily more involved when the legislative process is mass-mediated.* Deliberation is one part of the larger job with which Congress is charged—namely, representation. Political representation must balance acting in the constituents' interests and responsiveness to the constituents' own preferences and concerns.[100] Deliberating over the best legislative response must then ensure that represented citizens are taken into account, not merely as beneficiaries of wise public policies, but also as actors (real or potential) in the legislative process.

A central role for the news media does not guarantee a place for the public in deliberation; indeed, the former could even preclude the latter. News coverage is not a mere reflection of what people want. Reporters tend not to anticipate the public's preferences for the news. Their professional autonomy enables them to be inattentive to what readers and viewers prefer. They claim to provide the news their audience needs, not the news it wants. Ratings or circulation figures cannot reveal great satisfaction (or dissatisfaction) on the public's part with the content of the news. There are many reasons for the public to read a newspaper or watch a television broadcast: reassurance, topics for social conversation, entertainment, even sheer habit. The news is less directed by the public than shaped by the interaction of sources and journalists. The encounters of Washington reporters and senators are part of an inside-the-beltway game: "Washington news gathering, in other words, is an interaction among elites. One elite reports on another elite."[101] The public may well be out of the loop.

Nonetheless, the news is often taken as a surrogate for public opinion, even though the portrayal thereof can be quite distant from what polls might reveal. For one thing, mere inclusion in the news would seem to raise the appeal of agenda items, if senators then see the issues as affecting many people and as a serious problem.[102] More pointedly, explorations of political actors' concepts of public opinion have revealed that most members of political elites see media coverage as an accurate (not simply more immediate) indicator of public opinion.[103] The Pew Research Center in association with *National Journal* conducted a survey in 1998 of a representative sample of 81 members of Congress, 98 presidential appointees, and 151 civil servants in the Senior Executive Service.[104] Not only did relatively few respondents agree that "Americans know enough about issues to form wise opinions about what should be done," but they were likely not to rely on polls, even among members of Congress, generally the most favorable to the public.[105] Asked about their principal sources of information on how the public feels about issues (and allowed multiple responses), legislators pointed to personal contacts (59 percent), letters and phone calls (36 percent), and even the media (31 percent), before public opinion polls (24 percent). Moreover, 75 percent of presidential appointees and 84 percent of civil servants listed the media as a main source of information about public opinion.

In short, the media's impact on deliberation in the Senate is very much a mixed picture. Their presence may provoke legislators to think in the public interest. But the news media also push definitions of public problems that fit with journalistic production values above political concerns. They also work to speed up deliberation to favor the first available alternative—all without furthering the consultation of the public at large.

It is difficult to imagine, nonetheless, the Senate turning back to the time before 1986, when televised proceedings of the floor were launched, let alone to the 1950s, when powerful senators routinely tried to ignore the national news media. In this regard, the Senate's impeachment trial of President Clinton bears consideration. Recall the decision about whether to open the Senate's deliberations to the public (that is, to the news media). Examining the public record on the failed effort to suspend the rules present in the *Congressional Record* and in news transcripts and excerpts illustrates two points.[106] First, just about nobody saw the Senate as able to operate except in the spotlight. To be sure, Senate veterans such as Robert Byrd (D-W.Va.) and Strom Thurmond (R-S.C.) yearned for the good old days when senators did not have to wear microphones to speak. A handful of senators charged that the cameras in the Senate led to grandstanding and delay. But most senators who spoke out simply accepted the news media as a fact of political life. Even some of those, such as Charles Grassley

(R-Iowa), who voted to keep the processes closed, emphasized the exceptional nature of these deliberations when the Senate was operating almost as much as a jury as a legislature.

Second, legislative processes may not be easily changed simply by closing the doors to the news. Whether or not the closed sessions were really so different is doubtful. The evidence suggests that senators used up the full fifteen minutes allotted to them and tended to read speeches (many inserted in the *Congressional Record* at the end of the trial) rather than engage in discussion. In short, it is, at best, unclear if the Senate's process would be so different—and if deliberation would be better—if the news media were not there.

To sum up, then, the news media are not ancillary to, but key participants in, the legislative process in the U.S. Senate. As in past eras in the Senate, the news media have provided opportunities and resources that encourage senators to act in new and different ways within the institution when it suits their interests. But we have also seen how different understandings of what and who is news produces different opportunities for senators, and thus different possibilities for the Senate as a deliberative body.

The news is not solely the handiwork of reporters. But nowadays, the negotiation of newsworthiness, in which senators can and do participate, can and often does end up simply pushing journalistic values ahead of political values. And as the news becomes a way to get something done, senators and their staffs end up internalizing those understandings of how best to make news. While deliberation may well be assisted in crucial cases by encouraging greater attention to the public interest, the net result is more often to speed up the process, to downplay detail and nuance, and to embed news values into decisionmaking processes in spite of the fact that they have little or less to do with criteria for good public policy.

Under such circumstances, one may well wonder what is to be done. Working harder to manage the news media in their present guise seems misguided to me, because doing so enmeshes senators more deeply in trying to outsmart reporters at their own game by their own values. Likewise, proposals to have a nonpartisan information office, modeled on the Congressional Budget Office, to foster explanation of the institution itself, are valuable but incomplete, since they only deal with one part of the problem and cannot be expected to influence decisions on newsworthiness.[107]

At the end of the day, the main culprit seems to be the definition of news itself. Today, as this chapter has shown, journalists have collective power precisely because of the widespread agreement among them on who makes news, on what is news, and on the production values by which news is shaped—all of which leads to unfortunate side effects in politics as a whole and in the Senate's deliberations in particular. Yet this homogeneity is by no means merely something that happened to happen; it is the result of official policies and practices, which can be altered if the public wants to have a different, particularly more diverse news media.[108] As the historical evidence demonstrates, shifts in the understanding of news encouraged senators, and thus eventually the Senate, to alter how it went about its job. If the Senate is to regain its position as a deliberative body, one move is certainly to reassess the procedures, rules, and norms of the chamber itself. But we should not neglect another line of approach: to rework the institutions around it, and that includes the news media.

## Notes

A Division II grant from Williams College funded the research assistance of Emily Small. Thanks go to my partner Jack Yeager for a couple of close reads, to my colleague Marc Lynch for a well-timed conversation on deliberation, and to an audience at the Shorenstein Center for the Press, Politics and Public Policy at the Kennedy School of Government at Harvard for their comments.

1. See, for instance, Eric M. Uslaner, *The Decline of Comity in Congress* (University of Michigan Press, 1993).

2. Donald R. Matthews, *U.S. Senators and Their World* (University of North Carolina Press, 1960).

3. Ibid., p. 217.

4. See especially Barbara Sinclair, *The Transformation of the U.S. Senate* (Johns Hopkins University Press, 1989); Steven S. Smith, *Call to Order: Floor Politics in the House and Senate* (Brookings, 1989); and Sarah A. Binder and Steven S. Smith, *Politics or Principle? Filibustering in the United States Senate* (Brookings, 1997).

5. Timothy E. Cook, *Making Laws and Making News: Media Strategies in the U.S. House of Representatives* (Brookings Institution, 1989); Cook, "The Negotiation of Newsworthiness," in Ann N. Crigler, ed., *The Psychology of Political Communication* (University of Michigan Press, 1996); Cook, *Governing with the News: The News Media as a Political Institution* (University of Chicago Press, 1998).

6. Douglass Cater, *The Fourth Branch of Government* (Boston: Houghton Mifflin, 1959), especially chap. 1, which provides the earliest, and in some ways the best, argument along these lines.

7. Matthews, *U.S. Senators and Their World*, p. 206.

8. Cook, *Governing with the News*, chap. 3.

9. Exemplars within the literature on the Senate include Sinclair, *Transformation of the U.S. Senate*; Elaine K. Swift, *The Making of an American Senate:*

*Reconstitutive Change in Congress, 1787–1841* (University of Michigan Press, 1996); and Sarah A. Binder, *Minority Rights, Majority Rule: Partisanship and the Development of Congress* (Cambridge University Press, 1998).

10. Samuel Kernell and Gary C. Jacobson, "Congress and the Presidency as News in the Nineteenth Century," *Journal of Politics,* vol. 49 (November 1987), pp. 1016–35.

11. See Jeffrey Tulis, *The Rhetorical Presidency* (Princeton University Press, 1987).

12. Swift, *Making of an American Senate.* To be sure, the Senate was very much in line with precedent, to judge from the examples of the British Parliament, colonial legislatures, the Continental Congress, and the Constitutional Convention, all of which met mostly behind closed doors. See Charlene Bangs Bickford, "Throwing Open the Doors: The First Federal Congress and the Eighteenth-Century Media," in Kenneth Bowling and Donald Kennon, eds., *Inventing Congress: The Origins and Establishment of the First Federal Congress* (Ohio University Press, 1999), pp. 166–90.

13. Elizabeth G. McPherson, "The Southern States and the Reporting of Senate Debates, 1789–1802," *Journal of Southern History,* vol. 12 (May 1946), pp. 223–46.

14. Swift, *Making of an American Senate,* p. 61.

15. Quoted in Noble E. Cunningham Jr., *The Process of Government under Jefferson* (Princeton University Press, 1978), pp. 259–60.

16. See Swift, *Making of an American Senate,* fig. 7.1, appendix B. Swift (p. 176) concludes that the Senate continued to have a greater public profile from the 1830s on, based on three later years from the *New York Times,* but Kernell and Jacobson ("Congress and the Presidency as News," table 4) analyze selected years from 1820 through 1876 of Cleveland newspapers and see greater variability, and possibly more of a focus on the House during and following the Civil War.

17. Swift, *Making of an American Senate,* p. 142.

18. See Donald Lewis Shaw, "At the Crossroads: Change and Continuity in American Press News, 1820–1860," *Journalism History,* vol. 8 (Summer 1981), pp. 38–50.

19. F. B. Marbut, *News from the Capital: The Story of Washington Reporting* (Southern Illinois University Press, 1971), p. 3.

20. Thomas C. Leonard, *The Power of the Press: The Birth of American Political Reporting* (Oxford University Press, 1986), p. 72.

21. Ibid., p. 76.

22. Gerald Baldasty, "The Press and Politics in the Age of Jackson," *Journalism Monographs* 89 (August 1984).

23. This was Representative James Elliot of Vermont, starting in 1808 for the *Freeman's Journal* of Philadelphia. Elliot's letters did continue past the end of his term in 1809 until 1812. See Marbut, *News from the Capital,* pp. 26–27.

24. Donald A. Ritchie, *Press Gallery: Congress and the Washington Correspondents* (Harvard University Press, 1991), p. 22.

25. See, for instance, Michael Schudson, *Discovering the News: A Social History of American Newspapers* (New York: Basic Books, 1978); Dan Schiller, *Ob-*

*jectivity and the News: The Public and the Rise of Commercial Journalism* (University of Pennsylvania Press, 1981); and Gerald Baldasty, *The Commercialization of News in the Nineteenth Century* (University of Wisconsin Press, 1992).

26. The fullest account is Frederick B. Marbut, "The United States Senate and the Press, 1838–41," *Journalism Quarterly*, vol. 28 (Summer 1951), pp. 342–50. See also Marbut, *News from the Capital*, chap. 5; and Ritchie, *Press Gallery*, p. 26.

27. *Congressional Globe*, vol. 7 (25 Cong. 3 sess.), January 5, 1839, p. 93.

28. Similarly, Senator James Buchanan (D-Pa.) lengthily distinguished the letter-writer from the reporter, "a person who gave a faithful historical account of the proceedings of the body, with full reports or fair abstracts of the speeches of its different members, from which the public could be made acquainted with the nature of the business transacted. Were the letter-writers reporters in this sense? Would any senator contend that they were? No; they did not themselves pretend to be so" (ibid., p. 94). However, other senators, such as William Campbell Preston (Whig-S.C.), accepted the new form of journalism: "He was of opinion that these letter-writers presented a more interesting sketch, a more faithful picture of the doings of the Senate, than the mere journal-like records of the official proceedings furnished by our city papers, however correct they may be" (ibid., p. 95).

29. Quoted in Marbut, "The United States Senate and the Press, 1838–41," p. 347.

30. Quoted in ibid., p. 349.

31. Quoted in ibid.

32. See Cook, *Making Laws and Making News*, chap. 2.

33. Leonard, *Power of the Press*, chap. 3.

34. Ibid., p. 84. This rethinking of political rhetoric is perhaps best encapsulated by a contrast of two famous politicians. In 1850 Henry Clay's last stump speech in Lexington, Kentucky, was initially prevented by his unwillingness to speak to constituents until an Associated Press reporter taking notes departed; he was furious when the reporter wrote an account of the speech from talking with observers and not consulting Clay at all. In 1858, however, Abraham Lincoln willingly delayed a debate with Stephen Douglas when a voice in the crowd told him, "Hold on, Lincoln, you can't speak yet. Hitt isn't here and there is no use of your speaking unless the *Tribune* has a report." See Ritchie, *Press Gallery*, p. 32; and Leonard, *Power of the Press*, p. 88.

35. See, for instance, Schudson, *Discovering the News*; Baldasty, *Commercialization*; and David T. Z. Mindich, *Just the Facts: How "Objectivity" Came to Define American Journalism* (New York University Press, 1998).

36. Michael Schudson, *The Power of News* (Harvard University Press, 1995), chap. 3.

37. Francis A. Richardson, "Recollections of a Washington Newspaper Correspondent," *Records of the Columbia Historical Society*, vol. 6 (1903), p. 34.

38. See George Juergens, *News from the White House: The Presidential-Press Relationship in the Progressive Era* (University of Chicago Press, 1981); Martha Joynt Kumar, "The White House Beat at the Century Mark," *Harvard International Journal of Press/Politics*, vol. 2 (Summer 1997), pp. 10–30; and Stephen

Ponder, *Managing the Press: Origins of the Media Presidency, 1897–1933* (New York: St. Martin's Press, 1998).

39. Joseph Cooper and David W. Brady, "Institutional Context and Leadership Style: The House from Cannon to Rayburn," *American Political Science Review*, vol. 75 (1981), pp. 411–25.

40. Ralph K. Huitt, "The Outsider in the Senate: An Alternative Role," *American Political Science Review*, vol. 55 (September 1961), pp. 566–75.

41. Dorothy Hartt Cronheim, "Congressmen and Their Communication Practices," unpublished Ph.D. dissertation, Ohio State University, 1957, p. 36.

42. See Leo C. Rosten, *The Washington Correspondents* (New York: Harcourt, Brace, and World, 1937), chap. 5; Matthews, *U.S. Senators and Their World*, p. 198; Stephen Hess, *The Ultimate Insiders: U.S. Senators in the National Media* (Brookings, 1986); and Cook, *Making Laws and Making News*, chap. 3.

43. One might have expected the so-called Republican revolution, ushered in by the change in party control of both houses of Congress in 1994, to have created a similar reconstitutive change, but the consensus of most scholars of Congress is that Republicans built on and perhaps accelerated an evolution—particularly in the centralization of party leadership—that was already under way under Democratic control. See, for instance, the essays in Nicol C. Rae and Colton C. Campbell, *New Majority or Old Minority? The Impact of Republicans on Congress* (Lanham, Md.: Rowman and Littlefield, 1999).

44. Timothy E. Cook, "PR on the Hill," in Christopher J. Deering, ed., *Congressional Politics* (Chicago: Dorsey Press, 1989), pp. 62–89.

45. Burdett A. Loomis, *The New American Politician: Entrepreneurship, Ambition, and the Changing Face of Political Life* (New York: Basic Books, 1988).

46. See Samuel Kernell, *Going Public: New Strategies of Presidential Leadership* (Washington, D.C.: CQ Press, 1986).

47. See Norman Ornstein, "The Open Congress Meets the President," in Anthony King, ed., *Both Ends of the Avenue: The Presidency, the Executive Branch, and the Congress in the 1980s* (Washington, D.C.: American Enterprise Institute, 1983), pp. 185–211; and Austin Ranney, *Channels of Power: The Impact of Television on American Politics* (New York: Basic Books, 1983).

48. Cook, "PR on the Hill," Fig. 4-2.

49. See Ronald Garay, *Congressional Television: A Legislative History* (Westport, Conn.: Greenwood Press, 1984); and Richard F. Fenno Jr., "The Senate through the Looking Glass: The Debate over Television," *Legislative Studies Quarterly*, vol. 14 (August 1989), pp. 313–48.

50. See especially Herbert J. Gans, *Deciding What's News: A Study of CBS Evening News, NBC Nightly News, Time and Newsweek* (New York: Vintage, 1979); and for a more recent example in Los Angeles television news, see Ronald N. Jacobs, "Producing the News, Producing the Crisis: Narrativity, Television, and News Work," *Media, Culture, and Society*, vol. 18 (July 1996), pp. 373–97.

51. See, for instance, C. Richard Hofstetter, "News Bias in the 1972 Campaign: A Cross-Media Comparison," *Journalism Monographs* no. 58 (November 1978); Timothy E. Cook, "House Members as Newsmakers: The Effects of Televising Congress," *Legislative Studies Quarterly*, vol. 11 (May 1986), pp. 203–26;

Holli A. Semetko, Jay G. Blumler, Michael Gurevitch, and David H. Weaver, *The Formation of Campaign Agendas: A Comparative Analysis of Party and Media Roles in Recent American and British Elections* (Hillsdale, N.J.: Lawrence Erlbaum Associates, 1991), chap. 5; and Marion R. Just, Ann N. Crigler, Dean E. Alger, Timothy E. Cook, Montague Kern, and Darrell M. West, *Crosstalk: Citizens, Candidates, and the Media in a Presidential Campaign* (University of Chicago Press, 1996), chap. 4.

52. W. Russell Neuman, Marion R. Just, and Ann N. Crigler, *Common Knowledge: News and the Construction of Political Meaning* (University of Chicago Press, 1991), chap. 3.

53. See, for example, Gans, *Deciding What's News*; and W. Lance Bennett, *News: The Politics of Illusion*, 3d ed. (New York: Longmans, 1996).

54. Ritchie, *Press Gallery*, chap. 9.

55. See, for instance, Michael J. Robinson and Maura E. Clancey, "King of the Hill," *Washington Journalism Review*, vol. 5 (July–August 1983), pp. 46–49.

56. See the afterwords to successive editions to Richard E. Neustadt, *Presidential Power and the Modern Presidents* (New York: Macmillan, 1990).

57. See, for example, Hess, *Ultimate Insiders*; Peverill Squire, "Who Gets National News Coverage in the U.S. Senate?" *American Politics Quarterly*, vol. 16 (April 1988), pp. 139–56; Sinclair, *Transformation of the U.S. Senate*, table 10.1; Stephen Hess, *Live from Capitol Hill! Studies of Congress and the Media* (Brookings, 1991); and James H. Kuklinski and Lee Sigelman, "When Objectivity Is Not Objective: Network Television News Coverage of U.S. Senators and the Paradox of Objectivity," *Journal of Politics*, vol. 54 (August 1992), pp. 810–33.

58. Two good statements of this shift can be found in Kernell, *Going Public*; and Sinclair, *Transformation of the U.S. Senate*.

59. Sinclair, *Transformation of the U.S. Senate*, p. 5.

60. See, most notably, Shanto Iyengar and Donald R. Kinder, *News That Matters: Television and American Opinion* (University of Chicago Press, 1987).

61. David E. Price, "Policy Making in Congressional Committees: The Impact of 'Environmental' Factors," *American Political Science Review*, vol. 72 (June 1978), pp. 548–74; and R. Douglas Arnold, *The Logic of Congressional Action* (Yale University Press, 1990).

62. Susan Herbst, *Reading Public Opinion: How Political Actors View the Democratic Process* (University of Chicago Press, 1998).

63. Karen M. Kedrowski, *Media Entrepreneurs and the Media Enterprise in the U.S. Congress* (Creskill, N.J.: Hampton Press, 1996), table 4.1.

64. Susan Heilmann Miller, "Reporters and Congressmen: Living in Symbiosis," *Journalism Monographs,* 53 (January 1978).

65. Richard F. Fenno Jr., "Adjusting to the U.S. Senate," in Gerald C. Wright, Leroy N. Rieselbach and Lawrence C. Dodd, eds., *Congress and Policy Change* (New York: Agathon Press, 1986), pp. 123–47.

66. Stephen Hess, *The Washington Reporters* (Brookings, 1981).

67. Most claim more coverage for the Senate. Examples include Susan H. Miller, "News Coverage of Congress: The Search for the Ultimate Spokesman," *Journalism Quarterly*, vol. 54 (Autumn 1977), pp. 459–65; Michael J. Robinson and

Kevin R. Appel, "Network News Coverage of Congress," *Political Science Quarterly,* vol. 94 (Fall 1979), pp. 407–17; Hess, *The Washington Reporters*; Richard F. Fenno Jr., *The United States Senate: A Bicameral Perspective* (Washington, D.C.: American Enterprise Institute, 1982); Ross K. Baker, *House and Senate,* 2d ed. (New York: W. W. Norton, 1995), chap. 5. However, two articles provide some caveats. See Charles M. Tidmarch and John J. Pitney Jr., "Covering Congress," *Polity,* vol. 17 (Spring 1985), pp. 463–83; and Lynda Lee Kaid and Joe Foote, "How Network Television Coverage of the President and Congress Compares," *Journalism Quarterly,* vol. 62 (Spring 1985), pp. 59–65.

68. Cook, "PR on the Hill," Fig. 4-3.

69. Hess, *Ultimate Insiders,* p. 91.

70. Cook, *Making Laws and Making News.*

71. Fenno, "Adjusting to the U.S. Senate," p. 140.

72. Gans, *Deciding What's News.*

73. Jay G. Blumler and Michael Gurevitch, "Politicians and the Press: An Essay on Role Relationships," in Dan D. Nimmo and Keith R. Sanders, eds., *Handbook of Political Communication* (Beverly Hills, Calif.: Sage Publications, 1981), pp. 467–93.

74. See, for instance, Thomas E. Patterson, *Out of Order* (New York: Knopf, 1993); and Just and others, *Crosstalk.*

75. Cook, *Governing with the News,* p. 98.

76. See, in general Patterson, *Out of Order.* Studies from news of the 1970s and the early 1980s say that the bulk of congressional news was neutral, but any evaluation tended overwhelmingly to be negative. See Robinson and Appel, "Network News Coverage of Congress"; Hess, *Washington Reporters*; Hess, *Ultimate Insiders*; and Tidmarch and Pitney, "Covering Congress." More recent studies include S. Robert Lichter and Daniel R. Amundson, "Less News Is Worse News: Television News Coverage of Congress, 1972–1992," in Thomas E. Mann and Norman J. Ornstein, eds., *Congress, the Press, and the Public* (Brookings and American Enterprise Institute, 1994), pp. 131–40; and Mark J. Rozell, "Press Coverage of Congress, 1946–92," in ibid., pp. 59–130. Lichter and Amundson's estimates of the increasing negativity of congressional news must be taken with a grain of salt since they only coded statements that clearly expressed a tone and overlooked neutral statements altogether. Similarly, Rozell's conclusions are also potentially unreliable inasmuch as he focused only on news analysis and editorials, not the news itself. Nevertheless, the pattern over time—if not the exact level—seems clear; see Lichter and Amundson's table 5-1.

77. Gans, *Deciding What's News,* p. 44.

78. Unorthodoxy is now typical. See Barbara Sinclair, *Unorthodox Lawmaking: New Legislative Processes in the U.S. Congress* (Washington, D.C.: CQ Press, 1997).

79. Jonathan Mermin, "Conflict in the Sphere of Consensus? Critical Reporting on the Panama Invasion and the Gulf War," *Political Communication,* vol. 13 (April–June 1996), pp. 181–94.

80. See, for example, Joseph N. Cappella and Kathleen Hall Jamieson, *The Spiral of Cynicism: The Press and the Public Good* (Oxford University Press, 1997).

81. Sidney Blumenthal, *The Permanent Campaign: Inside the World of Elite Political Organizations* (Boston: Beacon Press, 1980).

82. Patrick J. Sellers and Brian Schaffner, "More than Reelection: Senators and the News Media, 1985–1998," paper presented at the annual meeting of the Midwest Political Science Association, Chicago, April 1999.

83. Lawrence R. Jacobs, Eric D. Lawrence, Robert Y. Shapiro, and Steven S. Smith, "Congressional Leadership of Public Opinion," *Political Science Quarterly*, vol. 11 (Spring 1998), pp. 21–42.

84. See Matthews, *U.S. Senators and Their World.*

85. Patrick J. Sellers, "Manipulating the Message in the U.S. Congress," *Harvard International Journal of Press/Politics*, vol. 5, no. 1 (2000), pp. 22–31.

86. See, for instance, Stephen Hess, *The Government/Press Connection: Press Officers and Their Offices* (Brookings, 1984); and Howard Kurtz, *Spin Cycle: Inside the Clinton Propaganda Machine* (New York: Free Press, 1998).

87. See, for examples, Penn Kimball, *Downsizing the News: Network Cutbacks in the Nation's Capital* (Washington, D.C.: Woodrow Wilson Center Press, 1994); Stephen Hess, "The Decline and Fall of Congressional News," in Mann and Ornstein, eds., *Congress, the Press, and the Public*, pp. 141–56; and Lichter and Amundson, "Less News Is Worse News." To take one example, when I was studying the Capitol Hill press corps in 1988, CBS was typical in having one full-time correspondent (Phil Jones) to cover the Senate and another (Deborah Potter) to report from the House; nowadays, not only is there only one CBS reporter to handle Congress (Bob Schieffer) but he is known as "chief political correspondent" and often wanders far from Capitol Hill.

88. Kimberly Coursen Parker, "How the Press Views Congress," in Mann and Ornstein, eds., *Congress, the Press and the Public*, pp. 157–70.

89. Jack Knight and James Johnson, "Aggregation and Deliberation: On the Possibility of Democratic Legitimacy," *Political Theory*, vol. 22 (May 1994), p. 285.

90. Joseph M. Bessette, *The Mild Voice of Reason: Deliberative Democracy and American National Government* (University of Chicago Press, 1994).

91. John W. Kingdon, *Congressmen's Voting Decisions* (New York: Harper and Row, 1973).

92. Price, "Policy Making in Congressional Committees."

93. Arnold, *Logic of Congressional Action.*

94. E. E. Schattschneider, *The Semi-Sovereign People* (New York: Holt, Rinehart and Winston, 1960).

95. The distinction between recurring and discretionary agenda items is drawn from Jack L. Walker, "Setting the Agenda in the U.S. Senate: A Theory of Problem Selection," *British Journal of Political Science*, vol. 7 (October 1977), pp. 423–45.

96. Benjamin I. Page, *Who Deliberates? Mass Media in Modern Democracy* (University of Chicago Press, 1996).

97. Ranney, *Channels of Power.*

98. David L. Protess, Fay Lomax Cook, Jack C. Doppelt, James S. Ettema, Margaret T. Gordon, Donna R. Leff, and Peter Miller, *The Journalism of Outrage: Investigative Reporting and Agenda Building in America* (New York: Guilford Press, 1991).

99. Ibid., table 10.1.

100. Hanna Fenichel Pitkin, *The Concept of Representation* (University of California Press, 1967), esp. chap. 10.

101. Hess, *Washington Reporters*, p. 118.

102. Walker, "Setting the Agenda in the U.S. Senate" identifies these as two key determinants of the Senate's agenda.

103. Herbst, *Reading Public Opinion*.

104. Pew Research Center on the People and the Press, "Washington Leaders Wary of Public Opinion: Public Appetite for Government Misjudged," press release and data report available online at http://www.people-press.org/leadrpt.htm, 1998.

105. Not surprisingly, members of Congress were more positive toward the public, with 31 percent agreeing and an additional 17 percent volunteering that "it depends," compared with 13 percent and 7 percent respectively of presidential appointees and 14 percent and 3 percent respectively of civil servants. Ibid., p. 1.

106. The record was collected and examined by my research assistant Emily Small and myself. It is not a good example of "the Senate in the looking glass," because unlike the case of televising floor proceedings in the Senate, there was not equal participation on both sides of the question. Proponents of closed sessions were much less willing to talk on the record (after all, they had the votes to defeat the attempt, and the whole point was to expedite the process).

107. See, for example, Hess, "Decline and Fall of Congressional News."

108. Cook, *Governing with the News*, chap. 8.

# CHAPTER NINE

# The Senate and the Executive

ROGER H. DAVIDSON

COLTON C. CAMPBELL

THE TIES BETWEEN THE SENATE and the executive branch are complex and interdependent. The Constitution itself dictates a special relationship between the two entities. Presidential nominations of individuals to serve in both the federal judiciary and the executive branch must be approved with the "advice and consent" of the Senate. Treaties with other nations are negotiated by the president "provided two-thirds of the Senators present concur." Legislation is debated and approved on the Senate floor, but the president is involved in developing legislation and in devising legislative strategy to rally a winning voting bloc of members (especially in matters of foreign policy and national security policy), or he may veto it. And the participation of the United States in declared wars, formal alliances, strategic arms control accords, and international trade agreements is impossible without explicit Senate sanction. Simply put, it is difficult for one end of Pennsylvania Avenue to ignore the other.

Our discussion of this relationship begins with the various ways in which the Constitution fosters congressional-presidential interaction. The Constitution implicitly requires both competition and cooperation between Congress and the presidency. Historical patterns and individual attitudes have oscillated between conflict and compromise. Congress and the executive at times work as "tandem institutions" that need each other's support or acquiescence to succeed.[1] At other times they compete fiercely, as when legislators see the executive as contemptuous and arbitrary, or when executive officials view the Senate as inefficient and intrusive.

We then explore shifting partisanship and presidential relations in the Senate. The contemporary Senate has become a partisan body, despite the facade erected by norms of courtesy in debate and civility between senators. From the evidence of both voting patterns and the testimony of individual senators, this heightened partisanship has had a profound effect upon the body. A driving force behind the current political state in the Senate is the changing character of its members. Senators known for compromise, moderation, and institutional loyalty seemingly have been replaced with more ideological and partisan members who see the chamber as a place to promote their party's agendas. As a consequence, life on Capitol Hill has become, at least temporarily, more acrimonious.[2]

We also examine the politics of executive and judicial appointments. No political appointee to a federal agency can execute federal laws and regulations, no ambassador can represent the United States abroad, and no federal judge can be seated without having been confirmed by a majority vote of the Senate. Although congressional cooperation in appointments is more the rule than the exception, senators are increasingly prepared to exploit their prerogatives.[3] Some senators routinely take advantage of their leverage to thwart presidential nominations if they consider the nominees to be out of step with existing congressional majorities.[4] Others regard advice and consent not as a mere formality but as an important constitutional weapon guarding the independence of the Senate from the executive branch.

Finally, there is the matter of formal and informal communication between presidents and senators. All presidents since Franklin Roosevelt have sought to exercise legislative leadership in Congress, provide Congress with a primary wish list, and establish its legislative priorities.[5] Typically, however, such presidential leadership occurs at the margins. Senate leaders routinely provide presidents and other executive officials with informal advice, some of which can prove decisive.

## Invitation to Struggle

In the expectation that the Senate would be a deliberative body, the Founders gave the Senate a set of special policy prerogatives. In foreign policy, senators are granted the power to ratify treaties and to confirm the appointment of ambassadors. A wise and stable Senate, the Founders believed, would guard the nation's reputation in foreign affairs. Along with other provisions, these powers placed the Senate in a unique position, which was to "exercise an extra increment of influence over the executive and judicial branches."[6]

Unlike their House counterparts, however, Senate party leaders have far fewer resources with which to fashion coherent chamber responses to the executive. "Leading the Senate," reminisced former majority leader Howard H. Baker (R-Tenn.), "is like herding cats." The chamber's flexible set of forty-two standing rules provide only a skeletal framework for procedure, conferring no prerogatives upon the presiding officer and including neither a previous question rule to shut off debate nor a germaneness rule to prevent irrelevant or destructive attachments.[7] Even the physical structure of the chamber encourages individualism; senators choose their particular seats on the basis of their party and seniority. Such features generally assure individual senators of a high degree of independence.

Recent shifts in Senate personnel and practices have both enhanced the leadership's ability to advance partisan agendas and underscored the chamber's historic individualism. The growing assertiveness of the news media and hordes of policy-oriented interest groups combined with the rise of candidate-centered campaigns have turned the chamber into an assembly of self-promoting "policy entrepreneurs" who are often in collective disarray.[8] When in the minority, senators of both parties increasingly exploit floor amendments and dilatory devices—filibusters, nongermane floor amendments, and holds—to bring the chamber to a standstill. In response to this "new Senate," party leaders on both sides of the aisle are only intermittently able or willing to assert themselves in an "untidy chamber."[9] The result has been a noticeable erosion of the comity traditionally associated with the institution.

At the same time, gaping partisan cleavages in the contemporary Senate have forced leaders into playing the roles of field generals and publicists. The factors usually cited are the greater ideological homogeneity of the two parties and the concomitant decline in the number of "centrists" in the chamber.[10] Since the civil rights revolution of the 1960s, southern Democrats have become more like national Democrats, and conservative southern states and districts now elect Republicans more often than Democrats.[11] The main ideological cleavage in the contemporary Senate now parallels the division between the two parties rather than bisecting each party, as was the situation during the 1950s. In the 1980s and early 1990s the budget deficit was the major issue of domestic policymaking, provoking sharp debates between the parties over taxation and reducing the size of government. Partisan stakes were raised by the tendency to address the budget crisis through periodic deficit-reduction packages that effected major policy change while bypassing the authorizing process.[12]

During the 1990s partisan repositioning depleted the ideological center, with "Democrats . . . perched on the left, Republicans on the right, in both the House and the Senate as ideological centers of the two parties . . . moved markedly apart."[13] In other words, the two parties became more cohesive internally and farther apart externally than they were in the recent past. The percentage of party votes expanded under Presidents Jimmy Carter and Ronald Reagan, reached new highs in 1990 under President George Bush, and soared to 67 and then 69 percent—the highest percentages of any recent president—under President Bill Clinton.[14]

## Legislative Relations with the Executive

Legislative-executive relations are characterized by compromise, conflict, and flux. Presidents have a variety of choices available to influence their effectiveness with the Senate. Presidents find supporters in Congress even when they are opposed by a majority of either chamber. Both branches pursue support for their policy preferences from each other and from outside allies. Their relationship requires that the president engage in a continual process of legislative coalition building. This is a task made easier or harder, depending on the nature of the institutional environment, the contour of political forces, the accessibility of economic resources, and the substantive character of the policy problems on the nation's agenda.[15]

Although the personal legislative skills of presidents are relevant, many factors lead to variations in legislative success or failure with the Senate. Senators' constituency interests, policy preferences, and ideological dispositions, as well as public opinion and the number of partisan seats in the Senate, are important in shaping senatorial outcomes. As a result, White House liaison activities with the Senate, patronage services, and public appeals for support are some of the ways presidents enhance their bargaining power with senators.

One measure of presidential influence and effectiveness in the Senate involves calculating in various ways the percentage of times in a year that the Senate supports the president's publicly expressed positions in recorded floor votes. The simplest and most utilized measure, the *Congressional Quarterly's* presidential support index, has several obvious shortcomings. It makes no distinction between major and minor issues or between conflictual or consensual ones. It accepts White House statements or indications of support or opposition, when in fact measures subject to floor votes may be amalgams that imperfectly embody presidential intentions. President Clinton, for example, backed a 1997 Internal Revenue Service reorganization bill only after it became clear that Democrats as well as Republicans were going to vote for it. More fundamentally, the index falls short of measuring the full extent of a president's achievements or setbacks. Two of President Clinton's greatest failures, for example, did not reach floor votes: the comprehensive health care plan of 1994, and the renewal of "fast track" trade negotiation authority in 1997.

Nonetheless, the presidential support index manages to give "a rough indication of the state of relations between the president and Congress."[16] Several familiar generalizations about presidential success apply to Senate votes as well as to House-Senate averages. For example, success depends on the number of seats controlled by the president's party, and it tends to deteriorate in the later years of the president's term of office.

Presidential support scores over nearly fifty years of the modern presidency also reveal elements of the special relationship between the Senate and the White House. Of the nine presidents who have served since 1953, all but two (Lyndon Johnson and Richard Nixon) enjoyed higher mean support levels in the Senate than in the House (see table 9-1). And since Gerald Ford's first full year in office in 1975, occupants of the White House have had more support in Senate votes than in House votes in all but two years. During Clinton's only years with a Democratic Congress (1993–94), he won slightly higher proportions of floor votes in the House than in the Senate. But in those two years Clinton's overall success rates in both chambers were the highest since the Kennedy-Johnson era.

Recent presidents have received far gentler treatment at the hands of senators than representatives, measured by success in floor votes. In two of the most recent years, 1997 and 1998, Bill Clinton's winning percentages of Senate votes were nearly twice those of the House. Along with predecessors Reagan and Bush, Clinton prevailed in about two-thirds of the Senate's presidential support votes. In the House, these three presidents' success rates were well below 50 percent.

An obvious explanation is that *Congressional Quarterly's* index for the Senate includes a number of presidential nominations, and at that only those that make it to the floor. These nominees for executive and judicial positions are normally, though not invariably, confirmed by the Senate. In 1997 and 1998, for example, Clinton's Senate victory records were enhanced because he won confirmation of all forty-five nominees who were

Table 9-1. *Presidential Victories on House and Senate Votes, 1953–98*[a]

| President and years | House (percent) | Senate (percent) | Difference (percent) |
|---|---|---|---|
| Eisenhower | | | |
| (1953–60) | 68.7 | 73.0 | +4.3 |
| (1953–54) | 87.0 | 85.3 | −1.7 |
| (1955–60) | 65.0 | 70.5 | +5.5 |
| Kennedy (1961–63) | 83.7 | 85.3 | +1.8 |
| Johnson (1964–68) | 86.5 | 79.8 | −6.7 |
| Nixon (1969–74) | 72.7 | 63.0 | −9.7 |
| Ford (1974–76) | 51.0 | 64.2 | +13.2 |
| Carter (1977–80) | 73.2 | 78.9 | +5.7 |
| Reagan | | | |
| (1981–88) | 43.6 | 66.5 | +22.9 |
| (1981–86) | 51.2 | 82.7 | +31.5 |
| (1987–88) | 33.0 | 60.6 | +27.6 |
| Bush (1989–92) | 40.6 | 64.7 | +24.1 |
| Clinton | | | |
| (1993–98) | 54.9 | 69.3 | +14.4 |
| (1993–94) | 87.3 | 85.5 | −1.8 |
| (1995–98) | 38.7 | 61.2 | +22.5 |

Source: Authors' calculations from Norman Ornstein, Thomas E. Mann, and Michael Malbin, *Vital Statistics on Congress 1997–1998* (Washington, DC: CQ Press, 1998), table 8-1. Recent figures are from *CQ Weekly* (Jan. 8, 1998), 13–17, 27–32; (Jan. 9, 1999), 75–78, 86–91.

a. Percentages indicate average numbers of congressional votes supporting the president divided by the total numbers of votes on which the president had taken a position. The final column indicates the differences between Senate and House averages for the years indicated.

voted on, while a group of controversial nominees remained bottled up in committee. When recomputed without these nominations, his Senate scores for those years were 57.1 percent and 47.1 percent, respectively, far more modest, though still well above his House scores. One reason for the president's high success rates in confirming nominees is the extensive and laborious White House process of vetting potential candidates before their names are sent to the Senate. (Nomination politics are considered later in this chapter.)

Another phenomenon is that Senate Republicans have been more supportive of presidents, regardless of party, than their House colleagues have been.[17] Senate Democrats have been less consistent in supporting presidents of their own party. Probably because of the large number of southerners in the party, Senate Democrats gave less support to Presidents Kennedy and Johnson than did House members of their party. Presidents Carter and Clinton received higher support from their own partisans, probably because of the declining numbers of southerners estranged from the Democrats' national agenda. That demographic shift also accounts for declining Democratic support for Republican presidents, though the trend is sharpest in the House.

It is essential to remember, however, that presidential support indexes measure only those votes actually taken on the floor and that those votes differ between the two chambers. A presidential initiative that is defeated decisively by the House may not reach the Senate floor at all; or the Senate may vote on a modified version of a presidential initiative that was originally turned down by the House. In either case, the Senate ends up with a more positive presidential support record than the other body.

## Advice and Consent: Treaties

The precise meaning of the Senate's duty to advise and consent in the making of foreign treaties is by no means unambiguous. One day in the summer of 1789, President George Washington appeared at the doorway of the Senate seeking the members' advice in person concerning a treaty with southern Indians. He recited seven propositions to which the Senate was to answer either yes or no. Following a great deal of discussion, someone suggested the matter be referred to a committee. As Senator William Maclay of Pennsylvania recounted in his celebrated *Journal*:

> The President of the U.S. started up in a Violent fret. This defeats every purpose of my coming here, were the first words he said, he then went on that he had brought his Secretary at War with him to give every necessary information, that the Secretary knew all about the Business—and yet he was delayed and could not go on with the Matter—he cooled however by degrees. . . We waited for him to withdraw, he did so with a discontented Air. . . the President wishes to tread on the Necks of the Senate. he wishes Us to see with the Eyes and hear with the ears of his Secretary only, the Secretary to advance the Premises the President to draw Conclusion. and to bear down our deliberations with his personal Authority & Presence, form only will be left for Us—This will not do with Americans. but let the Matter Work it will soon cure itself.[18]

Washington got the answers he sought the following week when he returned and in "a Spirit of Accomodation, declared his consent." Never again, however, has a president darkened the Senate's door in search of direct advice on a treaty.

The Senate rarely rejects a treaty outright. Since 1789, only twenty treaties have been formally rejected. More often the Senate attaches reservations to a treaty, amends it, or simply allows it to languish. Scores of treaties negotiated by various presidents languish without Senate approval.

Sometimes the Senate has rejected major treaties in order to force changes in international agreements brokered by presidents. The most notable example was the 1919 Treaty of Versailles and the establishment of the League of Nations. President Woodrow Wilson departed for the peace conference without seeking the advice of senators from either party; once there he insisted that his proposal for a League of Nations be incorporated into the peace settlement. When Wilson submitted the Treaty of Versailles to the Senate he announced that he was ready to confer with the members and provide them such information as he had. When nearly a week went by with no response to the invitation, Wilson reluctantly summoned individual senators to the White House for conferences.[19] Thirty-nine Republican senators, more than the one-third necessary to defeat the treaty, declared that the League was unacceptable. Although some opponents, including Foreign Relations Chairman Henry Cabot Lodge (R-Mass.), would have preferred to defeat the treaty outright, a majority pressed for a series of reservations aimed at protecting U.S. sovereignty.

Debate over the Versailles Treaty was one of the most rancorous confrontations between the White House and the Senate. Proud and unbending, President Wilson detested Senate opponents of the treaty, especially Lodge. For his part, Lodge accurately sensed that the president in the end would reject the reservations propounded by the Senate.

Another rejection—this one even more abrupt—was the Comprehensive Test Ban Treaty (CTBT), submitted by President Clinton in 1997. After two years of sparring between the White House and treaty opponents, Senate GOP leaders suddenly scheduled brief committee hearings and an equally brief floor debate. There was much posturing on both sides, but little attempt at serious negotiation or compromise of the type that had marked other controversial post-Versailles agreements. In the October 1999 vote, CTBT failed, 48–51, short of a majority, much less the required two-thirds. It was mainly a party-line affair: all but one Democrat supported the treaty, and all but four Republicans voted nay. The failure of leadership was equally evident at both ends of Pennsylvania Avenue.

The Senate continues to affect the president's foreign policy agenda. Indeed, modern chief executives typically inform key senators during treaty negotiations in the hope of avoiding the humiliation Wilson suffered.

Members of the Senate participated directly in negotiations with Panama over conditions attached to the unpopular Panama Canal treaties, negotiated by Presidents Gerald Ford and Jimmy Carter. Throughout debate on the treaties, a large segment of U.S. public opinion opposed "giveaway" of the strategically important canal. The Senate Foreign Relations Committee, along with its House counterpart, adopted the more flexible posture advocated by the State Department. Nonetheless, the Senate committee's published record of hearings and deliberations comprised four volumes totaling 2,423 pages. Senate floor debate continued for two and a half months, to the virtual exclusion of other business, the longest such debate since the Versailles Treaty in 1919. In the process, the senators offered some 192 changes to the treaties. Before the debate, almost half the senators visited Panama and talked to General Omar Torrijos. A group headed by Baker, then minority leader, advised the general that the treaty as signed could not be ratified and that U.S. rights for protecting the canal would have to be spelled out. These alterations, which removed ambiguities in the treaties, were accepted. Later, freshman senator Dennis DeConcini (D-Ariz.) successfully pushed an amendment allowing the United States to use military force in Panama or take other steps to keep the canal open after the canal passed out of U.S. hands. This amendment was adopted by the Senate and accepted by President Carter, even though it caused a furor in Panama and had to be clarified by yet another round of talks. Other senators were wooed by administration concessions on matters quite unrelated to the treaties. When Senate debate concluded in April 1978, the two treaty documents as revised were finally ratified by identical votes of 68 to 32.

The Chemical Weapons Agreement, negotiated and signed during President George Bush's administration, again showed the Senate's active role. Although the treaty had been signed by 161 nations and enjoyed broad bipartisan support, a group of senators—most notably, Foreign Relations chairman Jesse Helms (R-N.C.)—argued that the agreement had loopholes that would allow rogue states such as Iraq or Libya to make and use chemical weapons. To push the measure to the Senate floor, Secretary of State Madeleine K. Albright, encouraged by Majority Leader Trent Lott (R-Miss.), entered into negotiations with Helms. The administration agreed to twenty-eight clarifications demanded by conservative opponents. Other concessions—including a State Department reorganization, UN reforms, and submission of other arms control treaties to the Senate—would strengthen Lott's and Helms's role in future bargaining. During the floor debate, President Clinton and his aides worked the phones and sent a last-minute letter to Lott promising to withdraw from the treaty if it jeopardized U.S. interests in any way. Lott brought enough votes to ratify the treaty in April 1997.

## The Politics of Presidential Appointments

The Founders debated over where the appointment power should be lodged: in the entire legislature or in the Senate, wholly with the executive, or in some hybrid of legislative and executive responsibility. For James Madison, the Senate was more competent "as a less numerous and more select body."[20] But a proposal for shared responsibility was eventually adopted, calling for nomination by the president but leaving to the Senate the right of confirmation. Writing in support of this proposal, Alexander Hamilton stated that such an approach recognized "that one man of discernment is better fitted to analyze and estimate the peculiar qualities" for appointments, while also being mindful that "it would be an excellent check upon a spirit of favoritism in the President."[21]

Hamilton may have won the political moment, but the debate over the roles of the respective branches and the various interpretations of "advice and consent" has continued over more than two centuries. Some suggest the Senate has no formal responsibility in the nomination process and plays essentially a pro forma role in the confirmation process.[22] According to this view, the president is entrusted with the obligation to nominate those individuals who are confirmable, and the Senate is to refuse such choice only in the gravest and most compelling circumstances.[23] Others argue that the Framers sought to vest senators with an equally shared responsibility in the selection process.[24]

The modern presidential appointment process scarcely resembles its original design and intent. In fact, it differs dramatically from the way presidents made appointments as recently as the late 1940s. Senatorial prerogatives to block action apply to nominations as well as to legislation, but there was a certain presumption of success when the Senate received a presidential nomination.[25] By tradition, the president was afforded greater latitude over appointments than over legislation; the president often consulted key senators before sending his nominations to Capitol Hill.[26] Not until 1955 did testimony by a nominee at a hearing become established and effectively a mandatory part of the Senate's exercise of advice and consent.[27] Some nominees actually sat on the Supreme Court as recess appointments before their hearings were held.

Today's appointment process is much more formal and structured, longer, often many months longer, and more visible and consistently contentious than ever.[28] The confirmation hearings themselves, along with interest group lobbying and media coverage, are all part of today's landscape. In the last three quarters of the past century, judicial confirmation hearings appear to have evolved in roughly four stages: 1922–55, when senators infrequently questioned nominees; 1955–67, when nominees' appearances before the Senate Judiciary Committee became a routine part of the confirmation process; 1968–87, a transitional period; and 1987 to the present, in which hearings have become occasions for conflict and grandstanding.[29]

The Constitution does not require the president to justify why he makes a particular nomination, nor does it obligate the Senate to explain why it refuses to confirm a nomination. The presumption is that the respective roles of the Senate and the executive branch in the appointment process differ according to the kind of office under consideration.[30] In determining the acceptability of presidential nominees, the Senate historically has been guided by a number of recurring concerns; the foremost concern is with the nominee's policy and philosophical views and their effect on public policy. The confirmation process, Calvin Mackenzie writes, is dominated by policy and constituency considerations "because they are the dominant concerns of the Senate and because the confirmation process provides useful and often unique opportunities for expressing and implementing those concerns."[31] Presidents should expect that those they nominate to execute their policies will be scrutinized by the Senate with the presumption of confirmability.[32] In fact, of 1,464 important executive and judicial nominations from 1965 to 1994, fewer than 5 percent failed.[33]

Senators have three direct means of affecting appointments: the power to suggest candidates for executive and judicial posts; their actual votes on confirmations; and the "holds" they might place on scheduling confirmation votes. The custom called senatorial courtesy gives senators influence over presidential nominations to federal positions within their own states. Dating from 1789, the custom holds that senators may call upon the courtesy of their colleagues to reject nominees for positions within the senator's state, for example, federal district judges, U.S. attorneys, and U.S. marshals. In practice, this means that senators can directly influence the naming of certain officeholders, often selecting their own candidates in the hope that the president will nominate them. Nowhere mentioned in Senate rules or precedents, only linked to the Senate's tradition of extended debate, "holds" permit a single senator or any number of senators to delay—sometimes temporarily, sometimes permanently—action on a measure or other matter, such as the confirmation vote on a nominee.

Nearly all presidents have faced confirmation fights with the Senate. Of the fifteen cabinet nominations that failed to be confirmed, nine were rejected on the floor of the Senate and two were killed intentionally in committee. In addition, one died in committee because of insufficient time to process the nomination, and three were withdrawn for personal reasons, not because of Senate opposition. Of the eleven cabinet nominations that were formally rejected, seven failed because of policy and philosophical differences that senators had with the nominee and the president. The other four failed for a variety of reasons, including conflict of interest, character flaws, incompetence, and perceived disregard and disdain for the Senate.[34]

The average time required through Senate confirmation to fill policy positions in executive departments has increased in the last decade. In 1981 President Ronald Reagan took nearly five months, on average, to fill a full-time position requiring Senate confirmation. In 1993 President Clinton took nearly six months (or 20 percent longer), on average, to fill such a position. Both Reagan and Clinton faced a similar appointment process: the search for a candidate, investigation and clearance of the candidate before being nominated, completion of committee questionnaires and other possible forms before a hearing could be held, and full Senate consideration of the nomination.[35] Both presidents, incidentally, had the presumed benefit of a Senate controlled by their own party. From 1981 to 1993, the overall time for presidents to nominate candidates for appointment increased by twenty-one days; the average time to confirm appointees increased by eleven days; and the average time to fill executive positions increased by thirty-two days.

## The Vacancies Act

Originally passed in 1868, the Vacancies Act was intended to prevent the president from delaying sending forth nominations for advice and consent positions that could evade the Senate's confirmation prerogative and to provide the exclusive means for temporarily filling vacancies in covered positions unless Congress explicitly provided a superseding mechanism. Only two options were available under the statute: either a first assistant or a presidential designee who had previously received Senate confirmation would serve for a strictly defined and limited period. Before 1988 the limitation period was 10 days and then 30 days. In that year it was increased to 120 days.[36] However, the Department of Justice has taken the position that any executive department or agency whose authorizing legislation vests all powers and functions of the agency in its head and allows the head to delegate such powers and functions to subordinates in his or her discretion, does not have to comply with the Vacancies Act. As a consequence, during 1998 some 20 percent of the 320 advice and consent positions in departments were being filled by temporary designees, most of whom had served beyond the 120-day limitation period of the act without presidential submissions of nominations.[37]

The appointment in December 1997 of Bill Lann Lee by Attorney General Janet Reno as acting assistant attorney general for civil rights in the Department of Justice precipitated congressional hearings and the introduction of legislation to remedy a long-standing interbranch controversy over the legal propriety of the failure of executive departments and agencies to comply consistently with the provisions of the Vacancies Act.

Underscoring the importance of preserving the Senate's duty to advise and consent on presidential nominees, Senator Fred Thompson (R-Tenn.) declared in his introductory statement concerning S. 2176, the Federal Vacancies Reform Act:

> Mr. President, the Framers established a system for appointing important officials in which the President and the Senate would each play a role. Not only did the Framers wish to ensure that more than one person's wisdom was brought to the appointment process, but that the President, in selecting nominees, would be aware that they would face scrutiny. When a vacancy occurs in such an office, it is important to establish a process that permits the routine operation of the government to continue, but that will not allow the evasion of the Senate's constitutional authority to advise and consent to nominations.[38]

Under Thompson's guidance, the Senate Governmental Affairs Committee reported S. 2176 on July 15, 1998. Although the measure failed to survive a cloture vote on the floor, a compromise version was included in the fiscal 1999 Omnibus Consolidated and Emergency Supplemental Appropriations Act. The new Vacancies Act, rejecting the Justice Department's position, establishes itself as the exclusive vehicle for temporarily filling vacant advice and consent positions and prevents undue delay in the president's submission of nominees for Senate consideration.

## Ambassadorial Nominations and Foreign Policy

A similar level of confirmation success can be found with presidential nominations for ambassadorial positions. From 1987 to 1996, 91 percent of the 618 people named to ambassadorial positions were confirmed by the Senate. Of the 54 not confirmed, 37 had no hearings on their nominations. Many of these were instances in which the nomination was submitted late in the session or consideration was delayed for other reasons.[39]

In the extreme tactic of "hostage-taking," however, senators may place all designees on hold until the executive compromises or capitulates to lawmakers' demands. In the mid-1990s Senator Helms was lobbying for consolidation of three foreign policy agencies—the Agency for International Development (AID), the Arms Control and Disarmament Agency, and the U.S. Information Agency—within the State Department in order to downsize their operations. The Clinton administration was internally divided over the reorganization proposal. Although certain key figures in the White House and State Department favored consolidation, the affected agencies and their allies were, predictably, fiercely opposed. Especially vocal was AID administrator J. Brian Atwood, a close friend of the president and first lady.

Ambassadorial nominations were halted during much of 1995 by the stalemate, because Helms placed holds on nominations (and other actions) to prevent them from being considered on the Senate floor. At one point 15 percent of all U.S. embassies worldwide were left without new ambassadors. The standoff ended in 1997 when the administration, apparently in capitulation, offered its own foreign agencies' reorganization scheme. (As a reward for his spirited defense of AID, Atwood himself was denied an ambassadorial position. After announcing his resignation from AID and being nominated by President Clinton as ambassador to Brazil, he asked in May 1999 that his name be withdrawn after it became apparent the Foreign Relations Committee would not act on it.)

Chairman Helms and the Clinton administration clashed again over the October 1997 nomination of James Hormel as ambassador to Luxem-

bourg. Hormel's status—heir to a meatpacking fortune, prominent phi-
lanthropist, and political contributor—might have made him an obvious
choice for such an honorific noncareer posting. (This is, after all, the post
once held by Perle Mesta, the colorful "hostess with the mostest.") But
Hormel was also an openly gay man who had contributed an important
collection of gay and lesbian literature to the San Francisco Public Library. Several conservative senators placed holds on Hormel's nomination
on the pretext that his life-style would be offensive to Luxembourg's overwhelmingly Catholic populace.

The conflict escalated when Clinton appointed Hormel to the Luxembourg post during Congress's 1999 Memorial Day recess. "President
Clinton has shown contempt for the Congress and the Constitution," fumed
Senator James Inhofe (R-Okla.), leader of the opponents. "He has treated
the Senate confirmation process as little more than a nuisance which he
can circumvent whenever he wants to impose his will on the country."[40]
To back up his words, Inhofe placed holds on seven judicial and foreign
affairs nominations awaiting floor action. There was even a possibility
that the high-priority nomination of Lawrence Summers as treasury secretary could be held up.

Responding to Inhofe's actions, Democratic Leader Tom Daschle
(S.Dak.) threatened to block committee hearings and slow down the GOP
legislative agenda until the nominations were allowed to go forward.
Daschle warned that his retaliation would include "all of the options available to us, including refusing to allow committees to meet, including stop-
ping legislation."[41] He termed the blanket holds unprecedented and
dismissed the Republican suggestion that Inhofe was merely repeating a
tactic used by then-majority leader Robert C. Byrd (W.Va.) during a 1995
impasse over judicial nominations.

Clearly the war over nominations had gotten out of hand. The Hormel
imbroglio came at the same time as a long-running battle over judicial
nominees (discussed subsequently) and over such foreign policy nominees
as Atwood and UN ambassador-designee Richard Holbrooke. Majority
Leader Trent Lott (R-Miss.) signaled his displeasure with the situation by
suggesting that blanket holds might not be sustained. Under pressure from
several quarters, Inhofe then claimed his actions were not due so much to
Hormel's sexuality as to Clinton's precipitous action. The whole episode
seemed to be resolved by an exchange of letters between the White House
and Senator Lott. Clinton reportedly pledged to reinstate the practice of
giving the Senate prior warning of his intention to make a recess appoint-

ment, thus presumably giving senators an opportunity to act on the nomination in question.

## Judicial Nominations

Judicial appointments are a special type of senatorial confirmation. Judges are extensions of neither the executive nor the legislature, which means that both branches exercise equivalent influence. Such shared responsibility "holds the promise of increasing the commitment of each to maintaining a strong and independent branch."[42] For most of this century the confirmation process for the courts was distinguished by a strong presumption in favor of deference to presidential prerogative to fill vacancies on the Supreme Court. "So long as the nominee exhibited a basic level of competence and his political views fit within the narrow confines of acceptable American political discourse," the president's choices were typically confirmed by a voice vote, with no opposition on record.[43]

Senators increasingly use their advice and consent power to be heard, sometimes pressing for their own political objectives and to assert senatorial independence from the executive branch. Judicial appointees are queried about their legal qualifications, their private backgrounds, and their earlier actions as public or private figures. Other questions focus on social and political issues, the Constitution, particular Court rulings, current constitutional controversies, constitutional values, judicial philosophy, the analytical approach a nominee might use in deciding issues and cases, and partisan considerations.[44] Whereas nominees in the past tended to keep their distance from the appointment process, they are now active participants. During considerations of Supreme Court nominations, for example, the nominee's demeanor, responsiveness, and knowledge of the law may be crucial in influencing senators' votes on confirmation.

A recurring issue at recent confirmation hearings has been when a nominee should decline to answer questions that are posed by members of the Judiciary Committee.[45] Senators often try to elicit forthright views from nominees on various legal or constitutional issues. However, nominees cannot compromise their future judicial independence by appearing to make commitments on issues that could later come before the Court.[46] Nominees also worry that frank responses to certain queries might displease some senators and thus jeopardize their confirmation. Protracted questioning, occurring over several days of hearings, is likely when the nominee is relatively controversial or is perceived by committee members to be evasive or insincere in responding to certain questions.[47]

Aside from shedding light on the fitness of the nominee to serve, confirmation hearings are a vehicle for senators to press constitutional or other values upon the nominee, in the hope of influencing how he or she later might approach issues. In 1992 the Senate Judiciary Committee instituted the practice of conducting a closed-door session with each Supreme Court nominee to address any questions about the nominee's background that confidential investigations might have brought to the committee's attention.[48] In announcing this procedure, then-chairman of the committee Senator Joseph R. Biden (D-Del.) explained that such hearings would be conducted "in all cases, even when there are no major investigative issues to be resolved so that the holding of such a hearing cannot be taken to demonstrate that the committee has received adverse confidential information about the nomination."[49]

In considering judicial nominees, senators enjoy even greater leverage than in handling executive-branch positions. First, as already noted, the presumption in favor of the president is weaker than it is for executive appointments. Although presidents are expected to seek nominees who share their general approach to the law, senators have come to take seriously their right to reach independent judgments concerning such matters as judicial fitness and judicial philosophy. Second, the tradition of senatorial courtesy applies more broadly to judicial posts than to executive ones. Few executive posts considered by the Senate involve primarily a single state, whereas many judicial ones do, including federal district judgeships and some circuit judgeships, not to mention U.S. attorneys and marshals.

In practice, this means that administrations will draw a majority of their nominees from the ranks of their political parties and their traditional supporters, but that they will include moderates from the opposing party and a few individuals sponsored by key senators. Concessions to the opposition party are likely to be more frequent under divided party control, with its rise in holds and hostage-taking.

The maneuvering between the Clinton administration and the Republican Senate (during 1995–99) over judicial nominations presents an instructive series of case studies in contemporary White House–Senate relations. After the Republican takeover of the Senate in 1995, the administration's quest for suitable nominees—laborious at best—was complicated by the need to forestall implacable opposition by Republican senators. By the same token, Judiciary Chairman Orrin G. Hatch (R-Utah) was whipsawed by forces within the chamber. A conservative with an independent streak and a knack for occasionally forging alliances with Democrats, Hatch sensed an obligation to the judicial system (if not to the White House itself) to process the president's nominations and see to it that the courts are adequately staffed. His diligence, however, cost him support within his own party: a number of conservative senators have accused him of being too eager to process Clinton nominees and have sought to curtail his freedom to act.

The tension reached a peak in 1999, when Hatch proposed a political ally, Ted Stewart, for a federal district judgeship. Formerly head of Utah's Department of Natural Resources for five years, Stewart had fought constantly with environmentalists and had criticized federal land-use policies. His critics charged that he had favored business interests in development and conservation issues.

For months the White House declined to move the nomination. In response to Clinton's inaction, Hatch "essentially shut down the confirmation process for existing nominees."[50] From January through late June, no confirmation hearings were scheduled for the forty-two pending nominations for the federal bench. It appeared to be the first time in forty years that a senator had blocked all judicial appointments. (In 1959 then-majority leader Lyndon Johnson stalled President Dwight Eisenhower's nominations in order to force the nomination of one of his Texas political friends.) Political scientist Sheldon Goldman said of the 1999 standoff: "I couldn't say this is a perversion of the process. But I could say you are going to the brink of a constitutional crisis when you say, 'My man or nothing moves.' That's ominous."[51]

Intense negotiations between Hatch and the White House staff temporarily quelled the crisis.[52] The president agreed to begin the process by forwarding Stewart's name to the American Bar Association (ABA) and the Federal Bureau of Investigation. If the ABA rated Stewart "qualified" to serve, and if the FBI found no problems in his personal background, the nomination would go forward. Even before the agreement was revealed, a Judiciary Committee hearing was held and several nominees were subsequently approved for floor action. (Eventually, Stewart was nominated and approved by the Judiciary Committee, but environmentally minded senators slapped a hold on his nomination, which halted all judicial nominees yet again.)

The dynamics of appointment politics—both within the administration and between the administration and the GOP Senate—have dramatically slowed down the confirmation process. Whereas President Ronald Reagan filled 384 judicial seats during his eight years in office (George Bush added 190 in his single term), President Clinton had filled only 305 by mid-1999 and was unlikely to equal the Reagan record. In the meantime, conservative senators promised to organize against at least one controversial nominee (to the liberal Ninth Circuit); and there was heightened pressure among Senate Republicans to keep judicial seats vacant in the hope they could be filled by a president of their own persuasion after the 2000 election.

## Oversight

The duty to review actions of the executive branch, though not explicitly mentioned in the Constitution, is implicit in the law-making function. "The proper office of a representative assembly," declared John Stuart Mill, "is to watch and control the government, to throw the light of publicity on its acts; to compel a full exposition and justification of all of them which any one considers questionable."[53] And Woodrow Wilson remarked that "the informing function of Congress should be preferred even to its legislative function."[54]

The Senate rules contain special provisions relating to committee oversight of the executive branch.[55] First, every standing committee (except for Appropriations and Budget) is enjoined to "review and study, on a continuing basis, the application, administration, and execution of all laws within its legislative jurisdiction" (Rule XXVI, clause 8). Second, certain standing committees are given "comprehensive policy oversight" duties over larger topics that may lie partly outside their legislative jurisdiction (Rule XXV, clause 1a). Finally, all standing committees (except Appropriations) are required to prepare regulatory impact evaluations accompanying each public bill or joint resolution reported out (Rule XXVI, clause 11). These evaluations are supposed to include estimates of the legislation's effects on individuals and businesses, its impact upon the economy and personal privacy, and the amount of added paperwork that it will cause.

In addition, the Committee on Governmental Affairs has its own separate oversight responsibilities. The panel is to review and study the operation of government at all levels with an eye to economy and efficiency, to evaluate the effects of laws reorganizing various branches of government, to study intergovernmental relations, and to examine reports of the comptroller general and recommend action to the Senate.

Aggressive oversight of the executive is, however, a variable phenomenon. Some agencies are subjected to repeated and hostile scrutiny. For
example, the Internal Revenue Service, most people's least favorite government entity, is the object of the Senate Finance Committee's annual
hearings scheduled on or near tax day, April 15. Other agencies are tar-
geted when they are unable to fulfill vital services desired by senators. The
Federal Emergency Management Agency (FEMA) was such an entity. Long
a dumping ground for political appointees, the agency's tardy response to
Hurricanes Hugo and Andrew in the 1980s angered senators from the
affected states. Both congressional pressure and White House politics dictated that FEMA be reorganized and upgraded. Other agencies seem to
receive kinder treatment from their Senate committees than from House
counterparts. These include the Immigration and Naturalization Service
and the National Endowment for the Arts. In both cases the agencies'
statewide efforts are politically more palatable than their impact on local
communities and congressional districts. Finally, there are agencies that
fulfill the long-term concerns of individual senators or groups of senators.
The National Institutes of Health (NIH) is such an entity. Senators whose
personal or family lives have been touched by one or another serious dis-
ease are natural advocates of NIH research and treatment programs. Support for such programs defies partisan and ideological lines.

In short, levels of oversight activity vary greatly among federal agencies and programs. Moreover, periodic outbursts of elite or public concern
may trigger investigations by Senate committees. Some of these Senate-
executive confrontations are rancorous; more frequently, their relationships are mutually beneficial, with senators promoting rather than opposing
agency activism.

## Impeachment

Congress's most extreme sanction against the executive branch is its power
to impeach and remove the president, vice president, and other "civil officers of the United States" for treason, bribery, or "other high crimes and
misdemeanors" (Article I, Sections 2 and 3; Article II, Section 4). The
British parliament had fashioned this power to curb despotic monarchs;
rather than beheading the monarch, the lawmakers could attack and remove his ministers. Alexander Hamilton referred to impeachment "as a
method of national inquest into the conduct of public men."[56]

Despite historical precedents, the Founders were divided about whether the Senate should act as the court of impeachment. Opposing the role for the Senate, James Madison and Charles Cotesworth Pinckney asserted that it would make the president too reliant on the legislative branch. They suggested, as alternative trial bodies, the Supreme Court or the chief justices of the state supreme courts.[57] Hamilton and others argued, however, that such bodies would be too small and open to corruption. Hamilton explained the convention's decision in the following way:

> The Convention . . . thought the Senate the most fit depository of this important trust. Where else than in the Senate could have been found a tribunal sufficiently dignified, or sufficiently independent? What other body would be likely to feel confidence enough in its own situation, to preserve unawed and uninfluenced the necessary impartiality between an individual accused, and the representatives of the people, his accusers?[58]

Impeachment is exclusively the domain of Congress. Although the two chambers play distinctive roles in the process, it is the Senate that is the final judge of whether to convict on any articles of impeachment presented by the House. Even though the chief justice presides over Senate trials of the president, his rulings may be overturned by majority vote. The Senate is free to chart its own procedures in reaching its decisions. In the cases in which the House has voted to impeach, the time from when senators were sworn in at the beginning of the trial until the vote on the articles has ranged from three days for District Judge Alcee Hastings of Florida (1988–89) to 266 days for District Judge James Peck of Missouri (1830). The Supreme Court flatly refused to review the Senate's procedures when an impeached judge, Walter L. Nixon Jr. (no relation of President Richard Nixon), objected that although the full Senate had voted to convict him, the evidence in his case was taken by a committee rather than by the full Senate.[59]

As a legislative proceeding, impeachment is inherently political in character. The structure may appear judicial—especially the Senate's role as a trial court—but lawmakers themselves decide whether and how to proceed, which evidence to consider, and even what constitutes an impeachable offense. Treason is defined by the Constitution, and bribery by statute. Toward the end of the Constitutional Convention, however, George Mason complained that simply to bar those two misdeeds "[would] not reach many great and dangerous offenses," including "attempts to subvert the Constitution."[60] After rejecting as too vague such terms as "corruption," "maladministration," and "neglect of duty," the phrase "high crimes and misdemeanors" was added. Although open to interpretation, these are usually defined as (in Alexander Hamilton's words) "abuse or violation of some public trust"—that is, job-related offenses against the state, the political order, or the society at large.[61] Hence these can be either more or less than garden-variety criminal offenses. Both presidential impeachments (Andrew Johnson, 1868; Bill Clinton, 1998–99) were fiercely partisan affairs in which combatants disputed not only the facts but the appropriate grounds for conviction.

Impeachment has proven a blunt, unwieldy instrument for removing officials for the gravest of offenses. The two chambers, as we have seen, have many lesser ways of reining in wayward officials, and in any event presidents and vice presidents serve terms that are already strictly limited. (Gouverneur Morris, one of the wisest of the Framers, suggested that terms were short enough that impeachments would not be needed, but his view was swiftly overridden.) Still, although impeachment resolutions are frequently filed, only fifteen Senate trials have taken place, and only seven individuals have been convicted. Significantly, the seven who were removed from office were all judges, who, unlike executive officers, enjoy open-ended terms of office.

## Conclusions

This chapter has traversed various manifestations of the special relationship between the Senate and the executive branch. Both comity and conflict have marked this relationship throughout the nation's history. Most of the Senate's contacts with executive-branch officials are little different from those of the House. But the Senate's special constitutional responsibilities—advising and consenting to presidential nominations and to treaties—necessitate intensified negotiations with presidents and their staff assistants. The present state of this relationship can be summed up in the framework of three questions.

*Has Senate-executive comity deteriorated in the recent past?* As a general proposition, it seems unlikely that Senate-executive relationships have deteriorated significantly over time. The nation's history is replete with examples of tensions between the two institutions, starting with George Washington and continuing through the decades to the present day. Of course, these relationships have been negatively affected by the modern-day prevalence of divided party control of the Senate and the executive branch over twelve of the past twenty years.

*Do current political practices threaten Senate-executive comity?* Today's senators, like politicians at all levels, seem more prone to exploiting their prerogatives toward and even beyond their formal limits in order to achieve their political objectives, or even to demonstrate to the public their willingness to do so. Thus more frequently now are filibusters threatened (and sometimes implemented), holds placed on legislative matters or nominations, and even hostage-taking, that is, using the power of chairmanship or simply the ability to impose holds as a means of halting action until one's objectives have been realized.

*What might be done to promote comity between the branches?* Some of these techniques no doubt need to be reined in. The curious practice of holds, which has drawn criticism from both inside and outside the chamber, needs further curtailment. There seems no valid reason for tolerating the practice without severe limitations: at the least, strict time limits and requirements for public disclosure. The increasingly popular tactic of hostage-taking also seems overdue for swift retirement. It escalates interbranch disputes beyond their immediate boundaries and in the process jeopardizes governmental functions unrelated to the controversy.

More fundamentally, the procedures for nominating and confirming federal officials need to be radically rethought. Both the White House and the Senate have allowed the processes to become unnecessarily lengthy and cumbersome. Everyone involved in the process needs to "back off," to reinstate simpler and less adversarial rules of the game. The risk of approving unfit nominees is now clearly outweighed by the inevitable result of discouraging qualified nominees or humiliating those who are brave enough to allow their names to be put forward. Distressingly few federal nominees are unscathed by this bizarre process. In many cases, moreover, the flaws uncovered in candidates' backgrounds are either trivial or unrelated to the jobs for which they have been nominated.

In these and other points of contact, the executive branch and Senate leaders ought to abide by mutually agreed on rules of the game. No doubt these precedents may be threatened in the heat of controversy, but their existence will provide benchmarks to which reasonable individuals may repair.

# Notes

1. Mark A. Peterson, "The President and Congress," in Michael Nelson, ed., *The Presidency and the Political System*, 5th ed. (Washington, D.C.: CQ Press, 1998).

2. Eric Uslaner, *The Decline of Comity in Congress* (University of Michigan Press, 1993).

3. Louis Fisher, *Constitutional Conflicts between Congress and the President*, 3d ed. rev. (University Press of Kansas, 1991).

4. Peterson, "The President and Congress"; and Neil A. Lewis, "Clinton Has a Chance to Shape the Courts," *New York Times*, February 9, 1997, p. 16.

5. Michael Foley and John E. Owens, *Congress and the Presidency: Institutional Politics in a Separated System* (Manchester University Press, 1996).

6. Richard F. Fenno Jr., "Senate," in Donald C. Bacon, Roger H. Davidson, and Morton Keller, eds., *The Encyclopedia of the United States Congress*, vol. 4 (New York: Simon and Schuster, 1995), 1786.

7. Ibid.; Sarah A. Binder and Steven S. Smith, *Politics or Principle? Filibustering in the United States Senate* (Brookings, 1997).

8. Barbara Sinclair, *The Transformation of the U.S. Senate* (Johns Hopkins University Press, 1989).

9. Michael Foley, *The New Senate: Liberal Influence on a Conservative Institution, 1959–1972* (Yale University Press, 1980); and Norman J. Ornstein, Robert L. Peabody, and David W. Rohde, "The Senate through the 1980s: Cycles of Change," in Lawrence C. Dodd and Bruce I. Oppenheimer, eds., *Congress Reconsidered*, 3d ed. (Washington, D.C.: CQ Press, 1985).

10. See Norman J. Ornstein, Robert L. Peabody, and David W. Rohde, "The U.S. Senate: Toward the 21st Century," in Lawrence C. Dodd and Bruce I. Oppenheimer, eds., *Congress Reconsidered*, 6th ed. (Washington, D.C.: CQ Press, 1997); Steven S. Smith, "Forces of Change in Senate Party Leadership and Organization," in Lawrence C. Dodd and Bruce I. Oppenheimer, eds., *Congress Reconsidered*, 5th ed. (Washington, D.C.: CQ Press, 1993).

11. Nicol C. Rae, *Southern Democrats* (Oxford University Press, 1994).

12. Barbara Sinclair, *Unorthodox Lawmaking* (Washington, D.C.: CQ Press, 1997).

13. Sarah A. Binder, "The Disappearing Political Center," *Brookings Review*, vol. 15 (Fall 1996), pp. 36–39.

14. Norman J. Ornstein, Thomas E. Mann, and Michael J. Malbin, *Vital Statistics on Congress 1999–2000* (Washington, D.C.: American Enterprise Institute, 2000), p. 201.

15. Peterson, "The President and Congress," p. 494.

16. Ornstein, Mann, and Malbin, *Vital Statistics on Congress 1999–2000*, p. 191.

17. Ibid., p. 192.

18. Kenneth R. Bowling and Helen E. Veit, eds., *Documentary History of the First Federal Congress of the United States of America*, vol. 9: *The Diary of William Maclay and Other Notes on Senate Debates, 4 March 1789–3 March 1791* (Johns Hopkins University Press, 1989), pp. 128–31.

19. Thomas A. Bailey, *Woodrow Wilson and the Great Betrayal* (New York: Macmillan, 1945), p. 74.

20. Quoted in Max Farrand, ed., *The Records of the Federal Convention of 1787*, vol. 1 (Yale University Press, 1966), p. 21.

21. *Federalist* No. 76.

22. Robert A. Katzmann, *Courts and Congress* (Brookings, 1997).

23. John O. McGinnis, "The President, the Senate, the Constitution, and the Confirmation Process: A Reply to Professors Strauss and Sunstein," *Texas Law Review*, vol. 71 (February 1993), pp. 633–67.

24. See David A. Strauss and Cass R. Sunstein, "The Senate, the Constitution, and the Confirmation Process," *Yale Law Journal*, vol. 101 (May 1992), p. 1491; and Charles L. Black Jr., "A Note on Senatorial Consideration of Supreme Court Nominees," *Yale Law Journal*, vol. 79 (March 1970), p. 657.

25. Harold W. Stanley and Richard G. Niemi, *Vital Statistics on American Politics*, 6th ed. (Washington, D.C.: Congressional Quarterly, Inc., 1997), pp. 224–25.

26. Fisher, *Constitutional Conflicts between Congress and the President*; and Rogelio Garcia, *Cabinet and Other High Level Nominations That Failed to Be Confirmed, 1789–1989*, Congressional Research Service Report 89-253GOV (April 14, 1989).

27. Katzmann, *Courts and Congress*, p. 18.

28. G. Calvin Mackenzie, "The Presidential Appointment Process: Historical Development, Contemporary Operations, Current Issues," in *Obstacle Course: The Report of the Twentieth Century Fund Task Force on the Presidential Appointment Process* (New York: Twentieth Century Fund Press, 1996), p. 37.

29. Katzmann, *Courts and Congress*, p. 19.

30. Ibid.

31. G. Calvin Mackenzie, *The Politics of Presidential Appointments* (New York: Free Press, 1981), p. 186.

32. Katzmann, *Courts and Congress*, p. 12.

33. Glen S. Krutz, Richard Fleisher, and Jon Bond, "From Abe Fortas to Zoe Baird: Why Some Presidential Nominations Fail in the Senate," *American Political Science Review*, vol. 92 (December 1998), pp. 871–81.

34. Rogelio Garcia, *Cabinet and Other High Level Nominations*.

35. Rogelio Garcia, *Filling Policy Positions in Executive Departments: Average Time Required Through Confirmation, 1981–1993*, Congressional Research Service Report 98-641GOV (July 28, 1998).

36. Morton Rosenberg, *The New Vacancies Act: Congress Acts to Protect the Senate's Confirmation Prerogative*, Congressional Research Service Report 98-892A (November 2, 1998).

37. Ibid.

38. *Congressional Record* (105 Cong. 2 sess.), June 16, 1998, pt. 1 of 2, S6414.

39. Jonathan Sanford, *Senate Disposition of Ambassadorial Nominations, 1987–1996*, Congressional Research Service Report 97-864F (September 19, 1997).

40. John Bresnahan, "Holds Threaten Senate Agenda," *Roll Call*, June 10, 1999, pp. 1, 30.

41. Ibid.

42. Katzmann, *Courts and Congress*, p. 12.

43. Mark Silverstein, *Judicious Choices: The New Politics of Supreme Court Confirmations* (New York: W. W. Norton, 1994), p. 4.

44. Denis Steven Rutkus, *Senate Judiciary Committee Consideration of Supreme Court Nominations*, Congressional Research Service Report 94-479GOV (June 6, 1994).

45. Denis Steven Rutkus, *The Supreme Court Appointment Process*, Congressional Research Service Report 93-290 (March 4, 1993).

46. Rutkus, *Senate Judiciary Committee Consideration of Supreme Court Nominations*.

47. See Kurtz, Fleisher, and Bond, "From Abe Fortas to Zoe Baird"; and Rutkus, *Senate Judiciary Committee Consideration of Supreme Court Nominations*.

48. Rutkus, *Senate Judiciary Committee Considerations of Supreme Court Nominations*.

49. *Congressional Record* 138 (102 Cong. 2 sess.), June 25, 1992, S8866.

50. Joan Biskupic, "Orrin Hatch's Judgment Call," *Washington Post National Weekly Edition*, June 14, 1999, p. 12.

51. Quoted in ibid.

52. Neil A. Lewis, "Clinton Critic Is Key to Deal to End Tie-up on Judgeships," *New York Times*, July 3, 1999, p. A8.

53. John Stuart Mill, *Considerations on Representative Government* (London, 1861), p. 104.

54. Woodrow Wilson, *Congressional Government* (New York: Meridian Books, 1956), p. 297.

55. Congressional Research Service, *Congressional Oversight Manual*, Report RL30240 (June 25, 1999).

56. *Federalist* No. 65, p. 331.

57. U.S. Senate Historical Office, *The Senate's Impeachment Role*, Senate Briefings No. 6 (April 1998), p. 2.

58. *Federalist* No. 65.

59. *Nixon v. United States*, 506 U.S. 224, 1993.

60. George Mason, quoted in Max Farrand, ed., *The Records of the Federal Convention* (Yale University Press, 1913), vol. 2, p. 550.

61. *Federalist* No. 65.

# PART IV
## *Civility and Deliberation in Practice*

# CHAPTER TEN

# Civility, Deliberation, and Impeachment

## NORMAN J. ORNSTEIN

ON DECEMBER 19, 1998, House Minority Leader Richard Gephardt (D-Mo.) took to the floor of the House of Representatives, soon after Representative Bob Livingston (R-La.) had announced his intention to resign from the House before his impending election as Speaker of the House, and just before the House was prepared to vote for articles of impeachment of the president of the United States. Gephardt implored the House to "turn away from the politics of personal destruction and return to a politics of values." He said, "Bob Livingston is a worthy and honorable man . . . his decision to resign is a terrible capitulation to the negative forces that are consuming our political system and our country." He suggested, "We need to start healing."

Gephardt received a rousing, bipartisan ovation from his colleagues for his stirring words. But that ovation was one of precious few bipartisan moments in months of give-and-take in the House over the hyperdivisive issue of impeachment of a president.

## Conduct of the House and Senate

The process did start with at least a brief opening and hopeful sign for bipartisanship and civil discourse. On September 9, 1998, the day that Independent Counsel Kenneth Starr delivered the now-infamous boxes of materials to the House of Representatives, Judiciary Committee Chairman Henry Hyde issued a press release saying:

The solemn duty that confronts us requires that we attain a heroic level of bipartisanship and that we conduct our deliberations in a fair, full and independent manner.

Because of that requirement, let me say first that I intend to work closely with my Democratic colleagues on the Committee, and in particular, the Ranking Member of the Committee, John Conyers.

The American people deserve a competent, independent, and bipartisan review of the Independent Counsel's report. They must have confidence in this process. Politics must be checked at the door, party affiliation must be secondary, and America's future must become our only concern. I will not condone, nor participate in, a political witch-hunt. If the evidence does not justify a full impeachment investigation, I will not recommend one to the House. However, if the evidence does justify an inquiry, I will fulfill my oath of office and recommend a fuller inquiry.[1]

Hyde's call for bipartisanship continued that week, at least on the surface, with an overwhelming bipartisan vote of 363–63 in the House on September 11 to authorize an initial inquiry based on the Starr referral, and to release the bulk of the referral directly to the public by September 28. However, the huge margin obscured the fact that the 63 negative votes were almost all cast by Democrats, who blasted the plan to release embarrassing information, including raw files and grand jury material, without any serious vetting by the House itself. Within another week, the public tone in the House had changed, precipitated by the Republicans' strategy to short-circuit their own expedited plan to release the Starr documents by releasing even earlier the videotape of the president's grand jury testimony. On September 18, Minority Leader Gephardt stated:

At the heart of bipartisanship lies compromise. The spirit of bipartisanship cannot be "alive and flourishing" as Chairman Hyde has claimed, when party line votes decide issues of disagreement between the parties.

It is increasingly clear that the Republicans have absolutely no intention of conducting this investigation under the bipartisan principles that the Watergate investigation followed. In order to successfully carry out our constitutional duties, fairness must be our sole motivating principle. That principle did not guide Republicans in the Judiciary Committee today.[2]

Five days later, Chairman Hyde responded in kind to Gephardt:

The Democrats' mixed messages are thoroughly confusing and reveal a disturbing pattern:

On the one hand, they want an expeditious process, on the other hand they attacked us last week for moving too quickly.

On the one hand, they say we have all the materials we need to wrap this up in 30 days. On the other hand, they say we need more materials from the Independent Counsel's office before we can fairly resolve this matter.

On the one hand, they say we should follow the Watergate precedent (which took 9 months to do its work.) On the other hand, they want a timetable which was specifically considered and rejected by the House in 1974.[3]

Two weeks later, after two testy days of debate and votes, the House Judiciary Committee voted along party lines to authorize a full impeachment inquiry. The committee in the process rejected, on a strict party-line vote, proposals by the committee Democrats calling for a specific timetable and a debate on the meaning of "high crimes and misdemeanors" before the committee considered any of the specific evidence in the Starr referral. During the committee debate, Ranking Democrat John Conyers tried to praise Chairman Hyde while also separating him from his own party leaders and ideologues:

Mr. Chairman, over the past few weeks, you and I have worked together more closely than at any other time in our long careers, and I want to thank you for the many untold efforts you have made, including providing Committee Democrats the Watergate rules of operation which we sought. We have worked in a bipartisan matter on some of the issues that have confronted us, while your hands have been tied by your leadership on others. You know as well as I that whatever action the Committee takes must be fair and bipartisan for it to have any credibility. The American people deserve no less, and history will judge us by how well we achieve that goal.

Hyde did not view Conyers's comments as a compliment, and the attitude of the more ideological Republicans toward the Democrats' professed olive branches was reflected by Republican Bob Barr of Georgia: "Anyone who has made it their goal to hide the truth, obstruct this process or use it for political gain, should summon up whatever tattered remains of honor they have left, stand up, and walk out of this room." Referring to the Framers, American soldiers, teachers who have led their classes in the Pledge of Allegiance, and other noble Americans, Barr added, "Could you look into those faces, and tell them it really doesn't matter that the President abused his power, lied to the American people, perjured himself, and subverted the rule of law? Anyone who can answer yes to that question doesn't have the right to sit here today."

Less than a month before the 1998 elections, the full House took up the Judiciary Committee resolution. By a 258–176 vote, with 28 Democrats joining the Republicans, the House voted on October 8 to begin an impeachment inquiry. A statement from Minority Leader Gephardt that day established the tone: "Our problem is we don't trust each other."

A few days after the election, on November 9, the Judiciary Committee began preparations to hear witnesses pursuant to the impeachment resolution. On November 11, Democrats John Conyers and Robert Scott, the ranking minority member of the Subcommittee on the Constitution, sent a letter to Chairman Hyde that began, "On November 3rd, the American people sent a clear signal that it is long past time for this Committee to end its impeachment inquiry." Conyers and Scott then requested that Hyde hold a hearing, before calling any witnesses, on the standards of impeachment, and whether any of the allegations against President Clinton met those standards.

Hyde replied the next day: "It appears that you have already made up your mind and that you believe a rush to judgment is appropriate without any airing of the facts or thoughtful consideration of the evidence." He went on, "In your letter, you seem inclined to view this impeachment inquiry in any context except a factual one."

Through November and into December, hearings and deliberations continued, and partisan tensions increased. In mid-December, the Judiciary Committee took up debate of proposed articles of impeachment. With television cameras present, the public rhetoric tended to be relatively mild, although the rancor between the parties was barely contained. The most unrestrained Democrat, Representative Maxine Waters of California expressed that rancor more directly: "The impeachment tyranny by the right ignores the most profound document of our society, the Constitution of the United States. . . . This right-wing-driven assault on our Constitution poses a clear and real danger to our future. If the architects of this anarchy win, we surely place the rights of all American citizens at risk."

On party-line votes, the Judiciary Committee adopted four articles of impeachment on December 14. On December 16, former Senate majority leader George Mitchell (D-Maine) wrote in the *New York Times*, "Unfortunately, the hearings were more ferociously partisan than anything I have seen in nearly 25 years in Washington."[4]

The full House adopted two of those articles on December 19. Excerpts from minority members on the House floor that day reflect their general attitude: "totally misrepresented" (Martin Meehan, D-Mass.); "repeatedly saying an untruth doesn't make it true" (Jerry Nadler, D-N.Y.); "Spanish Inquisition," "Nazi Germany," "Gestapo tactics," "McCarthyism" (Bobby Rush, D-Ill.); "coup d'état" (John Conyers, D-Mich.); "a lynching" (Danny Davis, D-Ill.). Said Rep. Charles Rangel (D-N.Y.), "Friendships have been lost in the House today." He added, "There is a cloud on the House and I don't see how after the vote that suddenly the doors will be open." Minority Leader Gephardt said in his floor statement on the resolution to impeach the president, "the most important act" the Constitution asks the Senate to perform:

> The events of the last days sadden me. We are now at the height of a cycle of the politics of negative attacks, character assassination, personal smears of good people, decent people, worthy people. . . .
>
> We are deeply offended by the unfairness of this process. . . . You are doing this in a way that denies millions of Americans the trust and respect for our views that we afford to you.[5]

When a large group of combative House Democrats gathered with the president on the White House lawn after the House impeachment votes, it infuriated Republicans and underscored yet again the deeply divisive, even corrosive atmosphere that had pervaded the House.

On January 4, 1999, after a three-week holiday hiatus, Congress returned to the "shadow cast by impeachment" as the action shifted to the Senate. Majority Leader Trent Lott (R-Miss.) and Minority Leader Tom Daschle (D-S.Dak.) worked hard "to forge a compromise that would end a trial quickly and without witnesses." Mr. Lott tried "to weave a path between his party's moderates and conservatives [and] persuade enough Republicans on the bipartisan proposal by Senators Gorton and Lieberman to have an expedited trial with no witnesses."[6]

Over the break, moderate Democrat Joseph Lieberman (Conn.) and conservative Republican Slade Gorton (Wash.) talked regularly to try to find a bipartisan way to move the Senate quickly and without acrimony through an impeachment trial. Lieberman was known as a conciliator, one comfortable working with colleagues on the other side of the aisle. Gorton was more pugnacious. But the two were close friends through their years in the Senate, and they both believed the trial would end in acquittal for the president since there was little prospect for the higher Senate threshold of sixty-seven votes for impeachment being met.

The basic Gorton-Lieberman plan was to allow the prosecutors from the House of Representatives a day to make the case for the conviction and removal from office of the president. Then, the White House would have a day to make its defense. On the third day, senators would forward questions to each side. On the fourth day, the Senate would take a "test vote" on whether the articles of impeachment, *if proved,* rose to a level requiring removal from office. If the test vote did not produce sixty-seven votes in favor, the trial would be short-circuited, and the Senate would move to a consideration of censure of the president.

Underlying the plan was a fear of what would happen in the Senate if the impeachment debate dragged on for weeks or months. Lieberman said the Senate had "a very short window here to try to work out a procedure for this trial," adding, "If we don't we are going to descend, I fear, to the kind of partisan rancor that characterized the House proceeding."[7]

By most accounts, the Gorton-Lieberman plan, or some variation, had strong majority support in the Senate, starting with nearly all the Democrats. The majority Republicans were a different story. The plan was strenuously opposed by the House impeachment managers and did not reach consensus-level support among GOP senators. For Majority Leader Trent Lott, the choice on how to proceed was a difficult one. He decided to leave the decision to a caucus of his Republican colleagues, where opposition to proceeding without witnesses was evident among such senators as Phil Gramm (R-Tex.) and Arlen Specter (R-Pa.).

When it became clear that Republicans would not embrace the Gorton-Lieberman plan, a variety of options arose, most divided sharply along partisan lines, creating the prospect of a protracted partisan battle in the Senate. On January 7, the Senate tentatively scheduled votes on competing Democratic and Republican plans. But both Senate party leaders expressed openly their desire to avoid that outcome. Instead, they arranged a virtually unprecedented bipartisan Senate caucus for January 8 in the Old Senate Chamber, a ceremonial room in the Capitol that had served as the Senate chamber between 1810 and 1859.

At the bipartisan caucus, described by a range of senators as "extraordinary," Senator Chris Dodd (D-Conn.) reminded his colleagues that "one of the saddest moments in Senate history," the vicious caning of Senator Charles Sumner (Mass.) by Representative Preston Brooks (S.C.), had taken place in the historic room in which they were meeting. "Many historians feel that was when the comity of the Senate broke down, leading three and a half years later to the commencement of the Civil War," he added later.[8]

The feeling that the trial was a test for the Senate as an institution was widespread. Said Patrick Leahy (D-Vt.), "We have to preserve the Senate and give the country a sense of credibility." Added Mitch McConnell (R-Ky.), "I think there is a feeling in this situation that the Senate is on trial."[9]

The unanimous vote came for a plan initiated by an "odd couple," Republican Phil Gramm of Texas and Democrat Edward M. Kennedy of Massachusetts. Gramm and Kennedy spoke back-to-back in the caucus, agreeing with each other in basic principles, and their effort to strike a balance led in turn to a bipartisan negotiation. The plan accepted by the senators had deliberations beginning on January 13 with argument on procedural pretrial motions. That was to be followed by twenty-four hours in which the House was to present its case against the president, and another twenty-four hours in which the White House team was to present its case. Neither side would be allowed to present new evidence unrelated to the impeachment record presented in the House.

Those deliberations would be followed by debate and a vote on two motions, one to adjourn the trial and a second to call witnesses, each resolved by simple majority votes. If witnesses were accepted, they would first be questioned in depositions, with a second majority vote required to have testimony in front of the full Senate, for each potential witness.

Each side made significant concessions in the compromise. Many Republicans had wanted witnesses to kick off the trial, and House Republican managers wanted to include evidence of an uncorroborated allegation of a sexual encounter between the president and an Arkansas woman many years earlier, information that the managers had informally shared with several House colleagues as they lobbied for votes on the articles of impeachment in December. Democrats had insisted on no witnesses. Throughout their brokering, "Senators held to the idea that the impeachment trial was a historic moment for the Senate and that they had to rise to the occasion."[10]

If the process looked like a model of comity and bipartisanship on January 9 and 10, it did not stay that way. On January 14, before the opening arguments on the Senate floor, a story emerged that Republican senators had met secretly with House managers about witnesses, including the possibility, raised by Henry Hyde, of calling the president. Senate Majority Leader Trent Lott had quietly appointed three Republican senators, all of whom favored calling witnesses—John Kyl (Ariz.,) Jeff Sessions (Ala.) and Arlen Specter (Pa.)—to work with Hyde and other House managers.

When the story emerged, Senator Lott belatedly invited Senate Democrats to the meeting, an offer rejected by Minority Leader Tom Daschle as a breach of the overall bipartisan agreement to put off the question of witnesses.[11] As Senate deliberations began and Hyde mused publicly about calling the president as a witness, Senator Paul Wellstone (D-Minn.) said, "I'm fairly certain this won't be a bipartisan agreement. . . . This will be the point at which there is a parting of the ways. There's no question about it."[12]

Despite the strains, there was no parting of the ways. Deliberations continued through mid-January. On January 23 and 24, the Senate asked questions of both sides and privately agreed to allow three witnesses to be deposed. Sidney Blumenthal, Monica Lewinsky, and Vernon Jordan were subsequently deposed, and on February 4, by unanimous consent, the Senate put the three depositions in the record.

There were still strains, including the major question of whether and when the Senate would allow a vote on censure if conviction failed. But a compromise was achieved by unanimous consent to allow a motion by Senator Dianne Feinstein (D-Calif.) after the votes on the impeachment articles, but with the likelihood that any direct vote on the motion would take place only after a two-week recess.

On February 12, the Senate voted on the two articles. By a vote of fifty guilty, fifty not guilty, with five Republicans joining all forty-five Democrats on the not guilty side, the Senate rejected Article II, obstruction of justice. By a vote of forty-five guilty, fifty-five not guilty, with ten Republicans joining all forty-five Democrats, the Senate rejected Article I, on perjury before the grand jury. Afterward, Senate Minority Leader Tom Daschle issued a statement in which he said, "I believe that during this trial, the Senate fully and faithfully protected the Constitution and allowed both sides a fair opportunity to make their case."

## Why the Chambers Responded Differently

This brief narrative suggests a stark contrast between the House and the Senate in the conduct of the most serious and consequential matter each body considered in the 105th Congress, being "much harsher in the House than in the Senate, where it's layered over by a veneer of civility."[13] A slightly different reaction emerged from House Judiciary Committee Chairman Henry Hyde after losing the votes in the Senate: "If I have to criticize Senators, Republican senators, which I'm loath to do, they do make bipartisanship the ultimate ethic over there. The genuflection to bipartisanship has a certain ring of civility to it, but it means one side is disadvantaged, and we were."[14]

The stress of a presidential impeachment on a legislative institution is almost unimaginably high. The stakes are enormous, not just for the president and the Constitution, but for the reputation of the legislature and its members, the careers of the individual lawmakers, and party control of the chamber. The pressure to descend into bitter partisan acrimony is great and ever present. Clearly, in this case, both houses felt that pressure. So why, in a matter of such weight and significance, did one institution respond by unleashing all the partisan pit bulls and ending on the sourest of internal notes, while the other pulled back from the abyss and united across party lines in its institutional response?

As visitors to the Capitol often notice, a striking difference between the two chambers is "the apparent confusion and impersonality in the House chamber as contrasted with the relatively more informal and friendly atmosphere in the Senate."[15] In addition, House leaders appear to be more isolated from their colleagues, and there is "greater friction and more frequent violations of the spirit of comity in the House than in the Senate."[16]

Indeed, in many ways the Senate is different from the House. It is smaller, less formal, less hierarchical, more flexible in its rules, more deliberate in its actions, more personal, and more prestigious. Senators tend to know one another and see one another more regularly, creating interpersonal relationships across party lines. This makes it harder to demonize colleagues on the other side.

The informal, individualized rules in the Senate mean that every senator has some power over the agenda and the outcomes. The tradition of unlimited debate and the rules allowing filibusters underscore the power of the individuals but also make simple majorities less meaningful in the Senate. It takes sixty votes to do anything highly controversial. Since it is rare to find a party with sixty or more seats in the Senate, much important action requires by definition bipartisan supermajorities. This affects the mind-set of senators and their leaders; they have to deal on a daily or regular basis with members on the other side of the aisle, frequently converting today's adversaries into tomorrow's allies. The culture of the body, shaped by its greater prestige, tends to inculcate in members a sense of institutional loyalty.

That phenomenon has a particular resonance when it comes to impeachment. The House passed articles of impeachment by simple majority votes. It was theoretically possible for a pure partisan majority to impeach the president, and the actual result was not far from that. But it required a two-thirds vote in the Senate to convict. No conviction was possible without a significant number of members from the president's party. A strictly partisan vote in the House meant that, despite criticism and a heavy price, the majority could achieve its partisan goals. A strictly partisan vote in the Senate, on the other hand, would mean failure, added on to the costs of divisiveness.

The features above are enduring institutional factors. They are supplemented or influenced by more short-term trends. One is the seniority—or juniority—of membership. While both bodies have seen substantial turnover in the past decade, the Senate retains a larger core of more senior members, who represent the institutional memory and carry the institutional torch. In the 105th Congress, only 13 percent of House members had served twenty years or more, whereas 23 percent of the Senate had served comparable periods; and 56 percent of the 105th House had served six years or less compared with 40 percent of the Senate. Significant numbers of newer House members have limited their own terms to three or less, giving them little stake or interest in the underlying strength of their own institution. Several senior senators—most notably, Robert Byrd (D-W.Va.) but including Edward Kennedy (D-Mass.), Orrin Hatch (R-Utah), Pete Domenici (R-N.Mex.), and Richard Lugar (R-Ind.)—are highly institutionally minded and view themselves as keepers of the Senate torch.

The position of senator carries prestige and heft in itself, making majority or minority status less significant than in the House. But that fact has been reinforced by recent electoral patterns. Party control in the Senate shifted from Democrat to Republican in 1980, shifted back to the Democrats in 1986, and then reverted to the GOP in 1994. Thus the vast majority of senators in 1999 had served significant periods both in the majority and in the minority. All things being equal, each senator preferred the majority but understood the perspective of the other side, and lived quite comfortably in the minority. When party control shifted, the new majority was less able—and less willing—to stiff the other side in terms of staff, committee slots, or the rights to offer amendments and play a serious legislative role than in the House. Thus there was no deeper resentment, leading to no vow to do the same and more when the worm turned.

The House Democrats, on the other hand, had maintained a hammerlock on the majority for forty consecutive years. When Republicans took the majority in 1994, there was not a single Republican who had *ever* been in the House majority as a Republican, and only a single Democrat (Sidney Yates) who had ever been in the minority as a Democrat! Perpetual minority status had built in a disdain for the Democrats and a lack of loyalty to the House in many Republicans, regardless of ideology, even as it inculcated a smugness and condescension toward Republicans among Democrats.

Republicans publicly vowed when they took the majority that they would not be like the Democrats, that they would be fair and open. But the Republican majority began with the partisan drive to pass the Contract with America, and Republicans used every tool Democrats had to preserve partisan advantage. A few years of powerlessness in the minority had created among the Democrats a frustrated, seething unhappiness which they blamed on the nouveau riche Republican majority.

Ideologically, both houses had moved from classic "normal" distributions toward more bipolar distributions as more moderate members left and more ideologically driven members arrived. But the phenomenon was much more pronounced in the House than in the Senate. At least a third of Senate Republicans, including a higher proportion of more senior members, could easily be classified as moderate. The same categorization might apply to perhaps 10 to 15 percent of the Republicans in the House.

But if institutional differences and political trends have reinforced differences in culture between the House and the Senate, they did not mean inexorably that the House would dissolve into corrosive and bitter partisanship on impeachment, and the Senate rebound to bipartisan cooperation. The answer is not simply rooted in the deeper political culture, or the endemic responses of one house compared with the other. The 105th House of Representatives ended with the impeachment of the president. But it began with the ethics investigation of its own Speaker, Newt Gingrich, in a case with many fascinating parallels.[17] Speaker Gingrich had been charged with serious ethics violations, including willful violations of tax laws and repeated lying to House Ethics Committee investigators. He was teetering on the brink of disaster. It was not clear that he had the votes inside his own Republican caucus to continue as Speaker. He faced a possible censure, the equivalent for a member of Congress of an impeachment vote in the House, and an action unprecedented against a Speaker. Partisan tensions were at a peak.

On the House Ethics Committee, the relations between Chair Nancy Johnson (R-Conn.) and Ranking Minority Member Jim McDermott (D-Wash.) could only be described as poisonous. Democrats, armed with evidence from an illegal tape, accused Republican leaders like Tom DeLay of illegitimate pressure on Ethics Committee members and rank-and-file GOPers: obstruction of justice, in other words. Republicans charged McDermott with illegal manipulation of the intercepted cell phone conversation between Gingrich and other Republican leaders. While Republicans had a narrow majority in the House and might prevail in a showdown, it was clear that a purely partisan vote on censure for the Speaker would result in deep and lasting damage to the institution of the House and to any hopes for comity.

The tension was exquisite for weeks. But in the end, the House was able to vote in an overwhelmingly bipartisan fashion for a measured punishment for Newt Gingrich—a "rebuke," short of a censure, along with a $300,000 fine—that left the credibility of the institution intact and a widespread sense that justice had been served.

Why was the House—the same House—able to navigate through the treacherous shoals of the Gingrich case and emerge with bipartisan honor intact, while falling apart two years later on the Clinton case? There are three major reasons.

First, despite a weak chair and the impossible relationship between Nancy Johnson and Jim McDermott, the Ethics Committee saw that it *had* to find a bipartisan process to overcome the divisions. So the Ethics Committee created a subcommittee to conduct the Gingrich investigation. Four members with integrity and sensitivity, Republicans Steve Schiff (N.Mex.) and Porter Goss (Fla.) and Democrats Ben Cardin (Md.) and Nancy Pelosi (Calif.), were given the responsibility. Second, they worked with an independent counsel hired by the committee, Jim Cole, who had a mix of toughness, integrity, experience, fairness, and restraint. And third, they did their investigation quietly and privately, not releasing any documents or evidence to the public, but working behind closed doors together to evaluate the evidence and reach for consensus and compromise around a measured conclusion.

It would have been easy for the subcommittee Democrats to conclude that Gingrich had broken or evaded tax laws and lied repeatedly to the committee, justifying censure or expulsion; just as easy for the Republicans to argue that he had not lied, or if he had it was only technical, and in any case the offenses did not rise to the level of any serious punishment. But working with a nonpartisan counsel, they all decided not to push the charges of lying to the limit, or to deny clear-cut violations. They searched for a punishment they felt would be appropriate and balanced. Only after they had done their investigation and reached their bipartisan conclusion was the full committee convened, in public, to hear from Gingrich's lawyers and Cole.

At that hearing, all the parties rose to the occasion. Johnson presided in a fair and dignified manner. The four subcommittee members were superb. Cole was restrained and careful, laying out facts and conclusions without editorializing or lecturing the members. The committee's vote was thoroughly bipartisan. The only dissonant note came when a late addition to the committee, Republican Lamar Smith of Texas, dissented from the consensus.

Contrast all that with the House Judiciary Committee on impeachment. There was no bipartisan subgroup created, no effort by the committee chair Henry Hyde to bend over backwards to try a bipartisan approach to investigation or conclusion. The independent counsel Ken Starr had no aura of objectivity or fairness. The committee counsel, David Schippers, was in every important particular the opposite of Jim Cole: egotistical, opinionated, unrestrained, openly hostile to the Democrats on his committee, openly partisan in his allegations and conclusions. The committee's open deliberations had been preceded by the House releasing to the public the mass of materials in Ken Starr's referral, before most of the members had examined it themselves, including the unilateral premature release by the majority of the videotape of President Clinton's grand jury testimony. There was no opportunity to examine the evidence or work out any bipartisan approach outside of public view or away from partisan activist pressure. The die was cast before the committee itself met.

Individuals and individual decisions matter. Had Henry Hyde early on appointed a subcommittee consisting, say, of two Republicans and two Democrats, avoiding the more fiery and divisive personalities like Bob Barr or Maxine Waters, and told them not to come back until they had achieved a consensus on an approach to impeachment, we would likely have seen an outcome closer to the Gingrich one than the ultimate Clinton one. The choice by Hyde of David Schippers as his chief counsel had as much to do with the acrimony and the outcome as anything else. Had a Jim Cole been the chief staffer, the whole dynamic would have changed on the committee.

The role of Schippers was underscored in a remarkable interview he conducted in May 1999 with the ultraconservative newspaper *Human Events*. Schippers called the Senate process "a rigged ball game" and condemned roundly every senator who voted against impeachment and all the Senate Republican leaders. He emphasized the extent to which he tried to influence the votes of House members by giving them access to evidence that was not part of the official impeachment record or the articles. He said that if he had had more time, he would have subpoenaed "John Huang. I'd subpoena some people in the White House. I'd subpoena people in Little Rock. I'd subpoena a lot of lawyers. There's an awful lot of places to go." He stressed, "I would play hardball like nobody's ever played hardball. I already have and got nowhere."[18] It is hard to imagine another committee staffer with so much hubris and disdain for elected officials, but his aggressiveness and attitude clearly influenced the Judiciary Committee, and the whole House.

There is no reason to believe that Henry Hyde chose David Schippers, a longtime acquaintance from Chicago, deliberately to create a divisive outcome or to ensure an impeachment of the president on partisan lines. Nor is there any evidence that Republican congressional leaders or Judiciary Committee members came to contrary conclusions and were dragged to the outcome that emerged. But if there had been a determination from the beginning that a bipartisan process, and consensus outcome, were necessary, the chances are that Schippers would have been pushed aside or never hired, that a subcommittee would have been created, and a different outcome would have ensued.

Other circumstances contributed to the different House dynamic on impeachment. The desire for a negotiated, bipartisan outcome was greater among House Republicans when the target was their own leader than when it was the leader of the Democrats. Many House Democrats viscerally wanted Newt Gingrich's head as a fitting quid pro quo for the forced resignation, nearly a decade earlier, of Speaker Jim Wright. But other Democrats saw a deal that would keep a wounded and somewhat discredited Gingrich in charge as reasonable. And, just as significantly, Democrats, most of whom had spent most of their House careers in the majority defending the sanctity of the House, saw a bipartisan resolution of a difficult ethics matter as the best outcome for the House. That was particularly true of opinion leaders like Ethics Committee members Ben Cardin (D-Md.) and Nancy Pelosi (D-Calif.) and Minority Leader Dick Gephardt.

When impeachment arose, House Republicans, most of whom had spent most of their House careers in the minority excoriating their institution, did not think reflexively of its institutional character in their decision-making. And they were faced with weak leadership, in total turmoil. The 1998 election had resulted in an embarrassing setback for the Republicans: they became only the second nonpresidential party since the Civil War to lose seats in a midterm election. Conventional wisdom had been that a Democratic gain in the House would ensure no impeachment of the president. But in fact, the Democratic gain infuriated the conservative wing of the GOP, caused the forced departure of Speaker Newt Gingrich and challenges to other leaders, and left a weak and uncertain leadership unable to resist the demands of conservatives not to sell out on impeachment.

The Senate elections also proved to be a major disappointment for Republicans: expected gains of five or six seats turned into no gains at all. But there was no challenge to Majority Leader Trent Lott, and a challenge to Senate Campaign Chairman Mitch McConnell (R-Ky.) was turned aside easily. Lott thus started out in a somewhat stronger position, and early on made a determination as impeachment reached the Senate to avoid the kinds of circumstances or dynamics that would have created more division and partisanship. To be sure, Lott was not a particularly strong or persuasive leader and served in an institution where strong leadership is not a given. And he did not jump quickly to fill the vacuum in December, to set rules in place before the Senate came back to convene formally on the impeachment trial. But he gave a green light to others, such as Gorton and Lieberman, then Gramm and Kennedy, to seek a bipartisan process, and when the consensus was threatened, he worked with Minority Leader Tom Daschle to move things back on course. He was also assisted greatly by the desire on the part of individual senators to give him some slack to find ways to reach some consensus, a desire influenced by the outcome in the House, one widely seen as embarrassing and damaging to the reputation of the House as an institution.

## Are the Differences Enduring?

The idea of enduring differences on matters such as comity and institutional patriotism between the House and Senate goes back at least to the 1960s and is now back with the differences on the handling of impeachment. But in between, the two houses were seen in another light. Analyst Eric Uslaner found the decline in comity from the 1970s on present in equal measure in both houses. He quoted Arlen Specter (R-Pa.) in the *Congressional Record* in 1988: "In a sense, the Senate is disintegrated or has disintegrated, because without comity and courtesy the United States

Senate simply cannot function and that is our status today." He noted that Senators Nancy Landon Kassebaum and Gary Hart had written op-ed pieces lamenting the decline in comity in the Senate, joining House Republican Leader Robert Michel in that regard.[19] He quoted Senator Joseph Biden (D-Del.) in 1982: "There's much less civility than when I came here ten years ago. There aren't as many nice people as there were before . . . ten years ago, you didn't have people calling each other sons of bitches and vowing to get each other."[20]

In some respects, indeed, Uslaner focused more on the Senate than the House. After quoting Biden and reinforcing it with a subsequent observation, four years later, by Senator Bob Packwood (R-Ore.), Uslaner notes, "Trust is in short supply in the House as well."

Of course, Uslaner's thesis dealt with the broader culture and its impact on Congress, not on the differential impact on the House and the Senate. I had suggested back in 1981 that the two houses were converging in their behaviors and roles compared with the 1960s, and that this was leading to more identity confusion, but also to more rancor and less comity generally, as both houses decentralized and democratized. The negative observations by the range of eighties-vintage senators above cited by Uslaner reflect that position.

There *are* enduring structural, political, and normative differences between the House and Senate. Those differences are reflected in more than the impeachment imbroglio. When Congress clashed with the president in April and May of 1999 over policy in Kosovo, the House took a sharply partisan turn, as Speaker Dennis Hastert explicitly rejected an overture from Minority Leader Gephardt to work out a bipartisan position, while Senate Majority Leader Trent Lott agreed to work with Minority Leader Tom Daschle and Republican Senator John McCain to try to devise a bipartisan agreement.[21]

But there are also indicators that Uslaner's basic thesis holds: that the overall culture generally, and the political culture specifically, are influencing both houses of Congress, and that comity overall continues to decline. One major reason in the Senate is the influx in the past few years of hard-charging, antipolitical renegades, especially some members of the class of 1994 who had previously served in the minority in the House.

Rick Santorum (R-Pa.) for example, in his first three months in the Senate, led an effort to strip Senator Mark Hatfield (R-Ore.) of his chairmanship of the Senate Appropriations Committee to punish Hatfield for his vote against a constitutional amendment to balance the budget. The effort failed, but Santorum said his intention was to "send a shot across the bow to the leaders of this conference . . . and it better be received."[22] The effort led Teresa Heinz, widow of Senator John Heinz (R-Pa.) to describe Santorum as part of a "worrisome breed" of politicians who "mock, belittle and vilify those who disagree with him."[23]

Later in his first year, Santorum's conduct led the Senate's senior Democrat, Robert Byrd of West Virginia, to take to the floor and make an extraordinary speech, in which he referred to Santorum in the following way:

> Another Senator, who is very new around here, made the statement—and I quote from last Friday's Record: "This President just does not know how to tell the truth anymore," and then accused the President of stating to "the American public—bald-faced untruths." The Senator went on to say that, "we are tired of stomaching untruths over here. We are downright getting angry over here"—the Senator was speaking from the other side of the aisle. Then he proceeded to accuse the President—"and many Senators"—of making statements that tax cuts have been targeted for the wealthy, "when they know that is a lie.". . .
>
> Mr. President, such statements are harsh and severe, to say the least. And when made by a senator who has not yet held the office of Senator a full year, they are really quite astonishing. In my 37 years in this Senate, I do not recall such insolence, and it is very sad that debate and discourse on the Senate floor have sunk to such a low level.[24]

Santorum is not alone; nor is he the first brash freshman willing to challenge his elders. But his early approach to legislative compromise, and his lack of interest in his institution's history and traditions, are becoming more, rather than less common. As long as the Senate is compared to the House, it will not be hard to look more civil and less corrosively partisan. But impeachment, a high-water mark in the Senate's approach to institutional integrity in recent years, may be met with fewer comparable examples in the future.

## Notes

1. Henry Hyde, Chairman, Office of House Judiciary Committee, press release, September 9, 1998.

2. Office of House Minority Leader, press release, September 18, 1998.

3. Henry Hyde, Chairman, Office of House Judiciary Committee, press release, September 23, 1998.

4. George Mitchell, "In Danger of Discrediting the House," *New York Times*, December 16, 1998, p. A35.

5. Office of House Minority Leader, press release, December 18, 1998.

6. Alison Mitchell, "Congress Returns to a Shadow Left by Impeachment," *New York Times*, January 4, 1999, p. 1.

7. Ibid.

8. Quoted in Alison Mitchell, "The Trial of a President: The Overview; Senate, in Unanimity, Sets Rules for Trial," *New York Times*, January 9, 1999, p. 1.

9. Ibid.

10. Ibid.

11. Alison Mitchell, "GOP Senators Meet Secretly with Prosecutors on Witnesses," *New York Times*, January 14, 1999, p. 1.

12. "The Trial of the President: The Testimony," *New York Times*, January 16, 1999, p. 1.

13. David S. Broder and Dan Balz, "A Year of Scandal with No Winners; Public Trust in Institutions Has Suffered, but Long-Term Damage Remains in Doubt," *Washington Post*, February 11, 1999, p. A1.

14. Guy Gugliotta and Juliet Eilperin, "House Managers Put Brave Face on Bitter Loss," *Washington Post*, February 13, 1999, p. A1.

15. Lewis A. Froman, *The Congressional Process: Strategies, Rules, and Procedures* (Boston: Little, Brown, 1967), p. 7.

16. Norman J. Ornstein, "The New House and the New Senate," in Thomas E. Mann and Norman J. Ornstein, eds., *The New Congress* (Washington, D.C.: American Enterprise Institute, 1981).

17. This section is adapted from Norman Ornstein, "The 105th Congress Began with Gingrich and Ends with Clinton," *Roll Call*, December 21, 1998, p. 10.

18. "Schippers Speaks," *Human Events*, May 28, 1999.

19. Eric Uslaner, *The Decline of Comity in Congress* (University of Michigan Press, 1993), p. 22.

20. Ibid., p. 24.

21. Helen Dewar and Juliet Eilperin, "Hill GOP Leaders Take Cautious Course on Kosovo," *Washington Post*, April 28, 1999, p. A20.

22. Kevin Merida, "The Freshman Who Raised the Fuss; Santorum Hopes Hatfield Episode Sends a Message to GOP Leadership," *Washington Post*, March 9, 1995, p. A27.

23. Ibid.

24. *Congressional Record*, December 20, 1995, p. S18964.

# CHAPTER ELEVEN

# The Senate Budget Committee: Bastion of Comity?

## JAMES A. THURBER

Life on the Budget Committee is a grueling game!

—Former member of the Senate Budget Committee

COMITY REFERS TO THE NORMS, such as reciprocity and mutual respect, that sustain cordial relations in legislative bodies and facilitate the bargaining essential in policymaking.[1] Some level of civility is essential to a member's willingness to listen to colleagues, to learn from other legislators, and to accept the outcome of deliberation, especially in the congressional budget process. There is now ample evidence that comity has declined in Congress since the 1970s. In the view of analyst Eric M. Uslaner, this change is due to the decline of consensus on core values in American society, such as American exceptionalism, individualism, egalitarianism, religion, and science.[2] Congress, he asserts, reflects the larger society. Other influential factors, says Steven S. Smith, are "policy preferences imported with members after each election and formal rules and informal rules that mold those preferences into new rules and public policy."[3] These observations lead one to ask: Do expensive and nasty campaigns create an environment that promotes lack of trust and uncivil behavior in the House and Senate? Do party and committee leaders, presidents, socialization of norms, interest group pressure, and ideology have an impact on trust and civility among members on committees and on the floor? Does comity vary among committees compared with the floor of the House and Senate?

Another important question to ask is whether that decline has occurred evenly across all committees, and if not, does it have anything to do with their membership and responsibilities?[4] Also, has it been a steady decline or have there been periods of improved relationships influenced by personalities, elections, and the nature of the public policy being considered? What has had the greatest impact on the decline of comity in committees: the decline in society's core values, election and rule changes, or other factors?[5]

This chapter sheds some light on these questions by examining the history of comity in the Senate Budget Committee (SBC), a unique but important case, and by comparing its situation with that in the House Budget Committee (HBC). Further analysis of this type for all committees would produce a more accurate picture of the complex mutual respect and trust in Congress as a whole.[6]

## The Roots of Comity in the Senate Budget Committee

The socialization of norms, specialization, reciprocity, trust, and comity in both the SBC and the HBC have been greatly affected by their structure and organization. Because the Congressional Budget and Impoundment Control Act of 1974 (P.L. 93-344; 88 Stat. 297-339) established the SBC without tenure limitations on committee members, this committee is quite dissimilar from the HBC, which has service limitations on members and the chair.[7] Also, the SBC does not provide for direct representation of other committees or the party leadership, as is the case in the House with the Ways and Means Committee, Appropriations Committee, and the party leadership that have automatic seats on the committee.

The SBC has not only grown in size but has continued to have a higher percentage of freshmen than its House counterpart (see tables 11-1 and 11-2). The number of freshmen on a committee often has an influence on the socialization of norms, specialization, and reciprocity. The more freshmen there are, the more difficult it is to maintain the norms of the committee, such as trust and civility. As table 11-1 shows, until the 106th Congress, House Democrats always had fewer freshmen on the Budget Committee than did the House Republicans. From 1975 to 1998, the Democrats had no more than two freshmen on the committee (0–5 percent). In 1998, four of nineteen members on the committee were freshmen. The highest percentage of Republican freshmen on the committee was 38 percent (or five out of thirteen members) in the 97th Congress. Since the

Table 11-1. *House Budget Committee Freshmen*

| Congress | Republican Number | Republican Percent | Democrat Number | Democrat Percent | Total Number | Total Percent |
|---|---|---|---|---|---|---|
| 94 (1975–76) | 0 of 8 | 0.00 | 1 of 17 | 5.88 | 1 of 25 | 4.00 |
| 95 (1977–78) | 0 of 8 | 0.00 | 1 of 17 | 5.88 | 1 of 25 | 4.00 |
| 96 (1979–80) | 0 of 8 | 0.00 | 2 of 17 | 11.76 | 2 of 25 | 8.00 |
| 97 (1981–82) | 5 of 13 | 38.46 | 0 of 17 | 0.00 | 5 of 30 | 16.67 |
| 98 (1983–84) | 1 of 11 | 9.09 | 0 of 20 | 0.00 | 1 of 31 | 3.23 |
| 99 (1985–86) | 1 of 13 | 7.69 | 1 of 20 | 5.00 | 2 of 33 | 6.06 |
| 100 (1987–88) | 2 of 14 | 14.29 | 1 of 21 | 4.76 | 3 of 35 | 8.57 |
| 101 (1989–90) | 1 of 14 | 7.14 | 0 of 21 | 0.00 | 1 of 35 | 2.86 |
| 102 (1991–92) | 1 of 14 | 7.14 | 0 of 23 | 0.00 | 1 of 37 | 2.70 |
| 103 (1993–94) | 6 of 17 | 35.29 | 2 of 26 | 7.69 | 8 of 43 | 18.60 |
| 104 (1995–96) | 6 of 24 | 25.00 | 2 of 17 | 11.76 | 8 of 41 | 19.51 |
| 105 (1997–98) | 3 of 23 | 13.04 | 2 of 19 | 10.53 | 5 of 42 | 11.90 |
| 106 (1999–2000) | 5 of 24 | 20.83 | 4 of 19 | 21.05 | 9 of 43 | 20.93 |
| Mean | | 13.69 | | 6.49 | | 9.77 |

Sources: *Congressional Quarterly's Politics in America* (Washington, D.C.: CQ Press, various years); *Congressional Directory* (Washington, D.C.: GPO, various years).

inception of the committee, the average number of Republican freshmen has been 14 percent. The Democrats averaged 6.5 percent freshmen during that period.

As table 11-2 demonstrates, a different story emerges for the SBC. Both parties have always had a high proportion of freshmen in the SBC, with an average of almost 48 percent for the Republicans and 36 percent for the Democrats, and an overall high of 63 percent in 1981–82 and a low of 25 percent in 1987–88. The number of freshmen on the SBC is greater than in the House, but the turnover on the HBC, because of the term limits rule placed on its members, undermined networks of reciprocity

Table 11-2. *Senate Budget Committee Freshmen*

| | Republican | | Democrat | | Total | |
|---|---|---|---|---|---|---|
| Congress | Number | Percent | Number | Percent | Number | Percent |
| 94 | 4 of 6 | 66.67 | 4 of 10 | 40.00 | 8 of 16 | 50.00 |
| (1975–76) | | | | | | |
| 95 | 4 of 6 | 66.67 | 5 of 10 | 50.00 | 9 of 16 | 56.25 |
| (1977–78) | | | | | | |
| 96 | 5 of 8 | 62.50 | 6 of 12 | 50.00 | 11 of 20 | 55.00 |
| (1979–80) | | | | | | |
| 97 | 9 of 12 | 75.00 | 5 of 10 | 50.00 | 14 of 22 | 63.64 |
| (1981–82) | | | | | | |
| 98 | 9 of 12 | 75.00 | 1 of 10 | 10.00 | 10 of 22 | 45.45 |
| (1983–84) | | | | | | |
| 99 | 5 of 11 | 45.45 | 1 of 10 | 10.00 | 6 of 21 | 28.57 |
| (1985–86) | | | | | | |
| 100 | 0 of 11 | 0.00 | 6 of 13 | 46.15 | 6 of 24 | 25.00 |
| (1987–88) | | | | | | |
| 101 | 2 of 10 | 20.00 | 6 of 13 | 46.15 | 8 of 23 | 34.78 |
| (1989–90) | | | | | | |
| 102 | 3 of 9 | 41.67 | 4 of 12 | 33.33 | 7 of 21 | 33.33 |
| (1991–92) | | | | | | |
| 103 | 4 of 9 | 44.44 | 2 of 12 | 16.67 | 6 of 21 | 28.57 |
| (1993–94) | | | | | | |
| 104 | 5 of 12 | 41.67 | 2 of 10 | 20.00 | 7 of 22 | 31.82 |
| (1995–96) | | | | | | |
| 105 | 6 of 12 | 50.00 | 6 of 10 | 60.00 | 12 of 22 | 54.55 |
| (1997–98) | | | | | | |
| 106 | 5 of 12 | 41.67 | 3 of 10 | 30.00 | 8 of 22 | 36.36 |
| (1999–2000) | | | | | | |
| Mean | | 47.88 | | 35.56 | | 41.79 |

Sources: See table 11-1.

and trust. In addition, retirements can destroy longtime friendships that help bridge partisan differences and thus weaken the Budget Committee by robbing it of expertise and specialization. Although the Senate does not place term limits on Budget Committee members, retirements and a high proportion of freshmen on the SBC may have helped undermine comity in the budget process. The great conciliators of the Senate—particularly the moderate to conservative southern Democrats known for working with both sides of the aisle—appear to be a dying breed. In the last decade, the Senate has lost many of its leading centrists, including Senators Sam Nunn, Paul Simon, Mark Hatfield, Nancy Landon Kassebaum Baker, Alan Simpson, David Pryor, Bill Bradley, Bob Packwood, William S. Cohen, J.

Bennett Johnston, and Howell T. Heflin (six were members of the Senate Budget Committee). These changes are making it difficult to maintain the norms of comity, reciprocity, and mutual respect in the budget process and are depriving new members of role models that kept these norms alive.[8]

Another structural difference is that the SBC does not have subcommittees with legislative jurisdiction. Nearly all legislation that it considers is initiated as part of the 1974 congressional budget process. Few bills are referred to the committee in comparison with all other Senate committees, but what the SBC does is highly important and often highly politically charged. The production of an annual concurrent budget resolution is probably the most significant legislative action in each session of Congress. The concurrent budget resolution, scheduled for adoption before the Congress considers spending or revenue bills, centralizes budget decisionmaking. Concurrent budget resolutions often bring spending discipline to the Congress by calling on other committees to stay within spending limits set by the SBC's resolution. This committee has a politically grueling annual task; in effect, it coordinates the various revenue and spending decisions that are made in the separate tax, appropriations, and authorization legislative measures.

Since 1975, when the modern congressional budget process was initiated, the Budget Committee's procedures have adapted to changing electoral and budgetary circumstances (such as the Gramm-Rudman-Hollings Acts of 1985 and 1987, the Budget Enforcement Act of 1990, and the changes to the budget rules in 1993 and 1997).[9] Even with the growth of the national deficit and debt in the 1980s and early 1990s shifting to the politics of surplus in the late 1990s and 2000, the role of the committee has remained unchanged but has increased in importance and visibility. It is still at center stage, owing in part to concern over how to handle the budget surplus starting in the late 1990s.

At the same time, the internal workings and comity within the SBC have changed dramatically since 1975. Because it is the most important Senate committee in defining policy differences between the two parties, presidents and congressional party leaders think its actions have electoral consequences. In other words, what the SBC does is directly entwined with partisan electoral strategies. Therefore, the members of the committee experience a great deal of external pressure from each party's caucus.

In the early years of the committee, under the leadership of its first chair, Edmund S. Muskie (D-Maine), and ranking minority member, Henry L. Bellmon (R-Okla.), the SBC was a model of courtesy, reciprocity, apprenticeship, and specialization.[10] By all reports from former members and staff, its members respected one another and a good working relationship was built among senators from both parties with different ideologies.[11] The personality and the political backgrounds of these two committee leaders help to explain how they established and reinforced the norms of the SBC.[12] Both were former minority party governors who treated each other with respect and civility. According to Carol Cox Wait, former SBC staff director, "The experience of the two former governors who were the first to be elected to state-wide office from a minority party, created a bond that helped to build trust and civility among the committee members." Muskie and Bellmon also built a strong bipartisan consensus on basic goals, norms, and policy directives on the committee. The SBC did not suffer the ideological split or the extreme partisanship that the HBC experienced.[13] The roots of comity in the Senate committee were reinforced by the close friendship and trust between Muskie and Bellmon even as comity in the Senate as a whole declined.[14]

As deficits grew and the debt loomed large in the mid-1980s, pressure on the SBC increased to balance the budget. And as the drive to balance the budget gained momentum and became a major electoral issue, presidents, Senate party leadership, and interest groups drew a bead on the SBC. To sum up, the efficiency of the committee and of the congressional budget process in general from 1975 to 1983 was aided by a set of formal and informal norms, including reciprocity, institutional loyalty, specialization, apprenticeship, and comity; these norms were reinforced by Chairman Edmund Muskie and Ranking Minority Member Bellmon. They were close friends with similar values and political experiences. Although the SBC had a high percentage of freshmen during that period, they helped to socialize and maintain comity among the members of the committee.[15] The strong norms of trust and comity made SBC decisionmaking easier from 1975 to 1980. When the budget battles got rough in the mid-1980s, these norms declined or disappeared. In addition, elections and rule changes had an impact on SBC comity, too.

## Elections, Rule Changes, and Comity

A variety of political, institutional, and electoral conditions affect budget decisionmaking and comity within the budget committees. Elections bring new members to Congress, who in turn bring new values, political calculations, responses to public opinion, altered policy analysis, and a push

Figure 11-1. *Democrats' Party Unity Scores: Full House and Senate and Respective Budget Committees, 1975–97*

Mean score

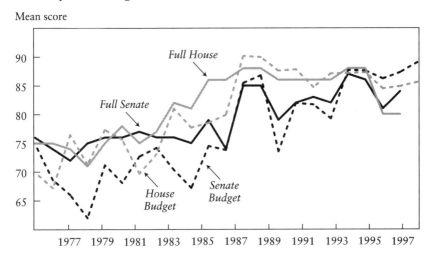

Source: *Congressional Quarterly Almanac* (Washington, D.C.: Congressional Quarterly Inc., various years).

for change in the budget process rules and budgetary policies. The history of SBC comity has been fundamentally transformed by almost annual rule changes in the budget process that were often directly influenced by the outcome of presidential and congressional elections. The major rule changes have been Gramm-Rudman-Hollings I and II, the Budget Enforcement Act of 1990, President Clinton's budget of 1993, and the Balanced Budget Act of 1997.

During the first five years of operation (1975 to 1980), the budget process inspired sharp partisan disputes in the House of Representatives, often to the point where many members in the House feared the process would collapse.[16] The Senate budget process was much more bipartisan, and the decisionmaking system was much more secure. One major reason for the cooperation in the Senate was the leadership and close working relationship between Muskie and Bellmon; another was the lower level of party unity among the Democrats in the Senate throughout the 1970s and early 1980s (see figure 11-1). The six-year terms in the Senate also insulated senators from the intense reelection pressures faced by House members, making it easier for senators to vote for budget resolutions. Also, since the SBC was a regular Senate standing committee, its members had more incentive to restrain partisanship as a means of protecting the prestige and influence of the committee.[17]

Reconciliation, one of the most powerful provisions of the Budget Act, was ignored in the 1970s.[18] Reconciliation is the process by which Congress (from the Budget Committees) includes budget resolution "reconciliation instructions" to specific committees, directing them to report legislation that changes existing laws, usually for the purpose of decreasing spending or increasing revenues by a specified amount by a certain date. In 1979, for example, efforts to use reconciliation to dramatically reduce spending were rejected by a coalition of committees. After the 1980 election, however, congressional leaders reported a reconciliation bill that reduced spending by some $8 billion. More significantly, it had strong bipartisan support in the SBC and established an important precedent for the use of reconciliation in 1981 (see budget resolution votes in table 11-3).

Elections have had a direct impact on the congressional budget process, its rules, and the SBC. The 1980 elections changed the presidency and the Senate. Republicans regained control of the presidency after a four-year hiatus and took control of the Senate for the first time since 1955. The size of the Democratic majority in the House was reduced from 117 to 51. With Republicans replacing Democrats as the majority in the Senate, Senator Pete V. Domenici (R-N.Mex.) became chairman of the SBC.

In his 1980 presidential campaign, Ronald Reagan promised three policy changes that had a direct impact on the committee: a rapid increase in defense spending, a significant reduction in taxes, and large cuts in domestic spending and entitlements. An important change in the congressional budget process helped Reagan accomplish his policy changes: the decision to move reconciliation from the end to the beginning of the budget process. Reagan had solid bipartisan Senate support for his position in a measure dubbed Gramm-Latta I, with a majority of both parties supporting the president's position in a vote of 78 to 20 (see table 11-3). This bipartisan support was greatly enhanced by the fact that the Republicans had a majority in the Senate and by the committee leadership of Domenici, who had been on the committee from its inception and had been influenced greatly by the bipartisan spirit of Muskie and Bellmon, and who continued to treat the minority with respect.[19]

After the infusion of conservative Republicans from the 1980 election, the Senate shifted distinctively to the right, also fundamentally shifting the SBC to the right.[20] Moreover, the SBC has always been more conservative than its House counterpart. The SBC has been closer to the mean conser-

Table 11-3. *Votes on First Budget Resolutions, 1975–85*

| | House | | | Senate | | |
|---|---|---|---|---|---|---|
| Date | Total vote Yes-No | Republicans Yes-No | Democrats Yes-No | Total vote Yes-No | Republicans Yes-No | Democrats Yes-No |
| 1975 | 200-196 | 3-128 | 197-68 | 69-22 | 19-18 | 50-4 |
| 1976 | 221-155 | 13-111 | 208-44 | 62-22 | 17-16 | 45-6 |
| 1977 | 213-179 | 7-121 | 206-58 | 56-31 | 15-17 | 41-14 |
| 1978 | 201-197 | 3-136 | 198-61 | 64-27 | 16-19 | 48-8 |
| 1979 | 220-184 | 9-134 | 211-50 | 64-20 | 20-15 | 44-5 |
| 1980 | 225-193 | 22-131 | 203-62 | 68-28 | 19-22 | 49-6 |
| 1981 | 253-176 | 190-0 | 63-176 | 78-20 | 50-2 | 28-18 |
| 1982 | 219-206 | 156-32 | 63-174 | 49-43 | 46-2 | 1-41 |
| 1983 | 229-196 | 4-160 | 225-36 | 50-49 | 21-32 | 29-17 |
| 1984 | 250-168 | 21-139 | 229-29 | 41-34 | 40-3 | 1-41 |
| 1985 | 258-170 | 24-155 | 234-15 | 50-49[a] | 48-4 | 1-45 |

a. Vice President George Bush cast the tie-breaking vote.

vative coalition average than the HBC has been to the House mean.[21] In 1977 the HBC was well below the conservative coalition chamber average of 51. From 1981 to the present, it has been close to the chamber average. The SBC has almost always been closer to the Senate chamber average than the HBC; thus the SBC has been a better reflection of the views of the Senate as a whole. As figure 11-2 shows, however, there are significant ideological differences between the HBC and SBC Republicans and Democrats as measured by the Americans for Democratic Action (ADA) scores. In the House, these differences are strong and statistically significant ($t = 34.024$, $p = .000$ significance). Similar differences were found in the Senate ($t = 18.953$, $p = .000$ significance). This is not surprising. Ideological differences on the two committees, as shown in figure 11-2, are extreme. Not only are they split ideologically, but members have been growing further apart over time. It is difficult to build a basis for trust, reciprocity, and comity when the members are moving apart ideologically.

With the Democratic gains in the House in the 1982 elections, the ability of Republicans and conservative Democrats to create a majority coalition virtually came to an end. Bipartisan voting on the budget resolution disappeared in 1983 when Senate Democrats and Republicans divided sharply over the budget, matching the partisanship of the House. This loss of bipartisanship was intensified in the SBC following the rapid growth in the deficit, which hit a record $208 billion in fiscal 1983. In the words of

Figure 11-2. *ADA Scores: House and Senate Budget Committees,
by Party, 1975–97*[a]

Score

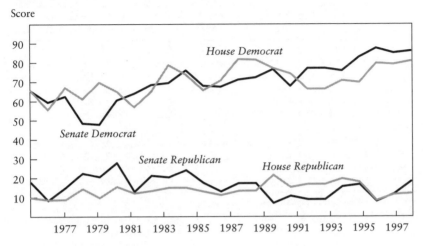

Source: *Congressional Quarterly Almanac* (Washington, D.C.: Congressional Quarterly Inc., various years).
a. ADA = Americans for Democratic Action.

Carol Cox Wait, an SBC staff director during that period, "The budget is
too important not to fight over it and it especially became important to
both parties in 1983 in the Senate Budget Committee. Civility in the budget battles started to fray that year." Rudolph G. Penner, former director
of the Congressional Budget Office, concluded that "deficits undermined
comity as Senate Budget Committee members searched for solutions that
would not cut their favorite programs and would not raise taxes." The
deficit remained at more than 5 percent of GDP through 1987. Given the
large budget deficits, the environment changed in the SBC, and there was
an impetus to revise the Budget Act in 1985.

Comity in the budget process declined in large part because of changes
in the rules of budgeting. The most dramatic of these occurred in 1985,
when Congress passed the Balanced Budget and Emergency Deficit Control Act (better known as the Gramm-Rudman-Hollings Act).[22] With strong
bipartisan support in the SBC, Congress created a mechanism for making
across-the-board cuts in outlays should the deficit targets not be met. It
also expanded the power of the SBC and party leaders at the expense of
the other spending committees. There was strong bipartisan support in
the SBC for this reform.

The growth of deficits and the debt brought new changes to the budget process and increased partisan pressure on the SBC, which led to heated rhetoric in the committee and comity among its members. Through 1986, Congress was unable to agree on how to fix a constitutional flaw in Gramm-Rudman-Hollings and was unable to meet the deficit reductions needed to meet the deficit targets. This led to the passage of Gramm-Rudman-Hollings II in 1987. An agreement reached in December 1987, covering fiscal years 1988 and 1989, was designed to meet the deficit targets through the beginning of the next administration. Reacting to eight years of partisan interbranch war over the budget and public opinion, the 1988 election of George Bush and newly elected members of Congress brought a more constructive engagement with Congress. After an agreement between President Bush and congressional leaders came unraveled over differences concerning taxes, social programs, and defense, the deficit targets were scrapped, and the congressional budget process underwent another major change worked out in a five-month-long budget summit. Led by Senator Robert S. Byrd (D-W.Va.) and Bush's director of the Office of Management and Budget, Richard Darman, congressional and White House leaders reached an agreement on a five-year, $500 billion deficit reduction package and revised budget process. The Budget Enforcement Act of 1990 (along with the Omnibus Budget Reconciliation Act [OBRA] of 1990) was the largest deficit reduction package ever, but it also included major reforms of the congressional budget act that changed the rules and the environment of the SBC.

During the early years of budgeting, spending and deficits in the budget resolution tended to be below those set by Congress in the resolutions drafted by the Budget Committee. As the level of disparity began to increase, the fights in the budget committees became more intense. The largest disparity occurred with the 1991 deficit: the concurrent budget resolution projected a $64 billion deficit, but the actual deficit totaled $268.7 billion. Working with the new rules established in the 1990 Budget Enforcement Act, the budget committee members were forced to make more realistic budget projections, and it brought increasing rancor to the committee.

Even with the critical changes in both policy and process that the 1990 Budget Enforcement Act (and OBRA) rendered, the deficit problem would not go away, and the internal environment of the SBC and the Senate in general became more partisan and less civil. After the election of Bill Clinton in 1992, projections showed that the deficits would remain in the range of $300 billion to $500 billion through the year 2000.

Clinton's victory in 1992 meant that one party would control both chambers of Congress and the presidency for the first time in twelve years. Clinton won only 43 percent of the popular vote, and Democrats lost ten House seats and broke even in Senate contests. As a result of the election and the large deficit projections, Clinton proposed a controversial five-year $500 billion deficit reduction package in 1993 that passed the House by one vote and was tied in the Senate. Not a single Republican in either chamber voted for the bill. Vice President Al Gore had to break a tie vote in the Senate in order to pass it. Bipartisan support for Clinton's proposal was nonexistent in the SBC and nonexistent on the floor of the Senate. Extreme partisanship over the budget had come to dominate the SBC and the Senate. The two largest deficit-reduction packages in the history of the United States, 1990 and 1993, were passed with great pressure on the SBC. This contributed to the continued transformation of the committee into a more partisan and less trusting and friendly entity. Comity was further undermined by the following external developments in the early 1990s: elections precipitated clear party and policy differences, interest groups and constituents pressured the committee not to cut their programs, and public opinion began calling for deficit and debt reduction.

## Partisanship and Comity

The election of 1994 brought simultaneous Republican majorities in the House and the Senate for the first time in forty years.[23] This also brought major change to the internal workings and relationships of the SBC. As the electoral margins closed to six seats in the House and five seats in the Senate in 1999, heated partisan rhetoric dominated the SBC, as it had from the beginning in the HBC. The SBC became a bastion of party electoral philosophy rather than a cohesive bipartisan panel working out the necessary compromises in a complex decisionmaking process. According to Carol Cox Wait, "The budget decision-making process and the SBC got more contentious because the budget and its impact got more real." Deteriorating personal relationships undermined the civility and comity of the committee that had been built so carefully in its first years. According to a current staff member, "Serious tension [developed] between chairman Domenici and ranking minority member Lautenberg based on political preferences, personality and style of leadership." Bill Frenzel, a former member of the House Budget Committee and cochairman of the Committee for a Responsible Federal Budget, notes, however: "The SBC is still

Figure 11-3. *Republicans' Party Unity Scores: Full House and Senate and Respective Budget Committees, 1975–97*

Mean score

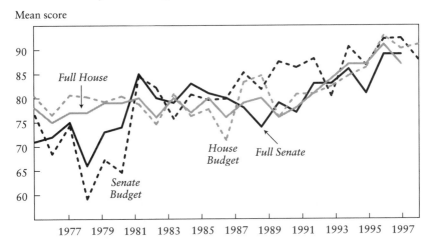

Source: *Congressional Quarterly Almanac* (Washington, D.C.: Congressional Quarterly Inc., various years).

more independent of the party caucuses, unlike the House Committee. The House Budget Committee is structured to guarantee partisanship."

Deficit-heightened partisanship has created delays and changed the budget process and the internal workings of the SBC over the past fifteen years. This is also reflected in the voting behavior of budget committee members in both the House and Senate, as shown by the party unity scores in figures 11-1 and 11-3. An important environmental factor of any committee is the loyalty of its members to the party and partisanship, as expressed through congressional party-line voting. Partisanship has increased in both the House and Senate Budget Committees over time. However, when Muskie and Bellmon were no longer leaders of the SBC, the party unity scores for both the Senate Republicans and Democrats increased dramatically. Generally, the percentage of party-line votes increases over time for the budget committee members of both parties, especially after each election. These figures represent the percentage of all recorded votes for both the House and Senate Budget Committees on which a majority of voting Democrats opposed a majority of voting Republicans. The Senate and House clearly show a pattern of increasing partisanship, with higher unity scores from 1980 to present. In general, SBC members have had lower party unity scores than the full House as well as Senate. Since the early 1980s, however, the Senate Republican Budget Committee members have been generally more loyal than their conference. They have had higher party unity scores than their counterparts in the House and the full Senate and House.

House members have generally been very close to the mean House party unity scores and were much lower than their counterparts in the Senate except in the early years of the budget process, 1975 to 1980. However, SBC Republicans were much more partisan than anyone after the 1987 Gramm-Rudman-Hollings reforms (see figure 11-3). Before Gramm-Rudman-Hollings II, the Democratic SBC members were well below their caucus and their House counterparts on party unity scores, most likely reflecting a realignment of the Senate Democrats through electoral losses in the South and the departure of moderate Democratic senators.[24]

According to one long-term SBC staffer, "The potential for partisan change in the Senate after each election heightened partisanship in the committee and undermined comity." Another SBC staff member said, "The complexity of reconciling competing budget and policy goals on the committee slowly ground down the civility and comity that was built in the first years of the committee." In the 1980s and early 1990s, SBC reciprocity changed from protecting each other's programs to "If I get screwed, you get screwed," says a current SBC staffer. Potential election "revenge" for making hard budget choices, trouble in reaching budget agreements because of seemingly insurmountable policy differences, large deficits (especially starting in the mid-1980s), and differences over spending the large surpluses for tax breaks, saving Social Security and Medicare, reducing the debt, or increasing social and defense expenditures in the late 1990s, have created a partisan environment that undermined civility, reciprocity, and comity in the SBC. As one staffer observed, "No one was muscling each other on the Senate Budget Committee until 1983 and then again in 1987 and again in 1990 (BEA). Every time there was a significant change in the budget process, new rules, the comity of the committee declined." In the absence of consensus and potentially rich electoral returns as a result of committee actions, comity declined and partisanship increased in the SBC.

## Divided Government and Presidential Influence on Comity

Pressure from presidents on budget committee members is another important influence on the internal workings of the committees. Figure 11-4 shows the mean support for the president and his programs by SBC mem-

Figure 11-4. *Presidential Support Scores: Full Senate and Senate Budget Committees, 1975–97*

Score

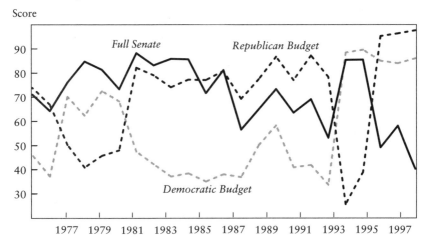

Source: *Congressional Quarterly Almanac* (Washington, D.C.: Congressional Quarterly Inc., various years).

bers by party and for all members of the Senate. Both parties have had high support for their respective presidents from 1975 to 1999. Senate Democrats have always been less loyal to the president until 1993. This was especially the case from 1975 to 1980, thus allowing for more bipartisan collaborations in building budget policy out of the Senate. Senate Republicans have been significantly more loyal to their president, as shown in figure 11-4 and in their vote for President Clinton's first tough deficit-reducing budget in 1993, when not a single Republican supported it. Figure 11-4 shows that 1993 reached the height of SBC Democratic loyalty to the president and SBC Republican opposition.

## Conclusions and the Future of Comity

Comity in the SBC has been directly affected by policy preferences imported with members after each election, turnover (number of freshmen on the committee and number of retirements in recent years), negative and expensive campaigns combined with perceived electoral vulnerability, partisanship, interest groups, public opinion, presidents, and of course the deficit or surplus and ideologically based differences over policy. These factors have led to deadlock over the budget, and that deadlock has undermined comity and trust on the budget committees. Partisanship and policy polarization from election battles have spilled over into the congressional budget process and the SBC. When power is divided between the two parties fairly evenly, the fight gets louder, the feelings grow more intense, and the differences between the parties are exaggerated for effect, especially in the zero-sum budget process. The partisan drive for electoral and political advantage in the budget process seems to have slowly undermined trust and comity among SBC members. The formal and informal rules that mold the member preferences into new rules and budget policy have also increased partisanship and undermined comity. Hyperpluralism, or the expansion of the community of lobbyists and interest groups, has increased conflict since the establishment of the budget committees. The intense pressure from groups has also contributed to the undermining of trust and comity among SBC members, placing incompatible demands for tax cuts and large spending increases on the committee. Divided party control of the White House and the Senate, the norm since 1976, has also reduced trust and civility on the committee by increasing pressure from presidents on SBC members to hold the line for or against the president's budgetary requests.

The intractability of policy preferences on the SBC when trying to balance the budget, decrease taxes, save Medicare and Social Security, reduce the debt, and increase social spending has led to distrust and uncivil behavior even in times of surplus. Often political rewards in the budget process go to those who obstruct, and the losses go to those who cooperate and compromise. Political leaders often wait for the opposition to make the first move in the budget process while continuing to use heated rhetoric that undermines trust, compromise, and comity. If the Senate Budget Committee returned to the days of Muskie and Bellmon when the committee was a bastion of trust, reciprocity, civility, and comity, it might again become a contagion of those norms for Congress as a whole.

## Notes

I am grateful to David Dulio, Michael Kaiser, Faith Passy, Leslie McNaugher, John McPhillips, and Christine Pollak for excellent research assistance. I would also like to thank Henry Bellmon, Sandy Davis, Bill Frenzel, Willis Gradison, William H. Gray III, Bill Heniff, G. William Hoagland, Robert Keith, Bruce King, James V. Saturno, Austin Smyhe, and Carol Cox Wait and the staff and members of the Senate Budget Committees for their time and observations about comity and the budget process. All unattributed quotations are from interviews conducted by the author.

1. See Donald E. Matthews, *U.S. Senators and Their World* (New York: Vintage Books, 1960); Eric M. Uslaner, *The Decline of Comity in Congress* (University of Michigan Press, 1993).

2. Uslaner, *The Decline of Comity in Congress.*

3. Steven S. Smith, "Review of the Decline of Comity in Congress," in *Congress and the Presidency,* vol. 21 (Fall 1994), pp. 155–57.

4. On the decline of comity, see Uslaner, *The Decline of Comity in Congress;* Kenneth R. Mayer and David T. Canon, *The Dysfunctional Congress?* (Boulder, Colo.: Westview Press, 1999); Steven S. Smith and Christopher J. Deering, *Committees in Congress,* 2d ed. (Washington, D.C.: CQ Press, 1990); Barbara Sinclair, *Unorthodox Lawmaking* (Washington, D.C.: CQ Press, 1997); and David Rhode, Norman J. Ornstien, and Robert Peabody, "Political Change and Legislative Norms in the U.S. Senate, 1957–1974," in *Studies of Congress* (Washington, D.C.: CQ Press, 1985).

5. Smith, "Review of the Decline of Comity in Congress"; and Uslaner, *The Decline of Comity in Congress.*

6. James A. Thurber, "If the Game Is Too Hard, Change the Rules: Congressional Budget Reform in the 1990s," in James A. Thurber and Roger H. Davidson, eds., *Remaking Congress: Change and Stability in the 1990s* (Washington, D.C.: CQ Press, 1996); and Daniel J. Palazzolo, *Done Deal? The Politics of the 1997 Budget Agreement* (Chatham House, 1999); and "Centralization, Devolution, and Turf Protection in the Congressional Budget Process," in Lawrence C. Dodd and Bruce I. Oppenheimer, eds., *Remaking Congress: Change and Stability in the 1990s* (Washington, D.C.: CQ Press, 1997).

7. James A. Thurber, "Congressional Budget Reform and New Demands for Policy Analysis," *Policy Analysis,* vol. 2 (Spring 1976), pp. 197–215; and John Ellwood and James A. Thurber, "The Politics of the Congressional Budget Process Reexamined," in Lawrence C. Dodd and Bruce I. Oppenheimer, eds., *Congress Reconsidered* (Washington, D.C.: CQ Press, 1981).

8. Eliza Newlin Carney, "Exodus," *National Journal,* vol. 28 (January 1996), pp. 108–13.

9. For a history of these reforms, see Thurber, "If the Game Is Too Hard"; and Palazzolo, *Done Deal? The Politics of the 1997 Budget Agreement.*

10. Ellwood and Thurber, "The Politics of the Congressional Budget Process Reexamined."

11. Thurber, "Congressional Budget Reform and New Demands for Policy Analysis."

12. Ross K. Baker, *Friend and Foe in the U.S. Senate* (Free Press, 1980), p. 58.

13. Ellwood and Thurber, "The Politics of the Congressional Budget Process Reexamined."

14. For further analysis of the importance of friendship networks in legislative assemblies, see Gregory A. Caldeira and Samuel C. Patterson, "Political Friendship in the Legislature," *Journal of Politics,* vol. 49, no. 4 (1987), pp. 935–75.

15. For a discussion of how legislative norms are learned, see Herbert B. Asher, "The Learning of Legislative Norms," *American Political Science Review,* vol. 67, no. 2 (1973), pp. 499–513; Robert Axelrod, "An Evolutionary Approach to Norms," *American Political Science Review,* vol. 80, no. 4 (1986), pp. 1095–1111; and Edward V. Schneier, "Norms and Folkways in Congress: How Much Has Actually Changed?" *Congress and the Presidency,* vol. 15, no. 2 (1988), pp. 117–38.

16. Thurber, "If the Game Is Too Hard," and "Centralization, Devolution, and Turf Protection in the Congressional Budget Process."

17. "Congressional Budget Reform and the New Demands for Policy Analysis."

18. Thurber, "Centralization, Devolution, and Turf Protection."

19. Thurber, "If the Game Is Too Hard."

20. Thurber, "Centralization, Devolution, and Turf Protection in the Congressional Budget Process."

21. Norman J. Ornstein, Thomas E. Mann, and Michael J. Malbin, *Vital Statistics on Congress 1995–1996* (Washington, D.C.: CQ Press, 1996).

22. Thurber, "If the Game Is Too Hard," and "Centralization, Devolution, and Turf Protection in the Congressional Budget Process."

23. On the impact of the 1994 election on Congress, see Thurber and Davidson, *Remaking Congress: Change and Stability in the 1990s*; and Dean McSweeney and John E. Owens, *The Republican Takeover on Capitol Hill* (Macmillan, 1998).

24. Sinclair, *Unorthodox Lawmaking.*

# Contributors

Ross K. Baker
*Rutgers University*

Colton C. Campbell
*Florida International University,
Miami*

Timothy E. Cook
*Department of Political Science
Williams College*

Roger H. Davidson
*University of Maryland,
College Park*

C. Lawrence Evans
*Department of Government
The College of William and Mary*

Gerald Gamm
*University of Rochester*

Burdett A. Loomis
*University of Kansas*

Walter J. Oleszek
*Congressional Research Service
U.S. Library of Congress*

Bruce I. Oppenheimer
*Vanderbilt University*

Norman J. Ornstein
*American Enterprise Institute*

Barbara Sinclair
*University of California
at Los Angeles*

Steven S. Smith
*University of Minnesota*

James A. Thurber
*Center for Congressional and
Presidential Studies
Department of Government
School of Public Affairs
American University*

Eric M. Uslaner
*Department of Government
and Politics
University of Maryland—
College Park*

# Index